BookshelF

A Guide for Librarians and Systems Managers

Written and edited by
Shelagh Fisher and Jennifer Rowley

Routledge
Taylor & Francis Group
LONDON AND NEW YORK

First published 1992 by Ashgate Publishing

Reissued 2018 by Routledge
2 Park Square, Milton Park, Abingdon, Oxon, OX14 4RN
711 Third Avenue, New York, NY 10017

Routledge is an imprint of the Taylor & Francis Group, an informa business

Publisher's Note
The publisher has gone to great lengths to ensure the quality of this reprint but points out that some imperfections in the original copies may be apparent.

Disclaimer
The publisher has made every effort to trace copyright holders and welcomes correspondence from those they have been unable to contact.

A Library of Congress record exists under LC control number: 92007152

Typeset in 11 point Plantin by Photoprint, Torquay

ISBN 13: 978-1-138-60965-5 (hbk)
ISBN 13: 978-1-138-60968-6 (pbk)
ISBN 13: 978-0-429-45984-9 (ebk)

Contents

Appendices

Acknowledgements

The authors would like to thank a number of people for their support in the production of this guide. Firstly, the contributors – Hilary Dyer, Peter Leggate, Karen Senior, Alastair Johnston, Stuart James, Barbara Salmon and Pat Darter – who produced their chapters so willingly, and on time. Particular thanks are due to Jonathan Willson, not only for his contribution, but also for his technical advice, given so freely, often in the wee small hours. Thanks are also due to colleagues in the Department of Library and Information Studies at Manchester Polytechnic for their patient support and friendship. Last, but certainly not least, sincere thanks are due to our families – Tony Oulton, Ruth, Jane, Peter Rowley, Shula and Zeta and our friends who undertook to ensure the relatively smooth running of our daily lives during the creation of the manuscript.

List of contributors

2 History and development

Peter Leggate, Bodleian Library, Oxford.
Hilary Dyer, Department of Library and Information Studies, Loughborough University.

3 Hardware and software

Jonathan Willson, Department of Library and Information Studies, Manchester Polytechnic.

10 BookshelF User Group

Karen Senior, Bolton Institute of Higher Education Library.

12 BookshelF in the Academic Library

Stuart James, Paisley College of Technology

13 BookshelF in the Public Library

Alastair Johnston, Dumfries and Galloway Public Libraries.

14 BookshelF in the Special Library

Pat Darter, Equal Opportunities Commission.

15 BookshelF in the Special Library

Barbara Salmon, Institute of Personnel Management.

List of figures

Part 1 Development and environment

1 Introduction

BookshelF is a computerized library management system marketed by Specialist Computer Systems and Software Ltd (SCSS). This guide is designed to introduce librarians and systems managers to the features of BookshelF. BookshelF has already been installed in over one hundred locations, and is enjoying an expanding market. BookshelF has established itself as a significant system in only the last few years. This rise in the market is partially due to the wide range of different sizes of system that can be configured. BookshelF offers systems that range from small systems of two to three workstations to networking for medium-sized public libraries.

BookshelF's other strengths lie in its origins in a British Library Research Project, which investigated the requirements of small to medium-sized libraries in respect of computerized library management systems. Specialist Computer Systems and Software Ltd have paid particular attention to user support, and this has been attractive to librarians who are implementing their first computerized library management system. In addition, BookshelF offers a wide range of modules. Modules include Catalogue, Acquisitions, Circulation and Serials. The Catalogue module incorporates a Thesaurus module which allows vocabulary control in indexing of a type that is not available in many other library management systems. In addition, this module offers facilities for Community Information. Facilities for Management Information are also available.

BookshelF, then, is an important library management system, but it is currently only installed in the United Kingdom. The future may see implementations in other countries, but the suppliers have chosen to consolidate their United Kingdom market before looking to other markets. This marketing policy is consistent with SCSS's commitment to user support.

This guide describes BookshelF in detail. Chapter 2 starts by exploring the development of the software and its emergence from a specification developed as part of a research project to a fully fledged multi-user system, with a large market share.

Chapter 3 discusses the wide range of hardware and operating systems platforms on which the system can be implemented. Chapter 4 identifies the key system parameters that need to be defined during implementation, and thereby demonstrates the range of options for configuring the system so that it meets the requirements of the individual library. Chapter 4 also includes an explanation of screen-handling functions. Other system parameters are established within specific modules, and these are further identified in the appropriate module.

Chapters 5, 6, 7, 8 and 9 describe the way in which specific modules of the system operate. In all of these modules the library has considerable choice in the way in which the system is configured to reflect local decisions concerning the management of the library and its resources.

A multi-site version of BookshelF has been implemented in several public library authorities, offering facilities for centralized or decentralized ordering and receipting processes, local or system-wide reservation procedures and stock transfer. Multi-site libraries can configure the system according to local requirements. Details pertaining to multi-site software options are included in the discussions of specific modules.

The Catalogue module is central to the system since it offers the opportunity to build the central bibliographic file. In supporting the creation of this file, the Catalogue module offers control over subject indexing terms via the Thesaurus and control over author headings and access points via Authority Control. Catalogue Enquiry offers a quick, command-based means of searching the catalogue, designed, primarily for library staff. The OPAC module offers a user-friendly interface for users, and may simply be used as an on-line catalogue, or additionally can provide access to community information. One of the limitations of BookshelF is that it was not originally a MARC-based system; this has been rectified recently with the introduction of a MARC-based catalogue conversion routine.

The Acquisitions module uses the central bibliographic file created in the Catalogue module. It offers all of the normal procedures associated with the ordering and acquisition of library materials. Orders can be created, using existing bibliographic records if appropriate, and added to the Order File. Orders may then be printed as forms or slips. There are also facilities for receipts and claims, and for control of budgets. The limitations of this module are two-fold: more sophisticated accounting information could be made available. (SCSS have, however, produced bespoke Accounting Modules on request from individual sites) and on-line ordering is not yet possible, although this is planned for the near future.

The Circulation module deals with circulation control, and offers all of the features that would be expected in such a module, including issue, return, reservations and fines control. A large number of different reader category codes can be set to cater for different locations, different kinds of library materials, and different reader groups. Each reader category code has its own Circulation rule within which is set parameters such as the maximum number of items on loan, the maximum days on loan, and the maximum number of renewals permitted. Moving from one function, such as Issue, to another function within the Circulation Control module is straightforward.

Serials control can subsume all of the processes associated with the control of serials in a library. Serials control systems differ from their equivalent for monographs in that they must control each issue of each copy of a given title. The Serials Control module in BookshelF focusses on serials acquisition, and has much in common with the Acquisitions Module for monographs. Where possible common procedures are adopted. The Serials module does not offer an OPAC-type interface to the Serials File, nor does it incorporate facilities for circulation control, other than routeing facilities for journal circulation to a pre-assigned user group. Both the Serials module and the Acquisitions module focus on the ordering and registration of incoming items. The Serials Module must however incorporate special facilities for dealing with serials subscription renewal, and the registration of each individual issue as it arrives. Claims and labelling correspondingly also become more complex processes, and there is a need for more detailed management information. BookshelF maintains serials records on a copy by copy basis, so that order and associated details have to be set up for each copy as it is ordered. Frequency codes must be assigned to each title, so that dates for expected receipt can be calculated. A Listing and Reports Menu offers a means to generate a number of reports, covering, for example, all titles, or titles on order from a given supplier, or all outstanding claims.

Chapter 9 reviews the management information and reports that are available within BookshelF. There remains much work to be done on the kinds of management information that library managers expect to derive from a transactional processing system such as a library management system. BookshelF does not supply all of the answers, but the two avenues to the production of management information do represent a powerful tool. A considerable number of reports can currently be produced simply by selecting a menu option in the appropriate BookshelF module, as indicated above in the discussion of the modules. Other reports can be generated through the use of the operating system, PICK or INFORMATION (depending on the type of machine on which the system is running). The use of the Query Language in PICK or INFORMATION allows any data element or data set to be correlated with any variable. Almost all of the imaginable analysis of the management information can be performed.

Chapter 10 outlines the establishment and achievements of the User Group. Although the suppliers encouraged its formation, the User Group is an independent body whose aims are to:

exchange information,
identify areas for development,
discuss problem areas, and
liaise with the vendor.

The chapter outlines how these objectives are achieved, and identifies areas in which the User Group has had a major impact on the development of BookshelF. There is a healthy relationship between SCSS and the User Group which has led to improvements in the product.

Chapter 11 reviews what are regarded by many users as one of the significant attractions of BookshelF, the support services. This chapter reviews the training programmes that have been offered, and the various help facilities that are available.

Chapters 12, 13 and 14 describe the way in which BookshelF has been implemented in a number of different environments. There are a number of different parameters that can be set and configurations can vary significantly depending on the nature of the library and its users in which the specific configuration has been installed. These chapters demonstrate how BookshelF works in practice, and illustrate the variations between specific implementations. Examples of libraries from the various sectors in which BookshelF might find an application have been chosen as case studies. In addition, case studies have been selected so that systems running on Primes under INFORMATION and other PICK-based systems have been included. These case studies also explore the systems requirements phase, and the problems associated with integrating a new system into the day-to-day operation of a library.

The first case study concerns the library at Paisley College. Prior to the acquisition of BookshelF, Paisley College had an automated catalogue and a manual issue system. After a detailed analysis of requirements, BookshelF was purchased in 1987, as a fully integrated system, based on a Prime 250. The Serials Control module was not purchased since these procedures were handled by in-house software.

The original specification for a library system for Paisley College is given in Appendix 3. Stuart James, the Chief Librarian and author of Chapter 12, emphasizes that if an analysis of requirements was undertaken at Paisley now (i.e. six years later) the specification would be rather different from the one included here.

Interesting developments outlined in this case study are worth noting. Paisley College have designed a limited electronic ordering system and are using this successfully to place orders with their major book supplier. The modifications to the standard BookshelF bibliographic record and experiments with the use of UDC as a subject access tool are unique to this implementation. The Circulation module has been used to allow much more flexibility in loan arrangements and to encourage students to make better use of library resources, but the changes made on the basis of the Circulation module have provoked wider debate about access to library services within the College. It took some time to successfully implement a pattern of overdue notices and a fines system. More recent developments are associated with the implementation of the Community Information and Thesaurus Modules.

Chapter 13 looks at the application of BookshelF in a public library. When Dumfries and Galloway Public Libraries entered the market for a library management system in 1988, they could not find a system to meet their specification. They sought a fully working, multi-site integrated library management system capable of handling everything from the potential record, to beyond withdrawal, with a combination of mobile and static service points, both off- and on-line. They chose BookshelF and developed it in partnership with the supplier, and they are now the proud possessors of a system that they regard as first class and which meets their requirements admirably. This chapter describes the development of the system to meet Dumfries and Galloway's specification and a number of enhancements that were added to make the product more attractive to the public library market in general.

Chapters 14 and 15 include two case studies which discuss the application of BookshelF in the special library. The implementation of the system in the Library of the Equal Opportunities Commission is a tale of responding to financial deadlines, and purchasing selected modules in the first instance, with plans to develop further later. The implementation started with Catalogue, Thesaurus and Serials Modules. The case study in Chapter 15 is based on the Library at the Institute of Personnel Management. In many respects this is a traditional 'special library' with a need to index items thoroughly and to loan items to users via the postal network. The Institute of Personnel Management uses the Catalogue, Acquisitions, Thesaurus and Circulation modules. Most interesting are the ways in which the Thesaurus module and the Circulation module have been tailored to meet the requirements of this application.

In Chapter 16, a rather different application of the BookshelF software is outlined. Students of Information and Library Management at Manchester Polytechnic have benefited from SCSS's sponsorship of the full suite of BookshelF modules for teaching purposes. Students gain an understanding of the principles of systems analysis, information retrieval, cataloguing and indexing by hands-on use of the system. Using BookshelF, students generate a range of hard-copy catalogues, indexes and thesauri to illustrate evaluative assignments on which they are assessed.

This book offers a thorough overview of the main modules in the BookshelF system, and demonstrates through the use of a limited number of case studies the way in which BookshelF has been implemented in different types of libraries. The book is written for any professional information worker or student who needs to assess different library management systems. It should provide an insight into the key features of BookshelF. Clearly, a book of this kind will date, and whilst the core features of BookshelF are likely to remain stable, it is a developing product and enhancements can be expected. This book is a starting point. Those who wish to know more will need to consult the journal literature and the supplier.

2 History and development

Peter Leggate and
Hilary Dyer

Origins

The well-stocked bar of the 8th Cranfield Conference on Mechanised Information Retrieval in July 1981 provided the venue for the informal discussions which gave rise to BookshelF. These discussions centred on the potential of the microcomputer to provide automation for the small library. The outcome was a successful application to the British Library Research and Development Department (BLR&DD) for a research grant to support a project based in the Cairns Library and headed by Peter Leggate. Hilary Dyer was appointed as research officer.

The objective of the project was to explore the possibility of developing a multi-user, integrated automation system for small libraries. The small library was defined pragmatically as one large enough to feel the need for automation but not large enough to be able to afford the existing turnkey or cooperative systems based on mini- or main-frames. As a rule of thumb this was taken to include libraries with total budgets for staff, stock and services in the range £25,000 to £250,000.

In 1981 most microcomputers available in the UK were 8-bit machines with 32 or 64k of RAM, floppy disks and single-user operating sytems. Winchester discs were being introduced but even a 5 Mb hard disc was a rarity. Names such as Apple, Commodore, Superbrain and Cifer dominated. Only a minority of libraries had microcomputers and almost no custom-designed software for library applications was available. Some innovative librarians had developed their own in-house software but the main use of microcomputers was for word-processing and cataloguing, often by producing catalogue cards. Fortunately for the success of the project, rapid developments occurred in the microcomputer market in the period 1981–83.

Against this background many small libraries as we had defined them were facing the same problems which had induced their larger counterparts to install automated systems using minis or mainframes. These problems included staff-intensive and error-prone filing of issue slips and catalogue cards; wasteful duplication in multiple typing of the same bibliographic records for orders, cataloguing and accessions lists; and user-resistance to the card catalogue. To these small libraries the microcomputer represented a dramatic lowering of the threshold for computer purchase and the potential for automation.

One computer application that was already established in small as well as large libraries was the on-line searching of remote databases from 'dumb' terminals. In the introduction[2] to the final report on the project, much emphasis was placed on the possibility that the same equipment could be used for both on-line searching and library automation. The report pointed out:

> The two types of application have much in common; both are concerned with the creation, filing, retrieving and manipulation of text records and to a lesser extent numerical data. We can view library automation as being concerned with internal records of library stock, and with operations in which information is added to the existing record of a *known* document. Information retrieval is more concerned with the retrieval of *unknown* records to a *known* subject. In practice these distinctions become blurred. A library may wish to search its own internal databases – of which its catalogue is one; external databases now include the catalogues of other libraries.
>
> Even though similarities outweigh differences, information retrieval and library automation applications had largely developed independently of one another and had been the concern of different people using different equipment and software. For example, the names of BLCMP and GEAC were associated with cataloguing and issuing systems, Lockheed and Datastar with information retrieval. Few people had expertise in both areas. This separation may have been encouraged by the internal organization of libraries which associated information retrieval with library services and library automation with housekeeping, and assigned them to different sections of the library.

We concluded that the lack of cross-fertilization between the two applications was undesirable and unnecessary. Closer links between the two became one of the major themes of the project.

A computer facility

Our declared objective was 'to explore the concept of a **computer facility** for small libraries, which would justify its cost by satisfying a range of library functions'.[3] The facility would be a multi-functional, multi-user system, based on the micro-computer. Functions would include:

Library automation applications:

- acquisitions
- cataloguing
- catalogue enquiry
- circulation control
- serials control
- management information

In-house database creation and information retrieval

Communications links for:

- on-line bibliographic services
- viewdata services
- telex to the British Library Document Supply Centre
- computers in other departments or libraries

Word-processing and spreadsheet applications

Though the original concept of the project was all-embracing, even grandiose, the realization was more modest, concentrating largely on library automation applications. A prototype linkage between information retrieval and library automation was established as part of the project, but the integration of the two functions was never realized in practice and the dichotomy remains in many libraries even in 1992.

Design principles

The design principles for the proposed integrated library automated system were:

- the use of common files, so that data is keyed in once only and then used for many different purposes;

access to all facilities from the same screen and with the same design philosophy for user interfaces.

It was recognized that, for any one function, a multi-functional facility might be less sophisticated than a custom-designed single function package. At the time we also suggested that the design philosophy for automation in the small library might be significantly different from that for a large one. A mixture of manual and computer systems might be the best solution for the small unit and an ‘all-singing, all-dancing’ approach might not be required. For example, a 1:200 exceptional event in a large library with 50,000 transactions represents 50 events per week and may require an additional software module. In contrast, in a small library with 25,000 transactions, a manual system could well be adequate to cope with the resulting two to three events per week. Subsequent experience has largely disproved this hypothesis: even the smallest unit requires the same singing and dancing as the largest. Much of the subsequent history of BookshelF has been devoted to acquiring the sophistication we had originally thought (or hoped) would be unnecessary.

The research project

The project started with two surveys:

(1) of the needs of small libraries for automation;
(2) of available hardware and software.

Seven small libraries of widely different character were studied to provide a more complete picture of need than would be offered by a single library. The seven libraries were those of:

The John Radcliffe Teaching Hospital (Cairns Library)
The Oriental Institute of Oxford University
Sir Alexander Gibb & Co., a firm of civil engineers in Reading
The Rutherford Appleton Laboratories, Didcot
The Central Veterinary Laboratories of the Ministry of Agriculture, Fisheries and Food (MAFF), Weybridge

Rothamsted Experimental Station
The Royal College of Surgeons, London

Data were gathered by one or more visits to each library and discussions with library staff.

Choice of software and hardware

Reference has already been made to the very limited penetration of the library market by microcomputers when the project started. The state-of-the-art in 1982 was defined in survey by Burton[4] of academic libraries, by Eyre[5] of Aslib members and by Singleton[6] of industrial library and information service. From our own survey of available hardware and software, it rapidly became evident that the key decision for the project was the choice of operating systems.

When the project started, most microcomputers used single-user operating systems and CP/M was the *de facto* standard, though MS-DOS was just beginning to make an impact. The choice was between a CP/M network or one of the multi-user operating systems which were now entering the microcomputer market: UNIX, OASIS or PICK.

A CP/M-based product which attracted attention was INMAGIC, a database/information retrieval package which is still widely used on MS-DOS machines. Network technology on several operational sites was assessed but was judged at the time (1983) to offer neither the reliability nor functionality required. It was therefore decided to seek a solution based on either UNIX or PICK which were competing for the microcomputer market. Both offered much of the power of mini/mainframe operating systems.

We had a strong preference to base the project on existing software but only one commercial product was available on either system: BRS/Search, an extremely powerful and sophisticated information retrieval package, running on UNIX, and based on the software used by the BRS on-line host in the United States. At the time, BRS/Search was marketed in the United Kingdom by Communication, Studies and Planning (CSP). It offered a flexible cataloguing and search facility but no other modules were available. Its use in the project would require the design and programming of circulation and acquisitions modules and their integration with the information retrieval software. In an exploratory experiment, CSP* created a prototype circulation module but the response times were too slow to offer any hope of success and BRS/Search was abandoned as a possible solution.

The remaining option was a PICK-based system. An Oxford based software house, Logical Choice, was interested in exploring the potential advantages of the PICK file structure in creating library automation software. They had developed a 4th Generation applications generator, CREATOR, which they proposed to use to write the necessary software. Given that no ready-made software was available, this approach had several advantages:

- the software could be developed according to our own design specifications.
- it could be designed from the beginning as an integrated system, rather than being created by adding modules to an existing single function package or by combining several existing modules from different producers. (The outcome was to be one of the first library automation products to be designed as an integrated system.)
- it would provide a test of the claimed advantages for library and information retrieval applications of the file structures and report-generating facilities of PICK.

Logical Choice agreed to produce the software without charging development costs in return for design specifications supplied by the project staff. A payment was made to Logical Choice which was judged equivalent to the price at which the product would be marketed as a commercial package for microcomputers. (Much to their regret, the authors did not ask for 5 per cent of any subsequent income.) At this point the name BookshelF was adopted.

After the event (1992)

It is of some interest to note the current (1992) status of the options considered in 1982–83. CP/M has been replaced by MS-DOS though one software package, LIBRARIAN, operated on a concurrent-CP/M (and subsequently MP/M) network until

* We wish to acknowledge the assistance and enthusiasm of Peter Gethin and Graham Seddon of CSP who wrote the prototype circulation module.

recently when it transferred to concurrent-DOS. A UNIX version is also being developed. Off-the-peg local area network (LAN) technology is now well-established and widely used, though libraries are only just beginning to instal networks and LAN-based library automation systems are not yet widely available.

UNIX is the dominant multi-user operating system with PICK established in more specialized areas. PICK has been the favoured system for library packages, examples of which are URICA and DYNIX. Recently GEAC, one of the longest-standing minicomputer-based systems, has been implemented on PICK. The competition between the two systems has in part been resolved by the development of 'PICK on UNIX' systems such as UNIVERSE and UNIDATA. These combine the communications and networking strengths of UNIX with the information retrieval capabilities of PICK. BRS/Search has now been developed into an integrated UNIX-based library automation package, UNICORN, which was recently (1991) introduced into the UK.

The 'typical' library

The analysis of the operations of the seven small libraries provided the specification on which Logical Choice based the design of BookshelF. Though it was hoped that the seven libraries provided enough variety to produce a package of general applicability, the analysis demonstrated that there was no such thing as a typical library. The range of libraries in which BookshelF was subsequently implemented demonstrated the converse: there was no such thing as a typical market for BookshelF. Present sites include public and further education libraries of a type never envisaged as potential users in the initial study.

Implementation in the Cairns

The Cairns Library was to be used as a test-bed for the new software and the available hardware. We were fortunate that, when we were ready to purchase hardware, 16-bit multi-user machines had just entered the market. Twelve months earlier, the project would almost certainly have used an 8-bit machine which had already provided evidence of serious degradation in performance in a multi-user environment. The hardware chosen was an Altos 586–40, a 16-bit machine, based on the Intel 8086 chip, with 512 kb of RAM, a 40 Mb Winchester disc, 4 ports expandable to 8, and a tape-streamer back-up. In 1984 this configuration, with 4 QUME terminals and the PICK operating system, cost £19,000!

The schedule for introducing functional modules was affected by the requirements of both the research project and Cairns Library management. Implementation was also influenced by the departure of the research assistant (Hilary Dyer) to take up a permanent post. Because of the resulting reduction in staff-time available for the project, full implementation was spread over several years and was not achieved within the lifetime of the project. The Project report to British Library gives a snapshot of the state of implementation at the end of the project period (September 1985).

At the start of the project, the perception of both Cairns management and the project staff was that the automation of circulation control was the most urgent operational need because of the high-cost in staff time and the high error rate of the manual system. In principle, a circulation control system could have been implemented using only bar-coded copy numbers. In practice, we decided that a minimum catalogue record including title and authors was necessary. Moreover, caution dictated that the implementation of a new, untried system should start with modules that had least direct impact on the end-user: cataloguing and acquisitions.

The catalogue of the short loan collection was the first function to be automated with the 800 records being input by keyboarding from a shelflist. This retrospective exercise provided the opportunity to identify and correct many of the teething troubles of the new software though at some cost to the library staff involved. It proved an ideal test collection with some 2 000 volumes representing 50 per cent of all loan activity. Acquisitions and *current* cataloguing, together with a Catalogue Enquiry module, came into operation in September 1984. All new orders and the corresponding catalogue records after that date were handled exclusively by the automated system.

Retrospective conversion of the remaining 11 000 items in the Cairns stock was accorded a relatively low priority. The Cairns is a 'current' library and the shelf-life of most of the bookstock is in the range of 5–20 years. In this case, retrospective conversion was a problem that would go away if left long enough.

In practice, conversion of all items available for loan was completed over a four-year period. Circulation Control was implemented for the short loan collection in August 1987, three years after acquisitions and cataloguing came on-line.

As soon as the Cataloguing module was implemented, the card catalogue was closed though still available for readers. A printed catalogue list, offering access to records by author, keyword and title, was created for all subsequent acquisitions. As the printed list increased in size, one of the concerns of library staff was that readers assumed that all stock appeared in the printed listing in spite of reader instructions drawing attention to the closed card catalogue.

An OPAC (On-line Public Access Catalogue) did not form part of the original specification (because of lack of time, not intention). The Catalogue Enquiry module provided with the cataloguing software was modelled on existing on-line information retrieval systems. It offered the functionality but not the ease-of-use of an OPAC and could have been made available to end-users. In the event, we decided not to do so, but to rely on printed listings until a custom-designed OPAC became available.

An OPAC was developed subsequently by SCG (see below) but implementation in the Cairns was postponed to allow testing of user reactions to experimental interfaces. An OPAC was not provided to Cairns users until 1989. In retrospect the less cautious approach of making Catalogue Enquiry available to users might have been preferable.

Conclusion

The lifetime of the project saw major advances in microcomputer technology. Price and size decreased while disc and RAM capacity increased; multi-user configurations became more widely available and the gap between minis and micros narrowed. A wider range of good quality software was becoming available and some suppliers were beginning to develop multi-functional library packages. By the end of the project the question: 'could the microcomputer offer automation for the small library?' had been answered in the affirmative. The questions now being asked were how a library could choose a system to suit its size and function.

There was little doubt that BookshelF constituted a viable system, a conclusion which was shortly to be tested in the market place. Toward the end of the project Logical Choice began to seek additional customers and BookshelF was implemented on three other sites: Harwell, the Fife Health Board and the Department of Library and Information Studies at Loughborough University of Technology. Continuing operational experience at the Cairns with the existing modules together with feedback from these new sites contributed to the further development of the software. In particular, a serials control module was developed, independently of the research project or the Cairns.

However, Logical Choice did not have the necessary marketing organization for selling to libraries and looked for another company to take over this responsibility. In 1987, they sold the exclusive UK marketing rights for multi-user installations to Specialist Computer Group (SCG), a company based in Stoke-on-Trent, in return for a royalty on each copy sold. SCG have made major improvements in the software though retaining the basic design structure defined in the research project. New modules include an OPAC, a Thesaurus and Management Information. As a result of the marketing and product development efforts of SCG since 1987, there are now 121 BookshelF sites (as of November 1991).

Logical Choice maintained an interest in the project by continuing the development of BookshelF-PC a single-user version running on REVELATION, which provides a PICK environment under MS-DOS. Marketing of BookshelF-PC has been largely targeted at the secondary school and college market. It has recently been made available as an MS-DOS network version and renamed HERITAGE.

BookshelF and BookshelF-PC (now HERITAGE) both derive from the same source but have been developed independently over the past six years to serve different markets.

References

1. Leggate, Peter and Dyer, Hilary (1987), *The development of a microcomputer facility for small libraries*. Library and Information Research Report 42, London, British Library Research and Development Department.
2. Ibid., pp. 4–5.
3. Ibid., p. 6.

4. Burton, P.F. (compiler) (1981), *Microcomputer applications in libraries and information retrieval: a directory of users*, The Library, Leith Nautical College.
5. Eyre, J., Personal Communication.
6. Singleton, A. (1982), *Information technology in industrial information services. A survey of what is available and how it is used*, Primary Communications Research Centre, Leicester University (ISBN: 0–906083–22–2).

3 Hardware and software

Jonathan Willson

The choice of operating system is a key decision in the development of a software product. It will determine which manufacturers' hardware and peripherals can be used as well as the wider range of applications software. To understand something of PICK is, therefore, essential to understanding the evolution of BookshelF.

PICK operating system

The PICK operating system provides the means to store, process and retrieve information whilst automatically taking care of the use of printers, terminals and hardware such as memory, disks and other storage devices. Since 1965 it has become an industry standard operating system for multi-user computers. It is distinguished by its data structure, multi-user performance, virtual memory management and ease of use.

PICK has highly efficient system usage which is optimized to suit the hardware configuration. Variable length data records keep storage volumes tight. The effectiveness of memory management means that large applications can be run on small kit. There is no limit to the number of files per system or per application. The virtually unlimited file size and variable fields and records make it particularly suited for business and commercial applications which support large databases. Many PICK installations in the United Kingdom are found in the health service, local government and libraries.

The emergence of PICK as an industry standard operating system is largely due to the close control which has been maintained over its implementation. The first commercial implementation of PICK came in 1972, known as the Reality operating system on Microdata hardware (subsequently McDonnell Douglas). It was later ported on the Honeywell Ultimate and during the same period development began of an emulation called Information, designed to run on Prime computers. The first implementation on IBM equipment came in 1981 and was rapidly followed by a number of major manufacturers including Altos, ADDS Mentor and General Automation. The release of the PC-XT version in 1984 and the PC-AT version the next year meant that PICK was now available on equipment ranging from the personal computer right through to large mainframes. The PC was turned into a multi-user micro that could support from three users and the large systems could handle many hundreds of users.

A unique combination

PICK is a database management system that is truly integrated with an operating system. It incorporates features that are found only as add-ons in other systems.

ACCESS — A relatively free format retrieval language that is used for database enquiries. English-like sentences containing verbs, file names, selection criteria and modifiers are used, for example, to extract, list, sort and total data. It is a very powerful feature that is quick to learn and simple to use.

ACCESS is known under various names depending upon the implementation of PICK: ENGLISH (McDonnell Douglas), INFO/ACCESS (Mentor), INFORM (Prime), RECALL (Ultimate).

BASIC — A powerful programming language that is easier to use than standard BASIC. It has the facility to interact with ACCESS. PICK/BASIC is also known as DATA/BASIC (McDonnell Douglas) and INFO/BASIC (Prime).

EDITOR — A line editor which allows on-line modification of the database. It can be used to create and/or modify any element of data within any file in a system, including PICK/BASIC programs, PROCs, datafiles and dictionaries.

PROC — A stored sequence of commands that can be executed by input of a single (word) command. PROCs can simplify day-to-day system management, and may comprise a complex sequence of events or be a regularly used ACCESS command.

RUNOFF A text processor that produces formatted documents such as letters or reports. It handles such things as justification, headings, page numbering and can automatically produce an index and table of contents.

TCL Terminal Control Language is the primary interface between the user and the computer system. All other processes such as EDITOR or ACCESS are invoked from TCL, as well as system utilities and an unlimited number of user-defined procedures. The environment can be tailored for each user. An alternative name is PERFORM (Prime).

Compatibility and portability

Available on micros, minis and mainframes, the PICK operating system offers the user upwards compatibility. The user seeking to protect a software investment can upgrade their computer hardware as use and demand require. The 'family' of PICK implementations also gives the user portability from one manufacturer's equipment to another. This hardware independence is a key feature that is shared with the other major industry standard operating system, UNIX. The user's investment in a particular software package is retained even if the hardware is changed. The links that can be established between machines to share files and application programs may also be considered an advantage. With a few exceptions, it is relatively easy to transport an application between different PICK systems.

PICK and UNIX

UNIX is fast becoming the standard non-proprietary multi-user operating system, be it one of the UNIX, POSIX or Open System Foundation AIX 'flavours'. As yet there is no single standard. The user is not tied to a single manufacturer or supplier and the operating system is available across the range of hardware from micros to mainframes.

Strengths of UNIX include portability, flexibility, networking facilities which are implicit in its design, the huge range of software packages available, suitability for office automation and PC links. Its weaknesses fall into the areas of system and network monitoring, back up, archive and restore functions, user-friendliness, machine sizing and security.

The success of UNIX in becoming the largest selling operating system has raised some concern about the future of PICK. With their respective strengths and weaknesses, PICK and UNIX can complement each other. Both can co-exist on the same machine. UniVerse and UNIDATA provide systems running under UNIX that are compatible with and can run PICK programs. UNIX may not be the top performer or the product most suitable for many applications but it has two major advantages: it is readily available and it is highly adaptable. PICK already exists as a single standard version and it integrates a database management system with programmer development tools. PICK is ideally suited for the end-user where UNIX requires considerably more programming work to achieve a similar flexibility of output.

BookshelF and the Specialist Computer Group

In 1987, the Specialist Computer Group (SCG) acquired the exclusive rights to market a multi-user version of BookshelF in the United Kingdom. Logical Choice would receive a royalty on the sale of each module covered by the agreement – Acquisitions, Catalogue, Circulation and Serials. SCG in turn was allowed to modify and enhance the existing modules and to go on to develop new modules and utilities.

It is often the case that when new software products are launched they are not fully developed. The library automation market is no exception. When SCG introduced the multi-user version of BookshelF to the market, it enjoyed the advantage that the key modules were already in place. Success followed quickly and by the year end 17 BookshelF systems had been sold to a variety of libraries.

The Specialist Computer Group is made up of a number of companies including: Specialist Computer Systems and Software (SCSS), Specialist Peripherals and Maintenance (SPM) and Specialist Digital Systems (SDS). BookshelF fitted into SCSS. As its name implies, SCSS is a systems and software house. Initially it had close links with Prime and in recent years has diversified. Libraries became one of a number of vertical markets in which the company specializes; amongst these are carpet distribution, institutes and membership organizations, retail travel, accounting and ledger systems. SCSS has also built up a reputation for bespoke software both within its existing markets and for one-off systems. This strategy has two principal benefits. The portfolio of products gives stability: SCSS is not subject to the conditions of a single market. The product teams contain a huge range of expertise: this expertise is available as a resource for all product development.

Specialist Peripherals and Maintenance was set up both to supply computer peripherals and to provide engineering support. The range of peripherals includes VDUs, lightpens, disk and tape drives, printers, modems, PCs and consumables such as printer ribbons, toner and magnetic tapes. Delivery and installation services are also available. Engineering support on-site is offered under maintenance contracts which may include fixed annual costs, minimum call-out or response times, and replacement equipment in the event of partial or total system failure.

The Specialist Computer Group can thus offer a total package of services to its customers. Typically, for a library choosing the BookshelF system, SCG can supply all hardware and software, deliver and install the equipment including cabling and telecommunications, provide hardware and software support and maintenance, and training. The company's location in Hanley, Stoke on Trent, is well-placed to serve customers throughout the United Kingdom. Access to the motorway network, mainline railway services and the proximity of Manchester airport ensures that personnel can arrive on site at short notice. BookshelF customers in Plymouth, Ipswich and Paisley are equidistant from Hanley. As the SCG customer base has expanded, staff have relocated. A new office and engineering base in Slough serves London and the South. Support librarians for BookshelF are currently based in Scotland, Slough and South Wales as well as Hanley.

Hardware

The multi-user version of BookshelF was developed to operate in the PICK environment. SCG could take advantage of the portability afforded by the operating system to install BookshelF across a wide range of hardware platforms. SCG has never been tied to a single hardware manufacturer although special relationships are maintained with a number of companies. Thus BookshelF has been marketed to the range of libraries in every sector. Hardware from different manufacturers can be configured to the precise needs of the customer rather than attempting to match every customer to a single manufacturer's range. BookshelF had been conceived as an integrated automation system for small libraries – SCG firmly believed that it was suitable for all types and size of library. BookshelF could be installed on minicomputers to serve public, government and large academic institutions, and on PCs to accommodate colleges, medical, special and other smaller libraries.

In practice the larger BookshelF systems were initially installed on Prime computers. SCG was one of the major VARs (Value Added Retailer) for Prime and received a high level of support. In particular, Prime already had a significant installed base in academic institutions and could thus provide an entry for BookshelF. The reputation of Prime for reliability and maintenance was an important consideration. Larger systems have also been installed on the ADDS Mentor range and at a single site on a Honeywell Ultimate.

At the lower end of hardware requirements, BookshelF has been installed on a wide range of PCs. These include models from Apricot, Arche, IBM (PC-AT and PS-2), Tulip and Zenith. The PC-based systems support from three to 17 users. PICK licences are available to support a greater number of users but the demands of larger systems are usually best handled by a minicomputer. A version of BookshelF, Mobile BookshelF, has been developed to operate on portable PCs or laptops, such as the models from Arche and Zenith. Mobile BookshelF is thus suitable for the mobile services of public libraries, for part-time service points and as a back up system. In the case of a total power failure, operation can be maintained by the use of battery packs.

Peripherals are chosen from the ranges of established and leading manufacturers. VDUs or dumb terminals installed across the range of BookshelF sites include Link 125, Visa MC-5, Televideo and Prime. Individual requirements, for example, to use existing customer hardware, can be met by terminal emulation software. Hardware is recommended based on monitoring by SPM. Reliability is assessed on the basis of component failure and other maintenance needs. It is worth noting that SPM has many maintenance-only contracts with companies and organizations throughout the United Kingdom. Across this wide base, any problems with the reliability of any product is rapidly identified so that, if necessary, remedial action can be taken or the problem can be raised with the manufacturer. Dot-matrix printers are usually sourced from Epson and laser printers from Hewlett Packard. SB Electronics is the one of the principal suppliers of barcode reading equipment.

The move to UNIX

BookshelF is now available under the PICK and UNIX operating systems. SCG has tended to design its software products around industry standard operating systems rather than proprietary systems. The move to UNIX is a natural and logical response to market trends. Increasingly, organizations are adopting a UNIX policy for all their computer-based systems. Suppliers to the Government, for example, must conform to the POSIX standard. The trend is seen in local government, educational institutions and the health service. Libraries which are normally part of a larger organization in turn are moving over to UNIX. More and more manufacturers are switching their production to UNIX-based systems, whether abandoning proprietary systems or other industry standards.

The first BookshelF UNIX-compatible systems were installed on the Prime UNIX range. The range of manufacturers' hardware has subsequently diversified and now includes Bull, Hewlett Packard, Sun and Unisys. It should be possible to install BookshelF on any hardware that supports a version of UNIX which is compatible with UNIDATA. UNIX brings to libraries many of the benefits of office automation. Increasingly BookshelF users access their system via PCs instead of dedicated dumb terminals. Facilities such as word-processing, electronic mail and on-line searching can be shared with normal BookshelF use.

Software

BookshelF in 1992 is substantially different from the BookshelF to which SCG acquired the rights in 1987. There are new modules and the functionality of the original modules has seen many advances. A few general observations are appropriate before discussing specific areas.

SCG acquired the rights to develop a multi-user version of BookshelF. The needs of larger single-site libraries could thus be accommodated. As a prerequisite to breaking into the large systems marketplace, multi-site capabilities had also to be introduced. Many of the features demanded of larger systems have also become available to the smaller BookshelF user. SCG has up to the present maintained a policy that all BookshelF users should operate on the same software release. Thus BookshelF customers in smaller libraries enjoy the same level of functionality as the largest systems. The functionality is also shared across the different operating environments. The port of BookshelF to UNIX has proved relatively easy and has not required a major system rewrite.

In addition to the standard implementations of BookshelF – single and multi-site – a significant number of customers have bespoke modifications and other unique features. This option is usually only available to organisations with an adequate financial resource and which may also place a high premium on having the product tailored to their specific needs. That said, there are numerous smaller sites where minor changes have been made to meet local operational requirements.

Major developments and new modules

The section that follows is intended to give a brief overview of the major developments and new modules. Many of these are dealt with in greater detail in subsequent chapters. [Note that this chapter describes developments into the early part of 1992.]

Thesaurus

Thesaurus was the first new module to be developed by SCSS. Designed to integrate with Catalogue and Enquiry, the module provides the structure for each library to set up a thesaurus based on the keywords assigned to records. The thesaurus can be used to validate the input of keywords on new records. In Enquiry, the thesaurus feature is activated by keyword searching and helps the enquirer to refine their search strategy.

MARC Catalogue

BookshelF was originally developed as a non-MARC based library automation system. Prospective users can opt for either a

MARC or a non-MARC Catalogue module. The MARC Catalogue module ensures the integrity of MARC records whilst retaining the functionality of the other BookshelF modules. A unique feature is that the cataloguing environment can be set to any MARC standard such as UKMARC, LCMARC, OCLC-MARC, AUSMARC and so forth. The environment is tailored by MARC tag definition tables which also accommodate local tags. The MARC Catalogue system is also used for importing MARC records to a BookshelF system, both on-line by downloading records captured on a PC or off-line from magnetic tape. The tag definition tables act as a precise filter so that imported records require a minimum of editing. MARC records can be imported to MARC and non-MARC BookshelF databases.

Authority control

All versions of the Catalogue module feature a subjects file and are compatible with the optional Thesaurus. The Catalogue is separately available with Author authority control. Personal and Corporate Authors are keyed on an acronym which provides efficient access to the authority file and significantly reduces the amount of keyboarding required of staff. Preferred, non-preferred and related headings are maintained. The index features a sophisticated browser and global updating of headings. New and variant headings in records imported to the authority system are automatically tagged for the attention of staff. The MARC Catalogue module is also available with a modified form of authority control.

Multi-site BookshelF

The Acquisitions, Circulation and Serials modules are available for single and multi-site operations. Developments have been made not only to meet the requirements of public libraries automating multiple service points, but also academic and other libraries operating on multiple sites. There are a number of shared systems, that is, different libraries sharing the same processor. In one case, a BookshelF system is shared between a library in Sheffield and two others in London. The multi-site version will support any number of service points and which may be arranged by group or area.

Some features associated with multi-site are illustrated:

Acquisitions	Centralized ordering with centralized receipt and processing; Centralized ordering with decentralized receipt and processing; or Decentralized ordering with decentralized receipt and processing.
Circulation	Issue, renewal and return of any item to any service point; Site-specific borrowing entitlements; Reservations system-wide, within a given area or group, or restricted by site.
Serials	As Acquisitions, centralized and decentralized ordering and receipt.

Enquiry and OPAC

Enquiry is the command-driven interface for searching a BookshelF database. Initially, BookshelF was unusual amongst library management systems in featuring only this command mode; other systems offered OPAC only or both OPAC and command interfaces. The command interface features an extensive Help sub-system and a user-definable tutorial but this did not allay the criticisms of some potential customers. The view was frequently offered that a library's users would not adapt readily to such an interface. The experience and observations of actual customers did not, however, support this argument.

In response to market expectations the menu-driven OPAC was launched. The menus, including help screens, are fully user-definable. The Help system is also context sensitive. Any number of sets of OPAC screens can be created; in effect, the OPAC can be terminal specific. For example, in a multi-site system, the OPAC displayed at each library can be individually tailored to the site and offer different types of search facilities. Different levels of support can be built in, to create search options which are often termed 'novice' or 'expert'. For ease and speed of OPAC creation, a Screen Designer was developed. The OPAC can be extended to accommodate local or community information facilities.

Enquiry, OPAC and the Screen Designer are integral to each version of the Catalogue module. Unlike some library management systems, they do not have to be purchased as additional modules. In the current development phase, the Help sub-system in Enquiry has been made user-definable, and the help messages and instructions are displayed in small windows. The facility to place reservations via the OPAC has been made available, and library users can also access their borrower details. Security of access is safeguarded by the use of a PIN number. Enquiry and OPAC usage by staff and borrowers can be optionally logged, to produce statistics on levels of use, the types of search strategies, the proportion of failed searches and as an indicator of subject requirements.

OPAC on CD-ROM

SCSS have developed the facility to reproduce the catalogue on CD-ROM. OPACs in this format are soon to be available in a number of BookshelF sites. Disks will carry bibliographic data for the library's holdings, but no loan details due to the transient nature of circulation data. It will be possible, however, to switch between the CD-ROM and the real-time system if a user requires status information pertaining to specific copies of a title.

The CD-ROM may be used in either novice or expert mode.

'Windows' interface

BookshelF can now be supplied with the Microsoft Windows user interface, allowing the user to switch between programs and packages by clicking on an icon, using a mouse. Thus, for example, a user may switch rapidly between the Issue program to Catalogue Enquiry and then to a word processing or spreadsheet package – and back to the Issue program. With the click of the mouse, the system will return precisely to the point at which the user started.

Enhanced management information

The adoption of the Windows environment has considerably enhanced the presentation of the management information which may be generated from BookshelF (See chapter 9). Statistical data can now be presented in graphic form, ie pie-charts, graphs and histograms.

For example, Figure 3.1 displays the number of issues which were made by each district in a public library system for the year 1990/91. Figure 3.2 illustrates a more detailed analysis of issue statistics for the Western district, which can be obtained by a click of the mouse on the 'Western' icon.

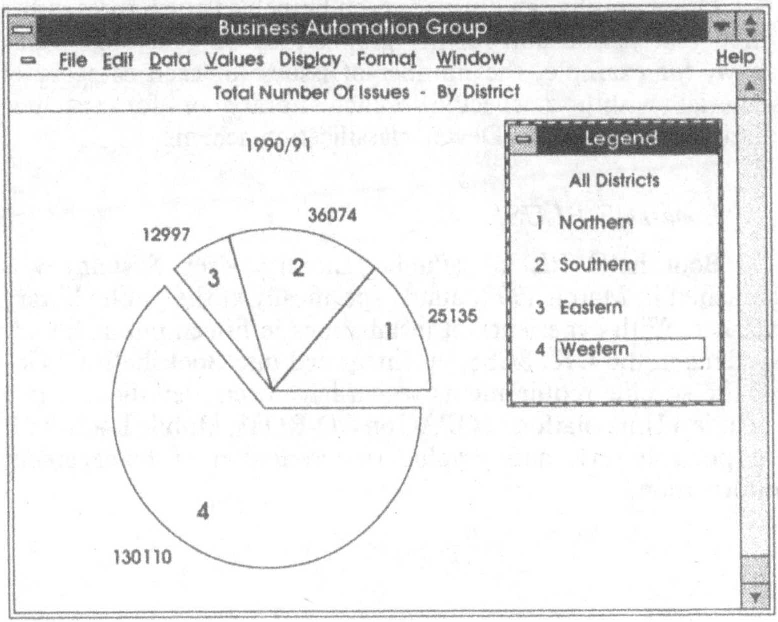

Figure 3.1 Issue figures for each district

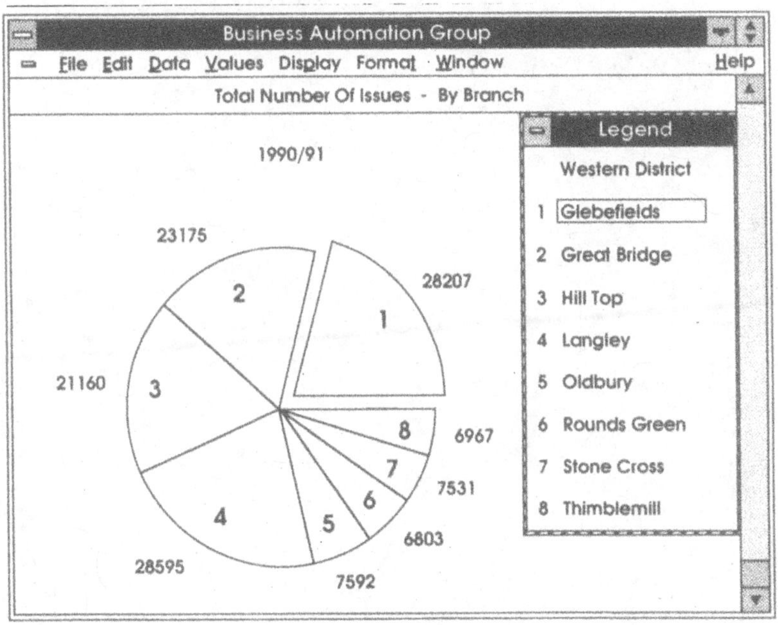

Figure 3.2 Issue figures for each branch

Other graphs can illustrate each branch's issue figures over a three year period and further graphs may be generated which show, for example, the number of issues for each category of material within a specific branch library or for specified disciplines within the Dewey classification scheme.

BookshelF PLUS!

BookshelF PLUS! (Public Library User System) was launched in March 1992, aimed specifically at the public library market. With experience of installations in fifteen public library systems in the UK, SCSS has integrated into BookshelF PLUS! all the specific requirements which have been identified. These include a Unix platform, OPAC on CD-ROM, Mobile BookshelF on portable PCs and graphic representation of management information.

Part 2 The BookshelF system

4 System-wide parameters and features

Introduction

Before examining the main modules available in BookshelF, it is useful to highlight system-wide, or global, features and perhaps answer the more general queries which prospective users may have. This chapter explains the fundamental aspects of the BookshelF library system which enable it to function effectively.

System security is addressed first. Libraries – especially large, dispersed organizations – often require the facility to assign differential access rights to specified users. This will range from read-only access for the public user, using the OPAC, to full access rights for the system manager.

Details of screen-handling functions are given next, to provide the prospective user with a perspective on the degree to which the system is user-friendly.

Finally, in this chapter, programs which pertain to the whole system, and not just to specific modules are detailed. System definitions are data which need to be defined in the initial stages of system implementation. Such definitions include media types, location codes, area and site codes (for multi-site versions of BookshelF) and subject definitions.

System security

It is desirable, particularly in large library systems, to maintain some control over access to BookshelF by library staff in order to maintain the integrity of the system. For this reason, users are provided with the facility to limit and control access to

the total system;
specific modules;
specific programs.

Security is enabled with the use of passwords to individual screens and program functions, and with the allocation of differential access rights to specified users. Passwords can be task-specific or person-specific. They can provide either read/write or read only access to specified data and program files.

There is also the potential problem of 'hackers' among the library's clientele who use the OPAC or Catalogue Enquiry. SCSS have pre-empted any occurrences of illegal entry to the system by creating Catalogue Accounts which are Read Only and entirely separate from the working datafiles and programs. These Accounts appear and function as the OPAC and are updated in parallel with the Catalogue database, but access to any other programs in BookshelF is denied to the OPAC user.

Screen handling

Function keys

The keyboards which are supplied with the BookshelF system have dedicated, labelled function keys as illustrated in Figure 4.1.

Help (F1) provides context-dependent help relating to fields in input screens. e.g. in Serials Control, codes for publication frequencies can be viewed on screen by pressing the Help function key.

Quit (F2) takes the user out of the current screen to the previous menu.

Whilst entering or editing text in fields, the operator can use *Insert* (F3) and *Delete* (F4) without having to retype whole lines and *Scan* (F14) will position the cursor at the end of a line with one keystroke.

Previous (F12) and *Next* (F13) allow the operator to move between fields while editing text and the arrow keys (F5,6,7,8) enable movement between lines of text in multi-value or multi-

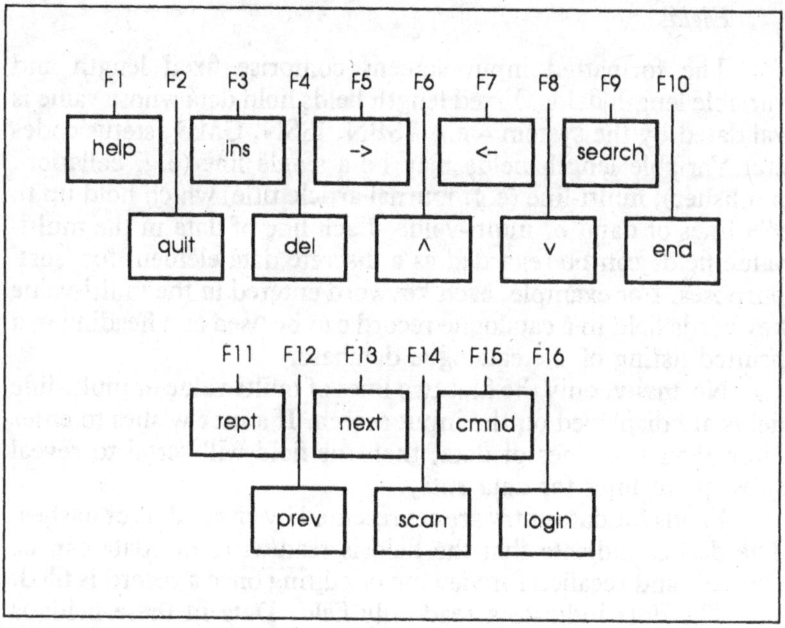

Figure 4.1 BookshelF function keys

line fields. *End* (F10) positions the cursor at the bottom of a record after editing, so that the amended record can be filed.

Repeat ('Rept' – F11) enables data entered in the same field in the previous record to be copied to the current record. The Repeat key obviates the need for re-keying if, for example, a set of books with the same series title is being catalogued.

The *Search* (F9) function key allows small files of data to be searched for specific values or to be displayed on the screen. For example, if a user wanted to check which Circulation rules had already been defined, the cursor would be positioned in the first field of the input screen, the Search key pressed, and the user would be offered the option to search for a specific rule or to display **all** Circulation rules. The Search function should not be used on large files, such as the Catalogue, as this process involves sequential searching of the file, and can be a relatively lengthy process.

The *Command* (F15) and *Login* (F16) function keys provide a short cut to invoking the BookshelF software. These keys are disabled for public use.

Fields

The formatted input screens comprise fixed length and variable length fields. Fixed length fields hold data whose value is validated by the system – e.g. ISBN, ISSN, GMD, status codes etc. Variable length fields may be a single line (e.g. collation, publisher), multi-line (e.g. journal article title) which hold up to 999 lines of data, or multi-value. Each line of data in the multi-value fields can be regarded as a discrete data element for 'sort' purposes. For example, each keyword entered in the multi-value keywords field in a catalogue record can be used as a heading in a printed listing of the catalogue database.

Normally, only the first two lines of multi-value or multi-line fields are displayed on the input screen. If a user wishes to enter more than two lines of data, then the field will scroll to reveal subsequent lines for data entry.

Fields for data entry are represented by either dots or dashes. The dashes indicate that the field is read/write i.e. data can be entered, and recalled for viewing or editing once a record is filed.

The dots indicate a read-only field. Data in these fields is entered in other relevant modules or options in the system, but is reflected in screens which carry related data, e.g. in Accession File Maintenance in the Catalogue module, a standard number is entered and allocated an accession number. The system automatically retrieves title information (using the ISBN) from Catalogue Maintenance, and is displayed in a 'dotted' field. Similarly, subsequent loan information for each copy is retrieved from the Circulation module, but reflected in the read-only field in Accession File Maintenance.

Editing data

Fields represented by dashes may be edited after the record has been filed, simply by typing the field number at the bottom of the screen and <Enter>. This positions the cursor at the beginning of the appropriate field. The system will not allow the editing of fields which are represented by dots.

System reference data

The establishment of module-specific reference data and system-wide definitions and parameters require some analysis of

SYSTEM DEFINITIONS MENU		
1. Locations	5. Accession status	A. Areas
2. Media	6. Accession streams	S. Sites
3. Default values	7. Order streams	U. Users
4. Last numbers	8. Subject definition	

Figure 4.2 BookshelF system definitions menu

Note: The (A)reas, (S)ites and (U)sers options are only available on BookshelF 'multi-site' software which is intended for organizations which share the same system but preserve decentralized Acquisitions or Circulation control. Some details of using multi-site software in Dumfries and Galloway public libraries are given in Chapter 13.

the library system by the acquiring organization. Any library or information unit which purchases a BookshelF system needs to investigate current practices and procedures and match these with the facilities afforded in BookshelF for setting parameters in line with local needs.

Each module in BookshelF includes a menu option labelled **'Reference data'**. The programs which are contained in these options enable the library to set up parameters to tailor the relevant module to the library's own requirements. Reference data which pertains to specific modules is explained in the relevant chapters. For example, **Indexed fields** allows the library to define which fields in the catalogue record should be indexed and therefore available on Catalogue Enquiry and OPAC. This option resides in the Catalogue module reference data. **Circulation rules** allows the system manager to define which categories of reader may borrow which media type and the period of loan. Thus, this facility resides in the reference data programs of the Circulation module. The facility to define codes and details of library suppliers resides in the Acquisitions module – and so on.

This section focusses on system-wide, or global, reference data i.e. parameters which pertain to all modules (see Figure 4.2).

These parameters must be defined before the BookshelF system can become functional. For example, until codes, descriptions and associated information are established in the system for 'Locations' (i.e. branch libraries or other units in the library organization), the library staff cannot:

(a) add individual copies of titles (see 'Accession File Maintenance – Catalogue module);
(b) order/receive copies of titles (see 'Order requests and catalogue update'; 'Orders: write, review, cancel' and 'Receipts' – Acquisitions module);
(c) set up circulation rules (see 'Reference data' – Circulation module), and
(d) add individual copies of serial titles (see 'Journal copy definition' – Serials module).

Some system definitions interact with each other or are dependent on module-specific reference data. This means that there is a pre-defined order for setting up definitions and codes in the system. The order is:

1. Area codes
2. Order streams
3. Site codes
4. Accession streams
5. Locations
6. Default values
7. Last numbers

Media and subject definitions are independent of extraneous codes and may be created at any time. User codes are dependent on area, site and location codes. They may also be dependent on the siting of terminals and Login identifiers. Accession status codes are pre-defined by the software and may not be altered by library staff.

System definitions – functions

Individual functions which are indicated in Figure 4.2 will be discussed in this section in the order in which it is required that they be defined in the system.

Area code definition

Area codes need only be defined by users of the 'multi-site' BookshelF software and they carry significance only in terms of Reservations within the Circulation module. It is likely to be used by public library systems in that it allows the library to choose whether to place reservations throughout the system i.e. targeting all branches, or to use the area codes to limit reservations to Sites within a particular area, or to limit reservations to its own site stock.

An 'area' refers to a group of one or more 'site' libraries (Option S). The way this is defined depends on the library organizations own perceived groupings – e.g. they may be geographical, or by institution served.

A one- or two-character code and a description of the code of up to 30 characters is defined by the library authority, e.g.

E	East Area
WL	Wigan and Leigh
CS	Central and South Areas etc.

'Areas' need to be defined before 'Sites' can be set up.

Order streams

A multi-site facility, this program is used to define prefixes for order numbers for use in the Acquisitions module. Separate prefixes, of up to three characters can be set up for each Site, or Area which is responsible for local acquisitions. If the Acquisitions procedure is fully centralized, then only one order stream prefix is needed. This program also allows the user to check the last order number used in a specified order sequence.

Site code definition

Site codes are significant for the Circulation and Acquisitions modules. Circulation rules (which reside in the Circulation Reference data) include location codes and the latter are attached to site codes. The system checks locations when an item is issued and returned. The library may also seek to satisfy reservations from site-wide stock. In the Acquisitions module, when an item is ordered or received, the system checks that the order stream and location match the Site. A 'dummy' location exists on the system from installation as a default to allow the user to 'get started'. This can be edited subsequently, and the user-defined codes substituted.

The data attached to the site code includes name of library, address, telephone, area code, order stream, and Default

GMD*Location (most frequently issued media type/busiest library).

Accession stream definition

This program is used to define prefixes for accession numbers. In BookshelF, accession numbers are unique numbers assigned to individual copies of titles. Indeed, any item which may be borrowed needs an accession number. The system performs a prefix check when the operator 'accessions' or adds new copies in either 'Accession file maintenance' (Catalogue) or 'Assign accession numbers' (Acquisitions). The accession number is also validated in the Circulation module when an item is issued or returned. If the stock is bar-coded, the accession number will be the bar-code number.

A minimum of one accession stream prefix is required by the system, but there is no upper limit. Prefixes may be alpha, numeric or a combination of up to three characters. Each location is assigned a single accession stream in the system, but the same accession stream may be assigned to different locations.

The meaning attached to accession stream prefixes is a local decision. For example, they may be used to signify different locations or different stock categories, or may indicate the year of purchase. SCSS advises that different prefixes are selected for pseudo-ISBNs, reader codes and accession numbers so that the operator can differentiate the numbers, at a glance, whether on the screen, written down, or on a bar-code label.

Locations

In BookshelF, the term 'location' may refer to (a) a physical location e.g. different library, separate room, closed access etc. or (b) a collection of items e.g. reference, local history etc. A location code is assigned to each individual copy of a title (i.e. accession). This may be changed on receipt of the item or at a later date, provided the item is not on loan.

A number of related parameters are attached to the location code and these can be specified on the same input screen. These include the budget code, accession stream, label class and site code. The budget code entered here appears as a default budget at the Ordering and Receipt of items stages. It is assumed that the budget code for the most likely budget will be charged when items are ordered for this location and that this will save keyboarding by the operator. The 'label class' code definition allows automatic formatting of spine, book and bar-code labels to a particular location's requirements.

Media

The GMD, or General Media Description, represents the type of material recorded in the database, e.g. (B)ooks, (V)ideocassettes, (C)artographic material, (S)ound recordings, (M)usic etc. Twenty-six GMD codes are available for the library to define according to local collection requirements. For example, a music library wishing to differentiate between audio-cassettes, compact discs, LP records and magnetic tape has the facility to assign separate GMDs to each medium.

The GMD is used subsequently in the Catalogue, Acquisitions and Circulation modules. It is a powerful tool. For example, when readers use the OPAC, a full description of the media type will appear prominently on the Enquiry screen whether the item is available, on-loan or on order. The library has a choice of which media codes to index for OPAC searching. Therefore specified media can be designated non-indexed and thus will not appear on the user's Enquiry screen – a useful facility for retaining confidentiality in documents which are for library use only. The GMD code is also used in combination with the reader category and location codes when establishing Circulation rules to determine which readers can borrow which type of material from which library – and for how long!

User number definition

A multi-site software facility, this program allows the library to specify the user number and location of each terminal/monitor in the system. Here 'location' is distinct from the 'location codes' as defined earlier. It means simply that the library can specify the precise locality e.g. 'J.R.'s' desk, reference counter, cataloguing room – processing table' etc. The user number definition allows a 'site' to be specified.

Last numbers

This option provides the facility for libraries to set the sequence of numbers, for example, to coincide with organization-wide order numbers. The last used number can be created or viewed in this screen. This program is used to define the sequence of numbers for

Numbers	*Relevant functions*	*Module*
Accession Numbers	Accession File Maintenance	CATALOGUE
	Assign Accession Numbers	ACQUISITIONS
	Issue/Return	CIRCULATION
Standard Numbers	Catalogue Maintenance	CATALOGUE
	Order Requests & Catalogue Update	ACQUISITIONS
	Catalogue Recommendations	CIRCULATION
ISSN	Serials Definition	SERIALS
Order Numbers	Orders: Write,Review,Cancel	ACQUISITIONS
	Process Order Requests	ACQUISITIONS

Accession status

Accession status codes are used to define the current status of individual copies of a title. They are reflected in Accession File Maintenance, Catalogue Maintenance and Catalogue Enquiry/OPAC and inform the operator or enquirer whether the copy is on loan, on order etc. The Accession status option allows the operator to view the available statuses , but not to add, amend or delete a status definition. These codes are pre-defined in the BookshelF software.

The following codes are used by the system

A	Available
B	Binding
H	Hold
I	Labelling/In process
L	On Loan
O	On Order
R	Reserved
T	In Transit

Subjects

This program maintains the definitive list of subjects into which the library catalogue may be categorized. In BookshelF, a subject relates to a broad subject category as distinct from a keyword which is more specific. Subject headings are assigned to individual catalogue records in Catalogue Maintenance and cannot be entered unless they have been pre-defined in Subject Definitions. Thus an element of authority control is provided. This program may also be used to provide a hard copy subject index showing class numbers, and scope notes.

Default values

This program allows the user to define the most commonly used, or preferred, values or codes and will display these automatically on the appropriate input screen. The most obvious benefit is that it saves the operator typing the same data repeatedly. So, for example, if the GMD for 'Book' has been defined as **B**, then it is sensible to create a GMD default as **B** as the book may be the most commonly catalogued item.

Twenty-five default values may be specified in the system. These include: bar-code type, claim delays (in number of weeks), currency codes, GMD, reader status codes, stamp dates (Issue program), routeing form for serials (i.e. type of route), discount percentages, label types etc.

5 Catalogue module

Introduction

The catalogue database is at the heart of the BookshelF system. It can be purchased as a stand-alone module if a library requires only bibliographic, indexing and enquiry functions. The Acquisitions and Circulation modules, however, are dependent on the Catalogue module, although these can be 'added on' at a later date. The relational nature of the system allows these three modules to be fully integrated and reference to features of other modules will be made in this chapter where appropriate.

The Catalogue module is not MARC-based although there is a facility available for downloading MARC records into the system from disk, tape, CD-ROM and on-line databases. The MARC conversion program is not a standard feature of the BookshelF Catalogue module and must be purchased separately.

This chapter will examine the detailed functions of the Catalogue module, identifying specific functions and fields within each of the menu options. The first section will provide an overview of each of these options and subsequent sections will examine elements of the input screens, processing programs and relationships between catalogue functions and other modules.

The Thesaurus module has been included in this chapter because of its strong links with Keyword indexing in Catalogue Maintenance and its role in searching the database in Catalogue Enquiry and OPAC mode. The Thesaurus facility enhances the already powerful retrieval facilities in BookshelF and is unique in its design among library management systems.

The OPAC screens and functions are shown alongside Catalogue Enquiry. The OPAC menus accommodate a Community Information option which can be rewritten and developed by librarians according to local requirements.

The Catalogue menu

There are eight main parts to the Catalogue module, as illustrated in Fig. 5.1. The user keys in the menu option number

CATALOGUE MENU	
1 Catalogue Maintenance	5 Execute catalogue indexing
2 Accession file maintenance	6 Labelling menu
3 Catalogue prints menu	7 Acquire from labelling
4 Catalogue enquiry	8 Journal article definition
A Acquisitions menu	R Reference data
C Circulation menu	F Finish

Figure 5.1 Catalogue menu

to select the appropriate program. The Acquisitions and Circulation modules can also be accessed direct from the Catalogue module.

Overview of options

Catalogue maintenance is the main program in which all bibliographic records are input to the system and where existing records can be edited. Catalogue maintenance provides a comprehensive bibliographic record, to which loan and order details are referenced. The data input to Catalogue Maintenance will be displayed in alternative formats when accessed through Catalogue Enquiry and the OPAC. Once a record added to the database has been filed, it can be recalled immediately in Catalogue Maintenance, but not in Catalogue Enquiry until it has been indexed. (Option 5).

Data may be input via the keyboard or may be downloaded into the system from existing electronic formats by SCSS. SCSS will provide assistance with, or undertake, retrospective conversion of existing manual or computerized catalogues according to the library's requirements.

Accession file maintenance is the program used to assign accession numbers to individual copies of a title. This allows the creation of a unique record for every book, journal article, videocassette etc. Information concerning individual copies e.g. location, order status and loan data is defined and updated with reference to this unique number.

Catalogue prints menu allows the production of a 'hard-copy' catalogue in a user defined format e.g. by class number, author, subject, keywords, media-type etc.

Catalogue Enquiry is the free-text information retrieval facility in BookshelF. It is a powerful enquiry system which allows global or field-specific searching, optional use of the Thesaurus, Boolean logic, and a wide variety of display options for screen or print output. The OPAC is the public interface to this enquiry system.

Execute catalogue indexing is an automatic routine which creates an inverted file of every word in every indexed field (see Catalogue – Reference data) in the Catalogue database. When a search is conducted in Catalogue Enquiry, terms are located in the inverted file from which pointers have been automatically set up to the appropriate bibliographic records. The Catalogue needs to be indexed before any new item added to Catalogue Maintenance or Journal Article Definition can be searched. The process of indexing the records requires that the contents of the Catalogue remain constant, therefore records should not be added, deleted or edited during this process. SCSS recommend that, for large databases, indexing should be undertaken when the library is closed and the program can be timed to do just this.

Labelling menu provides users with a range of options for defining and printing book labels, spine labels and bar-coded labels.

Acquire from labelling program is actioned after labels have been printed and automatically converts the status code of accessions from (I)n processing to (A)vailable.

The use of the labelling facility is optional, but it is a standard feature of the system.

Journal article definition is a specially formatted input screen to allow the inclusion of journal article details and abstracts on the Catalogue database. These details are integrated with the central database, created using Catalogue Maintenance.

Reference data

The Catalogue Reference menu allows users to tailor the catalogue module to their own requirements by

(i) defining which media-types and which fields of the catalogue records will be indexed and therefore accessible to users of Catalogue Enquiry and the OPAC;

(ii) creating a stop-list of specific words which are not to be indexed. The stop-list is a list of 'noise' words which commonly occur and which are unlikely to be used as access points in searching the database; and

(iii) creating files in which to store results of searches conducted on Catalogue Enquiry.

In common with other module-specific Reference Data and System Definitions (Chapter 4) there are some parameters which need to be established before the system becomes fully functional. In the following section, therefore, which details the features of each Catalogue menu option, Reference Data will be addressed first.

Fields and program functions

Reference data

The **Define Indexed Fields** input screen allows the user to specify which fields of the Catalogue records will be indexed. Indexed fields are defined for each different General Media Description (GMD) as shown in Figure 5.2. For example, all records with a GMD 'B' could be indexed on all fields or author, title and class number. Or all records with a GMD 'J' (journal articles) might be indexed on author, title and abstract.

Figure 5.2 illustrates the indexed fields which might be set up for a library holding (B)ooks, (J)ournal articles and (V)ideo-cassettes only. These media codes are pre-defined in Systems Definition (Chapter 4). The screen also shows the number of records on the database for each media type.

The **Index Stop-list Maintenance Screen** allows the user to add words or delete words from the stop-list. It may be modified by entering **W** at the prompt, and BookshelF will ask for the word to be entered. If a word is entered which already exists in the stop-list, the system will display the following message:

```
The word <word> already exists on the stop-list..
Its deletion would necessitate the re-indexing of the WHOLE catalogue..

Do you want the word <word> deleted? (Y/N)?
```

The user should proceed with caution from this point!

DEFINE INDEXED FIELDS

Fields available for indexing		GMD	Indexed fields	No. records
A = Author	Z=ISSN	A		
C = Class		B	ATCKY	27865
E = Editor		C		
F = Collation		D		
H = Edition		E		
I = Subjects		F		
K = Keywords		G		
N = Notes/Abstract		I		
O = Place		J	ATNY	3132
P = Publisher		K		
S = Series		M		
T = Title		O		
U = Input date		P		
Y = Year		T		
		V	ATFN	1267

Figure 5.2 Indexed fields definition screen (Reference data – Catalogue module)

The **User's enquiry file maintenance screen** allows the user to create a file to store search results from Catalogue Enquiry. A reader code (set up in the Circulation module) is attached to the filename and the reader's name will be displayed. The date on which the file was last used to store information is automatically generated by the system and the number of records saved is shown. The amount of disk space allocated for the file should also be stipulated by the system manager.

Catalogue maintenance

The Catalogue Maintenance input screen is two screens, or pages, in length and provides for a comprehensive display and input of bibliographic details and associated loan and order information.

Standard number is used to identify all records with the same title and edition statement. It can either be an ISBN or a number allocated in-house (with an alpha prefix) – a facility used mostly

```
BookshelF                CATALOGUE MAINTENANCE              09 NOV 91

1) Standard No ..............2) GMD ..........3) Class 1 ..........
                                                       2 ..........

4) Title 1 ................................................
         2 ................................................

5) F/names 1 .....................6) Surname 1 ................
           2 ....................            2 ................

7) Corp. Author 1 ...........................................
                2 ...........................................

8) Edition ........................9) Editor ....................
10) Place                  11) Publisher                 12) Year

   .....................    .....................         ....

13) Accession      Location          Status      Due date   No. of
                                                            copies
 1 ............    ...........         .        ...........
 2 ............    ...........         .        ...........   ..
 3 ............    ...........         .        ...........

   Modifications, FI(le), CL(ear), DE(lete) –
```

Figure 5.3a Catalogue Maintenance input screen – Page 1

for older material or non-book items. The system validates ISBNs to prevent miskeying. This is a mandatory field and is significant in that the ISBN is a key identifier throughout all the modules.

The *GMD* indicates the medium being catalogued. GMD codes are defined by the user in **System Definitions**. A default GMD, which automatically appears in the field, is defined by the library for the most commonly catalogued items to save keyboarding time. The GMD is also used in **Circulation rules**.

The *Class Number* field will accommodate any classification scheme and provides for added entry classmarks (up to 999!) – a facility which enhances the process of searching for subjects in the database. The multi-value class field also allows two or more libraries which are sharing the same system to use different classification schedules.

The *Title* field also allows up to 999 lines of information, all indexable and all with a searchable free-text facility. Enhanced titles might be entered to create additional access points. e.g. individual titles in collected short stories, titles of poems in anthologies, track titles on sound recordings etc.

BookshelF CATALOGUE MAINTENANCE Entry date .. 09 NOV 91

14) Collation ....15) ISSN ....

16) Series title ....

17) Series No. ....

18) Notes 1 ....
2 ....

19) Keywords 20) Subjects
1 ....1 ....
2 ....2 ....
3 ....3 ....

21) Recommenders 22) Reserves 23) Groups
1 ....
2 ....

24) Source ....25) Price ....

Modifications, FI(le), CL(ear), DE(lete) –

Figure 5.3b Catalogue Maintenance input screen – Page 2

The *Author's forename* and *Author's surname* will be displayed on the OPAC or in the hard-copy catalogue in its inverted form i.e. Cookson, Catherine as a heading. The field is multi-value therefore there is, in effect, no limit to the number of added entries which might be made. Thus, additional entries might be made for performers in sound recordings, films and video-cassettes, directors and producers, musicians etc.

The *Corporate author* field may be used instead of, or in addition to fields 5 and 6. Authority control is an available facility for this field, but it is not a standard feature of the basic system.

Editors may be entered in field 9, although the provision in the Author field for added entries might render the Editor field redundant.

Field 13 – Accession, Location, Status, Due Date, No. copies is a Read only field (indicated by the dots). This field exemplifies the relational nature of the system, in that the data is retrieved from other files and other modules in the system and displayed on the Catalogue Maintenance screen. *Accession* refers to the accession number assigned to each copy of a title. This is updated from Accession File Maintenance – Catalogue module, or may be updated from the Acquisitions module (Assign Accession Numbers). The *Location* of the copy (i.e. which collection; which library) is indicated by a code which has been pre-defined in **System definitions** and is updated from Accession File Maintenance.

Status refers to the availability of an item i.e. on loan, on order, in processing, reserved, available for loan, at binding. '*Due date*' does not always mean the date that an item is due for return. The meaning is dependent on the Status as follows:

STATUS		*DUE DATE*
L	(on loan)	Date due for return
A	(available)	Last date returned
O	(on order)	Claim date
I	(in process)	Claim date
B	(at binding)	Date due for return
R	(reserved)	Date by which should be collected
T	(in transit)	Last date returned
H	(on hold)	Last date returned

The *Collation* field allows only the briefest of entries e.g. number of pages. It is inadequate for some non-book media and for full physical description, as defined in *AACR2*. At present, cataloguers must use the Notes field for data which will not 'fit' into the *Collation* field.

ISSN is only used for periodical titles which are being input to the Catalogue database. The Serials module does not, at present, integrate with other modules, therefore separate input is necessary.

The *Entry date* is automatically generated when a record is entered and filed on the system. The Entry date is an indexable field and therefore can be retrieved in Catalogue Enquiry.

The *Series title* and *Series number* are entered in separate fields. If they are entered in parentheses, as instructed in *AACR2*, this should be taken account of when searching on the Series field in Catalogue Enquiry, as the system recognizes brackets as characters.

The *Notes* field allows for additional information. It may include elements of multi-level description e.g. contents listings, individual parts of series, etc. Information entered here, as with all other fields, may be retrieved in Catalogue Enquiry.

Keywords can be used for controlled or free language indexing. For controlled language indexing, the keywords field is linked to a thesaurus sub-module, which the user compiles from an existing printed thesaurus or from keywords allocated to the record at the indexing stage. The system alerts the user when a term is entered which does not exist on the Thesaurus and there is an option to add the term to the Thesaurus or to enter the term as a free language keyword. A search on the Keywords Field in Catalogue Enquiry will invoke the Thesaurus and offer a display of alternative search terms.

Terms entered into the *Subjects* Field must be pre-defined in Systems Definitions. *Subjects* is intended for broad subject headings related to specific disciplines e.g. History, Sociology, English Literature, etc. These subject terms are too broad for entry into the Keyword Field, but serve as headings in printed current awareness bulletins or new accessions lists.

The Price may be entered in sterling without the use of the £ sign.

Recommenders is a Read Only field which is updated either through the Circulation or Acquisitions module. It refers to readers who, at the ordering stage, have recommended that the library purchase a title.

Reservers is also a Read Only field and indicates the names of persons who have reserved a title, in order of priority. It is updated from the Circulation module.

Groups provides a method of grouping a number of titles together under one code. It is intended for reservation purposes. For example, it can be useful when there are several editions of a book, all with different ISBNs and the Reserver will accept any edition to satisfy the request. Codes used in this field are prefixed with the letter 'G' and followed by a number. New Groups can be set up in the Circulation module – reference data. Any number of titles can be added to a Group, using the ISBN as the key indicator.

The *Source* field may be used to indicate the source of the bibliographic details e.g. BNB, or if records have been downloaded from various sources, the database title might be entered.

Accession File Maintenance

The input screen is represented in Figure 5.4

The *Accession Number* is a unique identifier for individual copies of a title. It can be wholly numeric or be a combination of alpha and numeric characters. However, in order to enter an

```
SCSS                         BookshelF                       09 NOV 91

                      ACCESSION FILE MAINTENANCE

1) Accession No. ___________________2) Standard No. ____________

3) Author 1 ...........................4) Class 1 ....................
          2 ...........................          2 ....................

5) Title ..............................................................
         ..............................................................

6) Location __________7) Shelf Mark _________8) Status __
                      9) Trap _     10) Notes _________________

                              Loan Data

         Reader code ...............    Name .......................

      11) Due date ______________

      12) No. Renewals ___                 Max. Renewals ___

   Modifications, FI(le), CL(ear), DE(lete)
```

Figure 5.4 Accession File Maintenance – input screen

accession number a Stream Prefix (which may also be either alpha or numeric) must have been created in the System Definitions program.

It is also possible to set up the Stream Prefix so that when it is entered the next accession number in the sequence is generated. An accession number can be entered, therefore, in three ways:

i) by entering it in full;
ii) by reading it from a pre-printed bar-code with a light pen;
iii) by entering the Stream Prefix and keying <Enter>. This action will automatically generate the next available number in the sequence

The *Standard Number* (i.e. ISBN or pseudo) must already exist on the database. Once entered, the details of the item which were input in Catalogue Maintenance or Orders (Acquisitions), will appear on the screen.

The *Class, Author and Title* fields are Read Only to allow the operator to confirm that the details are correct.

Location refers to which library, section of the library or collection where this copy is to be stored. Location codes need to be created in System Definitions before details can be entered in this field. Default Locations, which are entered automatically, can be established for commonly occurring codes which the operator accepts at one keystroke or it can be overtyped with the preferred location code.

Shelfmark provides for any alternatives to the Class Number for shelf locations.

The *Status* code is one of the system's pre-defined codes. These are A(vailable), (H)old, (B)inding, On (L)oan, (R)eserved, (I)n process, (O)n Order. When creating a new accession record, it is only possible to enter the codes A, H, or I. B, O and R are updated automatically by the system. Only status A will allow items to be issued via the Circulation module.

If a *Trap* is required so that the operator is alerted when an item is returned from issue, the (H)old or (B)inding codes are entered. A Reservation will place an automatic trap on the first copy of a title returned from issue.

The *Notes* fields provide for any information concerning a particular copy e.g. reason for trap, copy faults. These Notes do not appear anywhere else in the system and are for internal consumption by library staff only.

Reader Code and *Name* allow staff to see at a glance to whom the copy is on loan. These are Read Only fields, automatically updated from the Circulation module.

Due Date is used in connection with the Circulation module and allows the facility to alter the date by which the copy should be returned from loan e.g. telephone renewals.

Number of renewals is also updated from the Circulation module. The field enables the operator to override the limit which has been stipulated in Circulation Rules. This limit is displayed in the subsequent Read Only field – *Max. Renewals*

Catalogue Prints Menu

The *Catalogue Prints Menu* provides options for the library to produce a hard-copy catalogue, sorted according to user defined criteria as represented in Figure 5.5.

Selection of options 1–4 displays a formatted screen with the value in the *1st Sort Field* entered automatically.

A *2nd Sort field* allows a sort on a secondary criterion. The most commonly used sort procedure is by Author and then by

	CATALOGUE PRINTS MENU
1	Sorted by Authors
2	Sorted by Title
3	Sorted by Subjects
4	Sorted by specified field
5	User defined print commands
T	Catalogue Menu
F	Finish

Figure 5.5 Catalogue Prints Menu

Title, but any field label may be entered e.g. by Subject then by Class Number. Any sort format may be entered providing the field label exists on the catalogue database.

Sort within media provides for grouping media types within the catalogue listing in alphabetical order of the GMD code.

Selected media allows specific media to be selected from the database for inclusion in the print-out. Thus a catalogue of sound recordings, including audio cassettes, compact discs and long playing records, excluding other media might be printed. Virtually any number of media types can be included for a selective listing.

Selected locations allows the printing of catalogues for specified locations e.g. branch libraries, sites etc. Any number of locations can be included.

Command name provides a facility for saving a complex sort/print specification for subsequent generation of print-outs. The allocated file name is automatically added to a table of *User Defined Print Commands*. In this latter option, commands are numbered and can be executed by simply entering the number of the file.

Catalogue Enquiry and OPAC

This program is the information retrieval facility in BookshelF. It is a Read Only program and therefore can be made available to library users.

Three modes of access to the Enquiry program are available:

i) *Command driven* – with Help facilities available 'behind' the screens on depressing the HELP function key

ii) *On Screen Help text* – in which the lower half of the screen is 'windowed' to provide 'pages' of instructions in narrative form. Enquiry remains command-driven, however.

iii) *Menu-driven OPAC* – in which help screens are formatted for user input and guide the user through a complex routine for performing searches. A standard default screen layout and OPAC instructions reside in the system, but libraries may rewrite and localize the text.

Command-driven Catalogue Enquiry

The *Command-driven Catalogue Enquiry* utilizes a simple command language. Indeed, some libraries using BookshelF prefer to retain the standard Enquiry mode for the public interface, because of its simplicity and speed. Its features and modes of searching are outlined in the following section.

Command language

Summary of commands

S <word>	to search the database
D	to display retrieved records on the screen
P	to output retrieved records to a printer
I <word>	to browse the index

Boolean operators

&	AND
!	OR
@	AND NOT

Searching the catalogue

Global or field-specific searches may be performed, e.g.

S DRUGS	will perform a global search i.e. of word in every indexed field in every indexed record
SA DICKENS, C]	will perform a search on author fields
ST, SC, SP etc.	will perform a search on title, class

	number, and publisher fields. Note that every field is indexable and therefore may be searched via Catalogue Enquiry (see Catalogue – Reference data – Indexed fields)
STK	will search title and keyword fields simultaneously. Any number and combination of search qualifiers (i.e. field label initials) may be specified
SK	will search the keywords field thereby invoking the Thesaurus

e.g. SK DRUGS will cause the system to indicate broader, narrower, related terms and synonyms if the keyword is also an entry in the Thesaurus.

Displaying retrieved records

A variety of record formats are available for the output of search results to screen or printer. In addition to bibliographic details, the searcher will be presented, according to the display format selected, loan details, number of copies in stock or on order, copy status (i.e. on loan, available, on order, at binding etc.), and location.

The default formats are displayed on screen, or printed, by entering **D** followed by a number between 1 and 7 as follows:

D1 ISBN (or in-house number), first Author, Title (1 line only)

D2 ISBN, Author(s), Title (in full)

D3 ISBN, Author(s), Title, Imprint

D4 ISBN, Author(s), Title, Location, Number of Copies

D5 ISBN, Author(s), Title, Location, Number and Status of Copies

D6 ISBN, General Media Description, Class Number, Title, Author(s), Edition, Editor, Imprint, Series, Series Number, Collation, Subjects, Keywords, Notes (2 lines), Accession Numbers, Status of Copies, Date due, Location

D7 will display the same details as format 6 but also show the full Notes or Abstract (in the case of journal articles)

Users may also define their own format for output, but this will only comprise bibliographic details, e.g.

DATC will display Author, Title and Keywords
DTPY will display Title, Publisher and Year
PCAT will print Class Number, Author Title etc.

The output appears on screen or from the printer in ISBN order. SCSS are currently upgrading the system so that the output of retrieved records will be printed or displayed in a more meaningful order, which may be user-defined.

Selecting records

If a search retrieves a large number of records, the user can select specific items from a list to create a new set of relevant records. Further details of each chosen record can then be viewed from a new list, obviating the need to view irrelevant records.

Search history

Search sets remain displayed on the screen and are numbered sequentially. Set numbers can be combined with each other or used in later searches in the same session using Boolean logical operators.

Boolean operators
ie. & AND , ! OR , @ AND NOT

e.g. *No. Search statement*

1	S	DRUGS & ALCOHOL	– will retrieve records which contain both the words DRUGS and ALCOHOL in any of the indexed fields.
2	S	DRUGS ! ALCOHOL	– will retrieve records containing DRUGS or ALCOHOL, or both.
3	S	DRUGS @ ALCOHOL	– will retrieve records containing DRUGS but not ALCOHOL

Set numbers may be used in subsequent searches e.g.

4	S	TEENAGERS ! ADOLESCENTS	
5	S	2 & 4	– will retrieve records containing DRUGS or ALCOHOL and TEENAGERS or ADOLESCENTS.

Note: Only one logical operator may be used in any single statement. There is no facility for 'nesting' terms.

Phrase searching

The system provides for searching on phrases (e.g. full titles)

eg. S THE MILL ON THE FLOSS
S CAMBRIDGE GUIDE TO ENGLISH LITERATURE

The Stoplist will contain 'The', 'on' and 'to', so in effect, searches will be performed for 'MILL & FLOSS', and 'CAMBRIDGE & GUIDE & ENGLISH & LITERATURE'.

Right-hand truncation cannot be used when conducting searches for phrases.

Truncation

The symbol for truncating terms is a right-hand square bracket.

e.g. S CAT] – will retrieve records containing the words CATALOGUE(S),-ERS,-ING; CAT(S); CATASTROPHE(S), -IC; CATALONIA, -N etc.

There is no facility for left-hand truncation or 'wild' characters.

Saving search results

Search results can be saved to disk either temporarily (i.e. until a subsequent login by a specific user) or permanently, in a user-defined file. At the end of each search session in Catalogue Enquiry, the system prompts:

End of session. Do you want to save your results? (Y/N)

If the user answers **N**, the system reverts to the Catalogue Menu. If the user answers **Y**, the following prompt is given:

Enter a codeword of your choice
Results saved under codeword
END OF SESSION

The system then returns to the Catalogue Menu. The next person to use Catalogue Enquiry will see the prompt:

A previous session's results have been saved. If they are yours then you may recover them by entering the codeword you chose.

In order to save search results permanently, i.e. to a user-defined file, the user types:

C <filename>

within Catalogue Enquiry. If no filename is given, a default file is created, using the line number of the terminal at which the search was made e.g. ENQ.L3

OPAC

As outlined at the beginning of the previous section, there are three types of Public Access Catalogue (OPAC) available in BookshelF viz:

- i) Command driven
- ii) On-screen Help text
- iii) Menu-driven OPAC

All OPAC interfaces are standard features supplied with the BookshelF Catalogue module.

The *Command-driven* 'OPAC' has been outlined as Catalogue Enquiry. All of the search facilities described here are also available in the OPAC modes, either with on-screen Help text or as a menu-driven facility.

Using the file editing facility in PICK or INFORMATION, specific terminals in the public area of the library can be defined for OPAC access only, presenting a user-friendly interface for accessing Catalogue Enquiry. System managers can be assured that these OPAC terminals can be rendered 'hacker-proof'.

On-screen Help text

This OPAC option remains command-driven, but the layout of the screen is slightly different from that of Catalogue Enquiry. The screen is divided into two sections. The top half shows the standard Enquiry screen with a simple prompt for commands. The lower half of the screen shows Help text on how to retrieve records (see Figure 5.6). The HELP text covers 26 pages and can be scrolled by pressing the NEXT or PREV function keys.

```
                    CATALOGUE ENQUIRY

Hits No.  Search Command
23   1    SA ROWLEY J)



>>

---------------------------------------------------------------

**************WELCOME TO BOOKSHELF**************

The program you are now using allows you to ask the computer if the library has
any items that may be of interest to you.

If this is the first time you have used this facility, or you're not sure what to do next,
please press the key laballed 'NEXT'. This will take you to the next help screen.

Press the NEXT key to see the next help screen.
```

Figure 5.6 On-screen help text for Catalogue Enquiry

The text can be re-written by library staff to suit the library's requirements.

Menu-driven OPAC

There are two formats for the menu-driven OPAC interface, in which one of the OPACs (OPAC1) is more explanatory and provides fewer options for field-specific searches than the other (OPAC2). OPAC2 also provides a Thesaurus facility, which OPAC1 does not. The hierarchy of the menu options for both OPACs is shown in Figures 5.7 and 5.8.

Whichever OPAC interface is used by the library, both include the facility to re-write or edit the screen text.

The default opening menu for both OPACs is shown in Figure 5.9.

On selecting the Library Services option, a reader will be presented with the option to search the catalogue, in addition to options to view details about opening hours, other branch or site libraries, mobile libraries etc. On selecting the Search option, a further menu is presented to the reader, requesting details of the search type (see Figure 5.10).

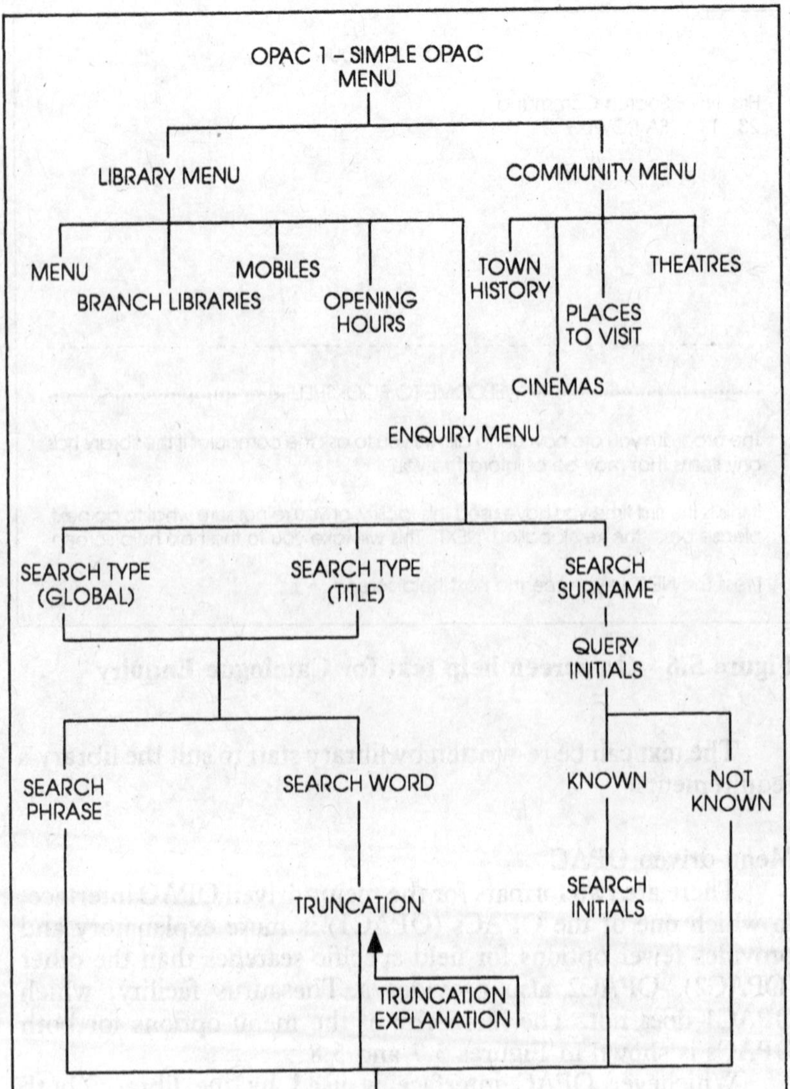

Figure 5.7 Hierarchy of functions – OPAC 1

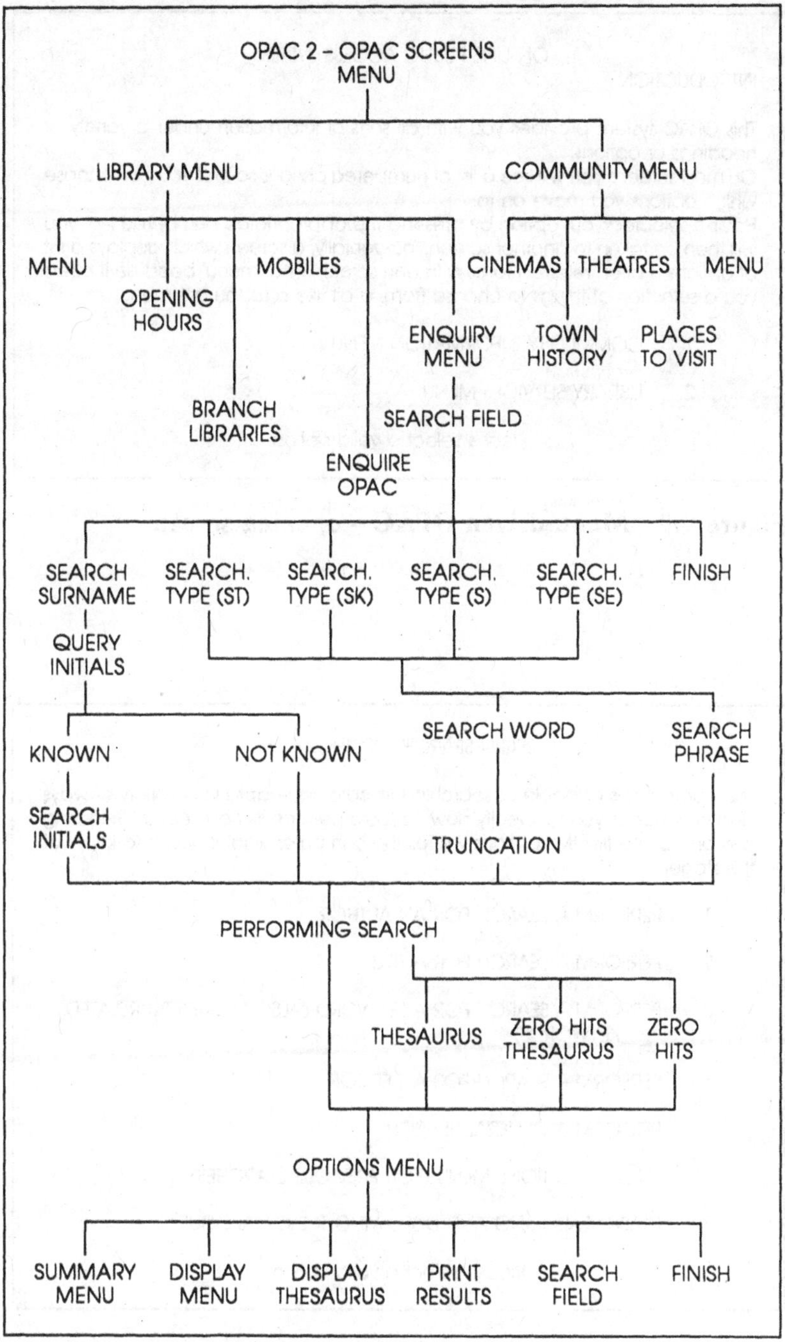

Figure 5.8 Hierarchy of functions – OPAC 2

ON-LINE PUBLIC ACCESS SYSTEM

INTRODUCTION

This OPAC system provides you with all sorts of information under a variety of headings or options.
On most screens you will see a list of numbered options so that you can choose which options you move on to.
Having selected your option by pressing the appropriately numbered key you will then be taken to another screen. Incidentally, a screen which displays a list of options is often referred to as a 'menu screen' or a 'menu' because it offers you a selection of things to choose from, a bit like a restaurant menu!

1 COMMUNITY INFORMATION MENU

2 LIBRARY SERVICES MENU

Please select a valid option

Figure 5.9 Menu-driven OPAC – opening screen

BEGIN SEARCH SPECIFICATION

The computer is capable of searching its catalogue data in a variety of ways and now needs you to specify how it should perform its next search. Selecting any one of the first five options will tell the computer what it needs to know at this stage.

1 PERFORM A SEARCH FOR AN AUTHOR

2 PERFORM A SEARCH FOR A TITLE

3 PERFORM A SEARCH FOR A KEYWORD (ALSO RELATES TO RELATED KEYWORDS)

4 PERFORM A SEARCH FOR AN EDITOR

5 PERFORM A GENERAL SEARCH

6 ENQUIRY OPTIONS MENU (FOR PREVIOUS SEARCHES)

7 FINISH SEARCHING AND DISPLAYING THE CATALOGUE

Please select a valid option

Figure 5.10 Search Menu – OPAC

DISPLAY RESULTS OF LAST CATALOGUE SEARCH

The computer allows you to display the catalogue records found in several different formats. The formats give varying degrees of information according to your requirements.

1 BRIEF BIBLIOGRAPHIC INFORMATION

2 BRIEF BIBLIOGRAPHIC INFORMATION (WITH HOLDINGS)

3 GENERAL BIBLIOGRAPHIC INFORMATION

4 DETAILED BIBLIOGRAPHIC INFORMATION (WITH HOLDINGS)

5 ENQUIRY OPTIONS MENU

Please select a valid option

Figure 5.11 OPAC display menu

COMMUNITY INFORMATION

1 TOWN HISTORY

2 PLACES TO VISIT

3 CINEMAS

4 THEATRES

Please select a valid option

Figure 5.12 Community Information menu

To view the search results, the user is presented with a menu which offers a number of display options, as illustrated in Figure 5.11.

It should be noted that both screen text and menu option text can be changed by the host library to suit local requirements.

Community Information

The second option on the opening screen of the OPAC allows users to select and view local information. The default menu and text, supplied as standard with the Catalogue module is shown in Figure 5.12.

LABELLING MENU	
1	PRINT LABELS
2	LABEL FILE MAINTENANCE
3	LABEL STATIONERY DEFINITION
4	LABEL CLASS DEFINITION
5	PRINTER CONTROL CODES

Figure 5.13 Labelling menu

Again the text and menu information can be changed to suit local requirements.

Execute Catalogue Indexing

BookshelF is a 'real-time' system, which means that when a record is added to the catalogue, it can be filed and recalled immediately. However, in order to use the Catalogue Enquiry facility (or the OPAC) the Catalogue Indexing program must be executed. This process creates an inverted file of every word from previously defined indexed fields (see Catalogue – Reference Data).

Option 5 of the Catalogue Menu invokes the Catalogue Indexing routine. It is recommended that the routine be run overnight, or when the library is closed, to avoid the interruption of work patterns or degradation of system performance. To facilitate this, the Execute Catalogue Indexing option allows either a delay or a time to be entered before the indexing process is initiated.

Labelling menu

As shown in Figure 5.13, the Labelling menu includes options which, together, allow the BookshelF user to print book labels, spine labels and bar-code labels.

The *Print Labels* option prints out any record which has its accession number in the LABEL file. These accession numbers will have been entered automatically for any records which have been brought into the system via the Receipts option in the Acquisitions module. However, option 2 – *Label File Maintenance* – allows records to be entered manually into the LABEL file.

Label Stationery Definition enables stationery formats for labels to be defined – i.e. label sizes and position of type on label. These specifications are assigned to a different label stationery codes for book, spine and bar-code labels.

Label Class definition allows the labelling requirements for each item-type to be specified e.g. book and spine labels, but not bar-codes for reference books.

Printer Control Codes allows the specification of a typeface for each type of label.

The use of the label production facility is optional and can be bypassed if not required.

Acquire from labelling

Option 7 of the Catalogue menu is the Acquire program. This should be executed after labels have been printed using the options in the Labelling menu.

This program is run to cause items to be Defined as (A)vailable after being processed through the Labelling routine, which is indicated by item status 'I' (In Process). The Acquire from Labelling program changes status 'I' items to status 'A', releasing them from Processing to make them available for loan.

The program will display on the screen the number of items it selects for this procedure and will list the item details to the screen or printer.

Journal Article Definition

The input screens for Journal Article Definition are illustrated in Figure 5.14.

This program allows journal articles to be catalogued and their records retrieved via Catalogue Enquiry. They share the same database with titles which are input to Catalogue Maintenance.

The *Control Number* is an in-house number used to identify each separate journal article, and comprises up to 10 characters. It is recommended that each number be prefixed with a 'J' to enable easy identification of such articles when searching the Catalogue.

General Media Description is automatically assigned the value 'J' to represent journal articles.

Entry Date is the date when the record was first entered on to the system. It is automatically assigned to this field. The Entry

SCSS BookshelF 09 NOV 91

JOURNAL ARTICLE DEFINITION

Control No .... Entry Date ....

1) Article 1 ....
   Title 2 ....

2) Forenames 3) Surname

1 ....

2 ....

4) Journal Title

....

5) Issue/Vol/Page ....6) ISSN ....

7) Keywords 1 ....

2 ....

3 ....

4 ....

Modifications, FI(le), CL(ear), DE(lete)

Figure 5.14a Journal Article Definition – input screen – page 1

Date is an indexable element in BookshelF and therefore may be used as a search term in Catalogue Enquiry.

The *Article Title* is a multi-value field which means that it can be of any length up to 999 lines. As is the case with all indexable fields in BookshelF, it has a free-text search facility.

SCSS BookshelF 09 NOV 91

JOURNAL ARTICLE DEFINITION

1) Abstract/ Notes

1 --

2 --

3 --

4 --

5 --

6 --

Figure 5.14b Journal Article Definition – input screen – page 2

Forenames and *Surnames* of authors are shown as separate fields but each line of the Surname field is linked to a corresponding line in the Forename field.

Journal Title, and *Issue/Vol/Page* fields provide for the Source information. These fields are single value, allowing only one line of information.

The *ISSN* (International Standard Serial Number) is validated by the system. In-house numbers (pseudo-ISSNs) may also be assigned. This field is not mandatory, so it may be left blank.

The *Keywords* field allows for subject terms or strings which may be assigned as additional access points. This field may be linked to the Thesaurus, if a controlled vocabulary is preferred.

The *Abstract* of the article may be input on page 2 of this option. This field is multi-value and indexable, and has a free-text search facility.

Thesaurus module

The Thesaurus module provides libraries with the means of controlling the index terms which are assigned to catalogue

THESAURUS MENU

1 DESCRIPTOR DEFINITION

2 SYNONYM DEFINITION

3 ENQUIRY

M BOOKSHELF MAIN MENU

F FINISH

Figure 5.15 Thesaurus menu

records. It also assists readers who are conducting searches on Catalogue Enquiry in the selection of alternative (broader, narrower, associated terms or synonyms) search terms.
The Thesaurus menu is shown in Figure 5.15.

Link with Catalogue

The Thesaurus is linked to the Keywords field in Catalogue Maintenance. Thus, when a catalogue record is created, and a term is entered into the Keywords field which has not previously been defined in the Thesaurus, the following prompt is displayed:

Term <term> is not on the THESAURUS file. Do you wish to enter it? (Y/N):

If **Y** is entered, the system will respond:

Term <term> will be added to THES.ENTRIES on filing the record

Thes.Entries is a file which contains all words and phrases which the operator has entered as a keyword in Catalogue Maintenance or in Journal Article Definition. These terms are held in this file until the user updates the Thesaurus file.

If **N** is entered, the term will be accepted in the Keywords field, but will not be linked to the Thesaurus.

```
SCSS                         Bookshelf                    09 NOV 91

                  THESAURUS DESCRIPTOR DEFINITION

      Word/phrase ......................Type _   Entered ............

      1)  Scope note

      ------------------------------------------------------------

  2) Broader terms        3) Narrower terms        4) Associations

     1 ---------------       1 ---------------        1 --------------
     2 ---------------       2 ---------------        2 --------------
     3 ---------------       3 ---------------        3 --------------
     4 ---------------       4 ---------------        4 --------------
     5 ---------------       5 ---------------
     6 ---------------       6 ---------------     5) Synonyms
     7 ---------------       7 ---------------
     8 ---------------       8 ---------------        1 --------------
     9 ---------------       9 ---------------        2 --------------
    10 ---------------      10 ---------------        3 --------------
```

Figure 5.16 Thesaurus Descriptor Definition – input screen

If a term is entered into the Keywords field in Catalogue Maintenance which has been defined as a synonym in the Thesaurus, the system will *not* allow the term and will prompt:

Term 'X' is a synonym to Term 'Y'

Thesaurus descriptor definition

On selecting this option from the Thesaurus menu the user will be prompted:

Do you want to update THESAURUS from THES. ENTRIES? (Y/N)

If **Y**, the system searches the Thes.Entries file, retrieves the first term which needs to be defined, and enters it automatically into the first field of Thesaurus Descriptor Definition screen which is shown in Figure 5.16.

If **N**, the system bypasses the Thes.Entries file and terms may be entered manually. These will be placed directly into the Thesaurus, once filed.

Term types

All terms defined in this screen are automatically given the marker **D** i.e. Descriptor. All terms which are subsequently defined as Synonyms are given the marker **S**.

Scope note

Each preferred term may be assigned a scope note to restrict or clarify the use of the term.

The user may enter as many *Broader Terms*, *Narrower Terms* or *Associated/Related Terms* in the respective fields as necessary. These are multi-value fields and will hold therefore up to 999 lines of data. These give rise to **see also** references, which the enquirer will see when using Catalogue Enquiry or OPAC.

Synonyms

Non-preferred terms are entered in the Synonyms field. These give rise to **see** references in Catalogue Enquiry or OPAC.

Synonym definition

A separate screen allows a single synonym to be defined for a range of descriptors, or preferred terms and the relevant Descriptor Definition screens will be updated automatically. Entries made in either Descriptor Definition or Synonym Definition will be reflected in the appropriate screens.

In Synonym Definition, it is only possible to enter a preferred term if it has previously been defined as a Descriptor.

Thesaurus Enquiry

Thesaurus Enquiry allows any terms whether Descriptors or Synonyms to be entered and viewed. Once a relationship between terms has been defined e.g. Broader, Narrower, this is reflected throughout the system.

Listing the Thesaurus

All terms entered into the Thesaurus may be listed alphabetically by Descriptor, to screen or printer using the command

SORT THESAURUS

The list will display every term in the context of its defined relationships.

6 Acquisitions module

Introduction

The Acquisitions module is implemented in conjunction with the following modules: Catalogue, Circulation, Thesaurus and Serials Control. The Acquisitions module operates closely with the Catalogue module.

Acquisitions is operated from the Acquisitions menu which is accessed from the BookshelF Main menu. The Acquisitions menu is shown in Figure 6.1. The Acquisitions Module covers orders, receipts, and claims.

The multi-site version of the Acquisitions module allows the user to opt for one of a combination of Order and Receipt processes. Thus, for example, the headquarters of a library authority may generate all orders for all locations (e.g. branch libraries, multi-site academic libraries) and perform all receipting functions for items received before despatching them to the branches/other libraries. Alternatively, sites/branches may be independent budget holders, responsible for generating their own orders and receiving new material in the home library.

Thus, the multi-site acquisitions software provides for the following situations:

1. centralized ordering with decentralized receipt of items;
2. centralized ordering with centralized receipt;
3. decentralized ordering with decentralized receipt;
4. decentralized ordering with centralized receipt. All of the operations associated with each of orders, receipts and claims for single-site systems are discussed below.

The functions of an Acquisitions module are basically to:

maintain records of items to be acquired;
maintain records of items on order;
print order, or otherwise order items;

check for overdue items and issue claims or chasers;
note the arrival of ordered items, or receipting, and prepare for payment;
maintain appropriate financial control;
produce various listings of books on order or recently acquired.

In order to support these functions the outputs from an Acquisitions module are:

printed listings of the order file;
a new accessions listing;
accounting information;
chasers or claims;
book cards and processing slips;
management reports.

Status flags

Throughout the Acquisitions module there are a number of operations being carried out on the processing of orders and receipts, and so status flags are displayed on the screen. These indicate the status of an order or the stage that it has reached in processing.

The status field on the order screens may be:

1. Blank – prior to an order being sent
2. H – hold which allows the order to be held.
3. S – sent.
4. C – completed order.

The status field on the receipt screens may be either S or C, as above.

The status of individual copies is reflected on Catalogue Maintenance and Accession file Maintenance as:

A	Available	L	On Loan
B	Binding	O	On Order
H	Hold	R	Reserved
I	Labelling/In Process	T	In Transit

1 Order requests and catalogue update

2 Process order requests

3 Orders: write, review, cancel

4 Prepare orders for printing

5 Print order slips

6 Print order forms

7 Receipts/claims menu

8 Assign accession numbers

9 New accessions listing

T Catalogue menu

C Circulation menu

R Reference data

F Finish.

Figure 6.1 Acquisitions menu

Acquisitions reference data

Before the other modules of Acquisitions can be used, data concerning suppliers and budgets must be created. Other reference data in respect of currencies and countries must be input if items are to be ordered from abroad. This reference data can be created and later reviewed through the Acquisitions Reference menu, which is shown in Figure 6.2.

Suppliers

Selecting Option 1 from the Acquisitions Reference menu will call up the 'Supplier Details' screen. The following fields are available for completion:

1 – *Code* – a code of preferably eight characters or less, for the supplier
2 – *Name* – name of supplier
3 – *Address* – comprises a number of sub-fields for entering the components of the address.

Acquisitions Reference Menu

1 Suppliers

2 Budgets

3 Currencies

4 Countries

A Acquisitions

F Finish

Figure 6.2 Acquisitions Reference Data menu

4 – *Claim delay* – there is usually a default period (in weeks), but this can be overwritten
5 – *Telephone*
6 – *Telex*
7 – *Currency* – filled with the code for currency, and details will be extracted from the Currencies Reference data.
8 – *Their ref.*
9 – *Notes.*

On completion of Field 9, the record can be filed, and the screen clears to allow a new supplier code to be entered.

Budgets

Selecting Option 2 brings up the Budget Code Definition Screen. This has the following fields:

1 – *Code* – Budget codes of one or two characters.
2 – *Description* – the name of the budget.
3 – *Balance* – This field includes:

Allocation – the total amount in any given budget
Balance – the total of the committed and spent sums
Committed – the amounts committed once orders are sent; cancellation of orders will return funds from committed to allocated.
Spent – when orders are received funds are moved from committed to spent.

4 – *Locations* – this is a display field and receives data from locations set up in Systems Definition.

Once a budget has been set up and locations assigned to it, it is not possible to delete the record.

Currencies

Currencies Reference data can be set up after the Countries data has been input via Option 4. The data entry screen has the following fields:

1 – *Code* – currency code of one or two characters.
2 – *Country* – country code as set up previously. Once the code is entered, the name of the country will be displayed.
3 – *Description* – name of the type of currency.
4 – *Exchange rate* – must be numeric.
5 – *Decimal point* – enter **Y** if a decimal point is required.
6 – *Last updated* – this is a display field that takes its input from the current date displayed and the field is completed whenever the exchange rate is changed.

Countries

Selecting 4 will bring up the Country Code Definition screen. This has two fields:

1 – *Code* – a one or two letter country code.
2 – *Name* – the name of the country.

Reviewing existing Reference Data

It is often useful to review data concerning suppliers, budgets, and sometimes, countries and currencies. This can be achieved through the use of the Search Function key. This involves:

Selecting one of the options: suppliers, budgets, currencies, countries;

pressing the Search Function key;

entering the number of the field in which you wish to do a search

The system then searches all entries and prepares a display.

It is also possible to search using the dictionary item name, but this is only recommended for experienced users, since the user must know the supplier or budget code.

Order requests and Catalogue update

Note: This section of Acquisitions uses the Catalogue Requests screen that is part of Catalogue Maintenance, which is described in Chapter 5.

Option 1 of the Acquisitions menu initiates ordering of items, at the same time as creating bibliographic records which will be added to the database.

Selecting Option 1 produces the Catalogue Requests screen (see Figure 6.3). The user first enters the standard number. If the number entered is one for which there is already a record on the database, the record will be retrieved and the data displayed on the screen. The cursor will move to field 11, Supplier code, awaiting instructions for the new order. If the order is for an item for which there is no record on the database, the user must enter the details as on the Catalogue Maintenance screen until reaching field 11.

The order fields are fields 11 to 17. Fields 11, 12, 14, 15 are mandatory. These fields should have the following data entered in them:

11 – *Supplier code* – A supplier code from one of the codes previously defined in Reference Data must be entered.
12 – *Item Price* – should be numeric.
13 – *No. Copies* – the number of copies for the location.
14 – *Location code* – A location code from one of the codes previously defined in Systems Definition must be entered. A default value will be displayed which can be overwritten.
15 – *Budget code* – A budget code from one of the codes previously defined in Acquisitions Reference Data must be entered. A default value will be displayed which can be overwritten.
16 – *Claim delay* – A default will have been set up via Supplier Details in Reference Data. This may be overwritten.
17 – *Order notes* – Any notes relating to the order can be entered, with one line of notes per order.

BookshelF CATALOGUE REQUESTS 09 NOV 91

1) Standard No .... 2) GMD .. 3) Class ....

4) Title 1 ....
2 ....

5) F/names 1 .... 6) Surname ....
2 ....

7) Corp. Author 1 ....
2 ....

8) Place 9) Publisher 10) Year

....

11) Supplier Code	Name	12) Item Price	13) No. Copies	14) Loc. Code	15) Bgt	16) Claim Delay
1	....	....	....	....	....	....
2	....	....	....	....	....	....

17) Order Notes
1 ....
2 ....

Page 1

Page 2
BookshelF CATALOGUE REQUESTS 09 NOV 91

18) Collation .... Entry Date ....

19) Edition .... 20) Editor ....

21) ISSN ....

22) Series Title ....

23) Series No. ....

24) Catalogue Notes ....

25) Recommenders	Names	26) Reservers' codes
1	....	1 ....
2	....	2 ....

27) Source ....

Modifications, FI(le), CL(ear), DE(lete) –

Figure 6.3 Order Requests and Catalogue Update

Once fields 11 to 17 have been completed page 2 can be called up and completed. This closely resembles the second page of Catalogue Maintenance. The only significant differences are:

25 – *Recommenders codes* – to record readers who recommend an item for purchase. A previously defined Reader code must be entered.
26 – *Reservers codes* – to record reservations for readers. A previously defined Reader code must be entered.

Filing of the completed record adds the record to the database. The next stage is for entries to be batched into suppliers. This is achieved by running Option 2 Process Order Requests.

Process Order Requests

Selecting Option 2 takes the user into the screen titled 'Acquisitions – Generates Orders'. The message on the screen will read: 'Enter the first unused purchase order number 'nn'.' Pressing <**cr**> will accept a number generated by the system. Alternatively, the user's own order number can be entered. For each order it is also necessary to enter the Supplier code and Supplier name. Once the order details have been entered new orders will be written to the order file. Option 4 Prepare Orders for Printing is the next batch process. Prior to executing Option 4 it is possible to change the Order details by retrieving the record as in Option 3.

Orders: write, review, cancel

Option 3 is an alternative method for ordering items. Option 3 can only be used once a bibliographic record has been created. Option 3 is the creation of an order for 'n' number of items from one supplier. Option 3 may be useful in that it separates the process of creating a bibliographic record from the process of ordering. In addition, Option 3 offers the opportunity to append internal notes, which is not available through Option 1.

Access to orders via Option 3 is by order number. A new number may be input; this may be a system generated number or a user's number. Input of an order number of an existing order will retrieve that order for review.

```
BookshelF                ACQUISITIONS – ORDERS                    09 NOV 91

1) Order          2) Supplier          3) Date of          4) Status
   number            code                 order

 .........         .........          .........            --

 Name................................Currency ..        Ref...............

5) Standard   6) Supp   7) Item   8) No     9) Loc   10) Bud   11) Claim   12) Ln
   Number        Ref       price     copies    code      code      date        Cancel

1 ........    ......    ......    ......    .....    .....     .......     .....
2 ........    ......    ......    ......    .....    .....     .......     .....
3 ........    ......    ......    ......    .....    .....     .......     .....
4 ........    ......    ......    ......    .....    .....     .......     .....

13) Supp.
    Notes 1 ......................................................
          2 ......................................................
          3 ......................................................

14) Int.
    Notes 1 ......................................................
          2 ......................................................
          3 ......................................................

                   Please enter the next order number
```

Figure 6.4 Orders – Write, review, cancel

The Acquisitions – Orders screen (see Figure 6.4) that is displayed in Option 3 includes the following fields:

1 – *Order number* – enter an order number.
2 – *Supplier code* – enter a supplier code.
3 – *Date of order* – the system will insert the current date, but this can be overwritten.
4 – *Status* – the status of the order; this is usually left blank, but there is the option to hold the order.
5 – *Standard number* – enter standard number of item(s) to be ordered. The author and title will be displayed at the bottom of the screen.
6 – *Supplier reference* – enter the identifying code set by the supplier, or the supplier's catalogue number.
7 – *Item price* – the price must be numeric and given to two decimal places.
8 – *No. of copies* – enter number of copies required.
9 – *Location code* – enter a pre-defined Location code.
10 – *Budget code* – enter a pre-defined Budget code.

11 – *Claim date* – enter date for claims; the system may default to a pre-set date.
12 – *LN Cancel* – line cancel; the system defaults to **N**.
13 – *Supplier notes* – Supplier notes relating to each order line. These notes may be printed on the order.
14 – *Internal notes* – for each order line.

Fields 5 to 14 are repeating fields, so that the details can be entered in respect of each item on the order. Once details of one item have been completed, the details of subsequent items may be entered. Once all items have been entered, pressing <cr> will file the order. Records can be deleted and cancelled, with two exceptions:

BookshelF will only allow orders to be deleted either prior to being sent or after they have been completed.

BookshelF will only allow orders to be cancelled after they have been sent. Once completed orders cannot be cancelled.

For orders that have not yet been sent i.e. those with null status, amendments are achieved by specifying the field number and line number, to bring the cursor to the point of data entry. Individual items on an order can be cancelled using the line order cancel facility at Field 12.

Prepare orders for printing

Option 4 assigns the status **S** to orders to show that they have been sent to printers. Choosing this option calls up the screen entitled: Process Orders for Sending. This offers the option to delete previous order slips. The screen also gives information which indicates that the order forms have been produced and the file in which they are stored, where they can be edited if so desired. Any queries are stored on the disk with Hold status and can be viewed and edited.

Printing orders

Orders may be printed as order slips by selecting option 5, or order forms by selecting option 6.

Order slips are generated for each title and are library definable. Typically they contain the basic information about the item that the supplier may require, such as:

ISBN
author
title
number of copies
imprint
price.

Prime users generate slips using RUNOFF. BookshelF sets up a file containing the order slips or forms. The Primos command RUNOFF may be used to create an appropriate Primos file for printing, and order forms and slips can be printed, using SPOOL.

Order forms are pre-defined and contain bibliographic and order details of up to 50 titles. The information for the supplier is as given above for order slips.

Both of the options 5 and 6 are batch processes and the user has only to confirm that they wish to run the routines.

Receipts/claims

Receipts and claims merit a separate sub-menu. This is displayed in Figure 6.5.

Receipting items

BookshelF allows users to receipt items ordered by two methods: Receipts Program 1 and Receipts of Bar-coded Stock Program 2. Receipts Program 1 was designed to receive items that has not been processed in any way by suppliers. The program assigns accession numbers, and it is necessary to use the Labelling menu in the Catalogue module. Receipts 2, Receipt of Bar-Coded Stock is used when the accessioning of items is carried out by the library or supplier. Most libraries will prefer one of these procedures and will not use the other. It is impractical to switch between the two options.

Receipts

Selecting 1 from the Acquisitions Receipts/Claims menu will display the screen entitled: Acquisitions – Receipts. Once an

```
                Acquisition Receipts/Claims Menu
          ______________________________________________

1  Receipts

2  Receipt of bar-coded stock

3  Claims

4  Print claims

A  Acquisitions menu

F  Finish.
```

Figure 6.5 Acquisitions receipts/claims menu

```
                              BookshelF
SCSS                   ACQUISITIONS – RECEIPTS                 09 NOV 91

Order Number     1) Supplier Code       Order date        Status

-----------      --------------         .................  ......................

  Name ............................................Currency ..........Ref ................

                      -------- Receipt details ---------

2) Standard   3) Supplr   4) Item   Copies    5) Now   6) Locn   7) Claim   Line
   Number        ref.no.     price  Ord/due      rec'd    code      date      Cancel

1  ---------  -------   -------...   ...      -----    -----    -------     .
2  ---------  -------   -------...   ...      -----    -----    -------     .
3  ---------  -------   -------...   ...      -----    -----    -------     .
4  ---------  -------   -------...   ...      -----    -----    -------     .

8) Notes 1 ---------------------------------------------------------------
         2 ---------------------------------------------------------------
         3 ---------------------------------------------------------------
         4 ---------------------------------------------------------------

Modifications: FI(le), CL(ear) –
```

Figure 6.6 Acquisitions – Receipts

order number has been entered, the details of the order will be displayed on the screen. To receive items type 5 comma and the line number of the order e.g. 5, 2. The cursor should now be positioned in field 5 and in the appropriate line. Enter the number of copies to be received.

To complete the receipting of items the record must be filed. To confirm that the record has been updated the order should be recalled. The field 'copies due' will reflect the amendments.

Multi-site version

When using the multi-site Acquisitions software, a check is performed by the system to confirm that the Location code is a valid code for that site when an item is received. For example, if a library operated a decentralized ordering system, then the Receipts program would only accept items to which valid location codes for the home library, or home site, were attached. 'Sites' can be two or more libraries which are grouped for budgeting or staffing etc. purposes. An explanation of codes for defining areas and sites is given in Chapter 4.

After receipting stock, the next options to follow are batch processes option 8 and 9, Assign Accession Numbers and New Accessions Listing, respectively.

Receipt of bar-coded stock

Selecting Option 2 from the Acquisitions Receipts/Claims menu, will display the screen entitled: Acquisitions – Receipt of Barcoded Stock.

When an order number is entered, the details of the order are displayed. The first screen shows order number, supplier code, order date, status, name, currency, invoice number and the details of the items on the order in terms of standard number, first author, title, location code and copies due. In order to receipt items it is necessary to enter

3, comma, and the line number.

This will bring up a window display. At this stage notes may be reviewed or appended, followed by input of invoice numbers and prices and locations. Press **<cr>** when ready to advance to adding an accession number.

The accession number can be inputted by using a light pen or by typing from the keyboard. The receipting process is completed by pressing the END function key with the cursor at the Acc No field. The screen will then clear to await a new order number. The record must be filed.

Receipt of unordered stock

Unordered stock can be received through the receipt screens. If the unordered items do not have an existing bibliographic entry on the catalogue it is necessary to have a bibliographic entry created before receipt.

To receive an unordered item **U** is entered. The receipt screen will allow input of a standard number. It is not possible to file details of unordered items, and recall the same record to add more items.

Claims

Selecting 3 Claims initiates the batch process associated with claims. The procedures are slightly different for Prime-based systems. The procedure for all other machines starts with a prompt that asks for confirmation that you wish to proceed. Next the cut-off date for claims must be entered. This is followed by the prompt:

> **Do you want the CLAIM.LETTER file cleared of previous letters [Y/N]**

The system will then process the letters and print out any errors or anomalies, but it is necessary to move to Option 4 Print Claims in order to print the letters.

Print claims

Printing claims is achieved via another batch process. Once you have confirmed that you wish to proceed, the Print Claims screen prompts for the entry of selected order numbers or an indication that all claims should be processed. The program then prints out the claim letters.

Process standing orders

Orders may be identified as a standing order through one of the fields on the order screen. Such orders are then processed through the Process Standing Orders option on the Receipts/ Claims menu.

Assign accession numbers

The procedure for executing this program is similar to all batch programs in BookshelF. First you are asked: 'Are you sure you wish to assign accession number [y/n]'. For machines other than Primes, the screen displays the selected items and a print out of accession numbers will be generated automatically. The listing will contain bibliographic details to enable users to match the physical items with the accession numbers. With Prime machines, the dialogue allows the destination of the print out to be specified.

New accessions listing

This program allows users to generate lists of new accessions.

The screen will prompt for a period start date and a period end date. You are then asked:

Delete this periods details once printed? [Y/N/Q(uit)]

Answering **Y** will allow the details to be printed out once and **N** the details to be printed out more than once. **Q** aborts the program.

7 Circulation module

Introduction

Circulation control is central to computerized library management systems. Many library managers attach considerable priority to the features that a computerized library management package might offer with regards to circulation control. Flexibility to tailor the processes to the policies of an individual library and to support changes in policies is important.

Circulation control modules must keep records to specify:

the items in the library stock;
the items on loan, and from whom or where they can be retrieved; and
when items on loan will next be available in the library for other customers.

In addition, most circulation control systems also:

recognize and trap reserved books on their return from loan;
prepare overdue notices;
notify over-borrowing and dubious borrowers;
facilitate the calculation and collection of fines; and
collect management information relating to circulation.

Circulation functions

Figure 7.1 shows the main Circulation menu for BookshelF. Options 1 to 9 cover the basic activities that might be expected to be encountered in a circulation control menu. These are organized with the most frequently used options first. For example, Issues is option 1, Returns is 2, and these are followed by Reservations. The remainder of the numbered options support various activities that are less likely to be conducted during issue, and which may be performed as batch jobs. In addition to the

SCSS		BOOKSHELF	09 NOV 91
		CIRCULATION MENU	
1	Issues	6	Catalogue Recommendations
2	Returns	7	Calculate overdues/fines
3	Reservations	8	Print overdue items
4	Reservation priorities	9	Reservation notifications
5	Readers	H	Display Circulation History
A	Acquisitions menu	R	Reference data
T	Catalogue menu	F	Finish
		Please select an option	

Figure 7.1 Circulation menu

numbered options there are options designated by letters. The Circulation History may be displayed, and reference data may be set or viewed. The other lettered options offer the opportunity to exit to the other menus and modules, such as Acquisitions and Catalogue, or to Exit and Finish.

The Circulation module of BookshelF operates entirely in real-time, interfacing with the Catalogue and Accessions File and the Reader File. Input is either through the keyboard or via a barcode reader. Changing from one operation to another is facilitated by the menu system. The Help function key at various levels within a program offers the facility to move between various Circulation programs by the input of a single character. The prompt is given in all cases at the bottom of the screen in the following format, when the Search key is pressed:

Commands: (R)eturn, Reser(V)e, (Q)uit.

Circulation Reference data

The Circulation Reference menu supports the initial establishment of a number of parameters that define the rules for

Circulation Reference Menu

1 Reader categories

2 Reservation groups

3 Circulation rules

4 Calendar

5 Dump circulation history

C Circulation menu

F Finish

Figure 7.2 Circulation Reference menu

circulation control for a specific library. These rules can also be reviewed and modified subsequently through the Circulation Reference menu. The Circulation Reference menu prompts the library manager to set Reader Categories, Reservation Groups, Circulation Rules, and the Calendar. The fifth option is to Dump Circulation History.

Reader categories definition

A number of reader categories must be defined so that each reader can be assigned a specific code. Each reader category is identified by a two-digit code. These codes must be set up before entering status information in respect of individual readers, and are displayed on the issues screen when the details of a reader are called up. The reader category code is accompanied by a description, which also appears on the issue screen. For each category the following parameters must be set:

1. Maximum number reservable is the maximum number of books that a reader assigned to this category can reserve.
2. Hold period is the maximum number of days which a reserved item will be held for this category of reader.
3. Overdue period and letter name. The librarian can set a series of overdue periods with associated overdue letters, so that,

when necessary, the system will trigger the printing of a series of overdue letters at the appropriate length of overdue period.

Circulation rules

Circulation rules must be established for each reader category code, and they must be established before any item from any location/collection can be loaned to a reader. Each set of Circulation rules has a code. This code is derived from a combination of reader status*GMD*location:

Reader status has just been discussed and will be defined in Circulation Reference Data, Reader Category.
GMD is defined in Systems Definitions, Media.
Location is defined in Systems Definitions, Location.

For each Circulation code, the following parameters must be set:

1. Maximum number on loan, or the maximum number of books that the reader can borrow under this rule. This will be displayed on the issue screen.
2. Maximum days on loan, or the loan period, will be reflected on the stamp date displayed on the Issue screen.
3. Maximum number of renewals permitted.
4. The fine table allows fines to be specified for various overdue periods. A number of different overdue periods can be defined, with associated fines rates. If desired a maximum fine can be set.

Calendar

In order that the system be able to calculate overdue periods, fines and other time-related parameters, it is necessary for it to have access to a definition of the days in which the library is open in any given year. A new calendar has to be set up at the commencement of each new year. The data that is stored is:

Days closed ie the days of the week on which the library is normally closed e.g. Sunday.
Dates closed, or any additional dates on which the library will be closed, such as Bank holidays.

Dates open, just to specify any dates which are exceptions to days closed e.g. if the library is open one Sunday in a year when it is not normally open on a Sunday.

Optional Reference Data

The remainder of the options that appear on the Circulation Reference Data menu are not mandatory. One optional feature is the use of the Group Definition code. A number of Group Definition codes may be set up. Each code serves to link a number of books in a group, by recording their ISBN, title and author. These groups can, for instance, be used when a student wishes to reserve all of the books on a reading list with the objective of merely borrowing the one that becomes available soonest. When one book has been borrowed he may wish to be taken automatically off the reservation list. This is accessed through the option Reservation Groups.

Dump Circulation History option is useful for keeping a copy of the circulation history. It dumps data from the Circulation History Files to the default back-up device, such as floppy disk or cartridge tape. Circulation history may also be restored from this device.

Issues

When Issue is selected the screen is cleared and the operator is asked for a reader code. In order to proceed a valid reader code must be input. This must be a code that has previously been set up using the Reader File. If there is some uncertainty about the reader code, such as in telephone renewals, the operator has the opportunity to input a surname, or, if that produces too many records, a postcode.

Once a valid code has been accepted, the following information is displayed:

Readers name;

Messages for or relating to the reader, as set up on the Reader File;

Expiry date of reader membership, if within four weeks of display date;

Stamp date;

Number of items on loan within category, and any loan stop that has been made;

Maximum number of loans allowed within category. If the maximum has been reached or exceeded 'LIMIT' is displayed.

The program now checks to see if a global loan stop has been placed. If it has, no loan is permitted until the stop has been removed.

Details of any reservations awaiting collection are displayed;

Details of unpaid fines;

Payment of fines can be made during issue. The use of the Help Key allows the operator to:

Display details of all items currently on loan to the reader, with the due date;

Go into the Returns Program;

Go into the Reservations Program;

Override the stamp date;

Quit the Issue program.

When the display has been read and acted upon, the operator presses the space bar, which erases the display of the reservation and fines information and replaces it with a prompt for the accession number.

Accession numbers may be entered through the keyboard or via a bar-code reader. Only accession numbers which are on the Accessions file can be issued. The Accessions file is maintained as part of the Catalogue module. The following data will then be displayed:

If the category of item is different to that defined on the default category for the reader, the appropriate details are displayed.

If issue of an item causes the maximum loan allowance to be exceeded, the operator is asked whether the transaction is to be operated or not.

The action to be taken depends upon the status of the item to be issued. Normally it will be available and issue can proceed. Should it be reserved and reserved for the reader to whom it is being issued, the transaction can continue and the reservation will be cancelled. If the book is reserved for another reader, the operator has to decide whether to proceed. Often the transaction will proceed, but with a shorter loan period or no renewal available. If the item is recorded as being on loan to another reader, it must first be returned, by transferring the Returns. If the reader is the one to whom the item is recorded as being on loan, the transaction is regarded as renewal.

When an item is issued using the multi-site version of the BookshelF Circulation module, a warning may be displayed on the screen to indicate that the item belongs to another library. The operator acknowledges this warning, but may proceed to issue the item. The multi-site version can also be parameterized to allow items to be borrowed from Library A and returned to Library B or Library C.

Renewals require a number of checks to be performed prior to registration of a renewal. The system will prompt the operator to consider whether the item is overdue, has been reserved, or causes the borrower's maximum number of renewals to be exceeded. The operator may also take the opportunity to shorten the loan period for a renewal, especially for reserved items.

Once one item has been entered, the operator is prompted for the accession number of the next item. When the return key is pressed, the program returns to the reader code prompt.

The multi-site Circulation software can be so defined as to allow renewal of an item at Library B, even though it was issued at Library A. Libraries may also adopt the Global Renewal facility, whereby a Borrower Enquiry function lists all items on loan to specific reader, and the operator has the option to renew all or selected items. This feature is particularly useful for libraries which offer a telephone renewals facility.

Returns

The Returns program prompts the operator to enter an accession number. Again, the use of the Help key allows the operator to move into Issue, Reserve, or to Quit. When an accession number is entered, the various checks are made. The possible status of the item are:

On loan;
Available, or not recorded as being on loan;

Labelling	–	the items needs to be sent for completion of labelling;
Binding	–	the item has to be bound;
Reserved	–	the item is placed on one side for checking of reservations;
Hold	–	the item has been trapped for housekeeping e.g. repair.

When a number of items have been returned by a reader, and fines are outstanding, the reader's name and amount outstanding are displayed on the screen, after the first accession number is read. The fines due on each item are cumulated into the total. Whenever there is an amount payable, the following prompt will be displayed throughout the transactions:

Press RETURN when all entries for this program are completed

When RETURN is pressed, the operator will be taken into the Fine Payment program.

Certain errors can occur when an item is returned. The most common of these are flagged by self-explanatory messages. Possible error conditions are that:

the item is not on loan;
the item is not on loan to this borrower;
reader code has not been defined;
accession number has not been defined;
circulation data is inconsistent.

These errors tend to arise because there has been some change in the data since the item was issued. This may have been a deliberate change, or error messages may be an early warning of the corruption of data. All errors of the above types are recorded in the CIRC.SIN or the CIRC.ERROR files, and should be examined later in order to identify the source of the error.

Multi-site version

When an item is returned to a library which was not the issuing site, the system alerts the operator that the item should be returned to the home library. The status code of the item is automatically changed to **T** (In Transit).

The receiving library processes the item in the Returns program, which checks for any 'stops' or reservations. This action generates reservation notification letters and automatically changes the status of the item to (A)vailable or (R)eserved.

Fines

Fines may be paid either in Issue or Return.

In Issue, when a reader code is entered, any amount owing is displayed at the bottom of the screen. The operator may accept full payment, part payment or no payment, and the amount paid is entered accordingly. A new amount due is calculated.

For flexibility, the payment of fines on return, can be treated in two different ways:

single reader, when all amounts due are payable by one reader.
multiple readers, when the reader is returning items on loan to a number of people.

Payment for a single reader is very similar to payment on issue. Payment for multiple readers builds up a report that shows a number of readers with the appropriate fines. The reader can then opt to pay the fines associated with selected readers only, and all accounts are updated accordingly.

The Fine Calculation and Update program updates the fines due and generates some general reports on the fine situation. It should only be run when all returns for the day have been entered through the Returns program, otherwise readers may be asked to pay fines on books that they have returned.

The program first asks whether fines are to be calculated for all categories or specific reader categories. Once a reader category has been defined, the program displays the running count of the number of reader items on loan, items overdue, and number of errors, before displaying the total of fine due. Once the total has been displayed, you are asked:

do you wish to produce overdue letters? [Y/N]

If the operator agrees to continue, the next screen also displays the number of overdue letters to be produced. When the operator presses the space bar, the Circulation menu appears.

Overdues

The production of lists of overdues and overdue notifications is clearly closely linked with fines, in that the two processes must draw on some common data. The Print Overdues option may be selected from the main Circulation menu. The associated program provides a checklist of overdues, for internal use, under the following headings:

Code
Reader name
Acc. No.
Due date
Fine

The program is intended for daily operation after the issues and returns for that day have been completed. It is independent of the running of the Fine Calculation and Update program.

Overdue letters are stored in the file OVERDUE.LETTER. They cannot be run from the main Circulation menu, but require the operator to Finish from that menu, and then to issue the appropriate RUNOFF commands.

Reader's file

This program controls the input of data on readers. Initially, the operator is prompted to enter a reader code. For new readers this can be generated automatically in sequence when a prefix is entered, or pre-printed bar-code labels can be read in.

The default expiry date is then displayed. This may be overwritten.

The operator is then prompted to enter the category of borrower, using one of those set up in the Reference Data files. Personal information relating to the reader, such as name, address(es), telephone number(s), year/course information for an academic library. Address fields are multi-value, and screen layout is to the library's own specification. This is likely to be the initial data entered.

Other data may be entered as the reader uses the library. Fields include:

Notes	–	Usually relating to any stops placed;
Instructions	–	Any messages that are highlighted on issue and reservation when that reader code is input;
Flag	–	Allows the operator the option of deleting any message defined in Instruction;
Loan Stop	–	May be indicated. Defaults to N if not required.
Reserve Stop	–	Operates as for loan stop.

The reader file can also be accessed by surname or by postcode, as described under Issue.

Catalogue recommendations

This program accesses the same screen as Catalogue Maintenance. It enables reservations to be placed for items that are neither in stock or on order, and are therefore, not on the database. The entry can be held on file until a decision concerning purchase or borrowing through inter-library loans has been taken. If the Acquisitions module is in use a catalogue recommendation can form the basis of an order.

The catalogue recommendation can also be used to control requests through inter-library loans, and even as a record of loans of items borrowed through inter-library loans.

The entries made using catalogue recommendations must be examined regularly to ensure that a lot of sub-standard bibliographic records do not remain on file.

Reservations

Reservations may be selected from the main Circulation menu. The operator is prompted to enter a reader code, surname, or postcode. Again, use of the Help key allows exit to Issue, Return or Quit back to the main Circulation Menu.

When a valid reader code is input, the reader's account is checked for any fines due, and the opportunity for payment is offered. If the expiry date for the reader has passed, or is within four weeks, this is displayed, together with any messages. The reservation information relating to the reader is displayed:

number of items currently reserved;
maximum number allowed;
'LIMIT' if the maximum has been reached.

The program checks that there is no reserve stop, and if there is no stop prompts for a standard number. The use of the Search Function key at this stage gives the following commands:

Issue
Return
Quit
List – provides a list of items reserved for the reader, with date of reservation;
Cancel – lists the standard numbers or groups reserved by the reader and prompts. Cancel can be applied to a line at a time or all.
Group – enables the reader to reserve a pre-defined group of items, as defined in Group Code Definition.
Prior – enables the operator to create a priority reservation (see below).

Only valid standard numbers present on the catalogue can be reserved. If any accession numbers are recorded as Available, the operator is informed and asked whether the reservation should be continued with. If there is more than one reader reserving a title, a waiting list is formed, which is accessed using Reservation Priorities (see below).

The Reservation Priorities program allows the operator to alter the order of a waiting list for titles. It should only be used by authorized personnel if chaos is to be avoided. The operator is prompted to enter a standard number or a group number. Details of the readers who have reserved the items are displayed on the screen, with each reader being assigned a line number in order of priority. Positions of lines may be adjusted, and thereby priority is adjusted. **E** ends the adjustments to priorities and reverts to the prompt for a standard number.

Reservation Notification produces notifications and, when relevant, a print-out of reserved items which have been available for issue to the reserver but which have not been issued. The program sorts the reader file, and then prompts the operator for a reader status/category. If reservation notifications for one specific category are required, the relevant status code must be entered.

Alternatively, all reservation notifications may be prepared. The number of notifications is then calculated and displayed along with the number of letters that are to be produced.

Multi-site software

When a reader places a reservation on an item, the library can seek to satisfy the request from stock which is in

1. a specified location;
2. a group of libraries in an area;
3. all libraries in the system.

For example, if the routine is set to search on an area-wide basis for a copy to satisfy the reservation, the system first displays details of the copies in stock at the reserving library. BookshelF then prompts the operator to indicate whether details of copies held in non-home libraries in the area should be displayed for inspection. The reserving library can then reserve specific copies of the title at whichever libraries the items are available or will be returned soonest. If a waiting list exists for a popular item, the holding library's reservations will take priority.

An optional 'Keep' program allows receiving libraries to keep the item once a reservation has been satisfied.

A daily report is printed in each library, giving details of which local items have been reserved, showing the status code (A)vailable or (L)oan. This serves as a shelf checking list for library staff.

8 Serials module

Introduction

The Serials module subsumes all of the processes associated with the control of serials in a library. The focus is on creating and maintaining a file of serial holdings and on order processing. Serials systems differ from their equivalent for monographs in that they must control each issue of each copy of a given title. The serials file on BookshelF is not currently available for access by the public via an on-line public access catalogue, but rather acts as an administrative tool. Further, the module does not cover circulation control, except in so far as it offers facilities for journal circulation systems. In some respects then, the Serials module draws together in one module all of the processes normally associated with the control of library material, but with only limited access to the Serials File for users and only routing facilities for circulation control.

The multi-site version of the Serials module allows the user to opt for one of a combination of Order and Receipt processes. Thus, for example, the headquarters of a library authority may generate all orders for all copies of serial issues for all locations and perform all receipting functions for items received before despatching them to the branch libraries. Alternatively, sites and branch libraries may be independent budget holders, responsible for generating their own orders and receipting material in the 'home' library.

Thus, the multi-site Serials Control software provides for the following situations:

1. Centralized ordering with decentralized receipt of items;
2. Centralized ordering with centralized receipt;
3. Decentralized ordering with decentralized receipt;
4. Decentralized ordering with centralized receipt.

The Serials module shares much in common with Acquisitions, and many procedures are common to both modules. Both

1	Serials
2	Copy definition
3	Issue registration
4	Issue label prints
5	Serials holdings
6	Generate expected issues
7	Review expected issues
8	Readers
O	Order Processing menu
L	Listings and reports menu
R	Reference data

Figure 8.1 Serials menu

1. Journal issues labels
2. Processing slips
3. Photocopying slips
4. Routing slips

Figure 8.2 Issue label prints menu

focus on ordering and registration of incoming items. The big difference is that for Serials the order is not sent once, but is often renewed for a subsequent year, and neither is it only receipted once. Registering serials issues involves recording each of the issues of the journal as it arrives.

Serials Reference Data

In order to make use of the Serials module it is necessary to define a collection of items in the Serials Reference Data. Where appropriate, Reference Data established in other parts of the

1 Supplier definition

2 Serials order entry

3 Prepare order forms

4 Print order forms

5 Check for forms

6 Review claim file

7 Prepare claims letters

8 Print claims letters.

Figure 8.3 Order processing menu

1 All serial holdings

2 Serial holdings concise

3 Titles with ISSNs, Codens, Abbreviations

4 Titles on order

5 Titles ordered (by budget code)

6 Titles on order from given supplier

7 New and overdue claims

8 All outstanding claims

9 Titles routed to a given reader

A Photocopying requests of a reader.

Figure 8.4 Listing and reports menu

system may be used. For example, countries must be defined in the Acquisitions module, as part of the Reference Data in this module. Locations are defined as part of the System Definition Reference Data. Also there is consistency in the codes used in the different modules. Thus, the status codes used elsewhere in the system i.e.

1 Issuing body

2 Publishers

3 Countries

4 Issuing frequency

5 Issue copy holding details

6 Change serial standard number

7 Budget codes

8 Reader categories

L Locations

Figure 8.5 Reference Data menu

A	Available	L	On Loan
B	Binding	O	On Order
H	Hold	R	Reserved
I	Labelling/In process	T	In Transit

are also used in the Serials Control module. Similarly, the budget data that is held for serials and monographs is recorded in a comparable format. The Reference Data includes the definition of a number of codes, the issuing frequency, issue copy holdings data, ISSN conversion procedure, the establishment of budget codes, and reader categories.

All codes must be defined in Serials Reference Data before they can be used elsewhere in the module, such as in Serials Definition. The codes to be defined are:

1. *Issuing Bodies* – A code must be established for every issuing body of the journal publications that are likely to be handled by the system. The code, together with the name of the body, is recorded.

2. *Publishers* – A code must also be established for every publisher. The code, together with the name of the publisher is recorded.

3. *Countries* – A code is defined for each country from which publications are to be received. The code is recorded with the name of the country.

4. *Locations* – Each location must have a code defined. The code will be stored with the description of the location and the default budget code for a given location.

5. *Issuing frequency* – It is possible to define the minimum and maximum number of issues expected in a year, the claim delay (in weeks) for this frequency and the valid issue description. This might for instance take one of the following three forms:

Date 12th April 1991
Month April 1991
Year 1991.

6. *Issuing copy holding data* – This screen allows the user to examine the status of issues received for specific locations, volumes, numbers and copies. Access is via the code of the full holdings item, and new codes can be established by entering a new code, together with the other appropriate details. The full code includes the ISSN/location/volume and part/copy number. The fields recorded and displayed are:

Description i.e. issue description e.g. April 1991;
Received – the date that the issue was received or registered;
Status code – to demonstrate the status of the item. The Codes are as indicated above and as used elsewhere in the system;
Bound – indicates whether or not the issue is bound;
Notes – an opportunity to enter any notes pertaining to this ISSN.

7. *Change Serial Standard Number* – This option supports the changing of an in-house number of an ISSN. Care needs to be exercised in executing this option. Before activating this option it is necessary to ensure that there are no new or active orders specifying the in-house code, so that systems integrity can be maintained and all files and print-outs use the same code.

8. *Budget code definition* – Codes can be defined and budgets identified through this option. A code, a verbal description, and the amount allocated to the fund must be entered initially. Actual and committed expenditure is calculated from the order program in a similar way to in the Acquisitions module.

9. *Reader categories* – Codes must be defined for the various categories of reader, so that readers can be registered, and, in general handled by the system.

Serials definition

Once the appropriate codes and other reference data have been defined the librarian can proceed to Serials Definition. Serials Definition creates the basic bibliographic record of the serial, which is used throughout the module. Existing records can be retrieved via ISSN, title coden or abbreviation (see Figure 8.6).

A new record for a new title can be created by entering the following details:

1. *ISSN or a local number for the serial title.* ISSN's are validated. Local numbers can be selected and input by the user or generated by the system which will offer the next unused number in the sequence.
2. *Full title* The full title can be taken from the chief source of information, which is the title page of the first issue, or, the first issue that is available. This is a multi-value field with up to 999 lines of text input available.
3. *Coden*, i.e. standard abbreviation for the title.
4. *Previous ISSN*.
5. *Continued ISSN*. This and the previous field offer the facility to indicate the relationship between the journal title being described and any immediately preceeding or superseding journal.
6. *Sort title, or key title*. The sort title brings together all of the entries for the journal when it has appeared under a number of different titles.
7. *Abbreviations*. This is the standard or in-house abbreviation for the title.
8. *Country*. This is the code for the country of publication.
9. *Language*, of the journal.

SCSS BookshelF 09 NOV 91

JOURNAL DEFINITIONS

1) ISSN ....2) Full title
1 ....
3) CODEN ....2 ....

4) Prev. ISSN ....
5) Cont. ISSN ....

6) Sort title ....

7) Abbreviations 1 ....
2 ....

Country .... 9) Language ....

10) Issuing body ....

11) Publisher ....

Modifications, FI(le), CL(ear), DE(lete) –

Page 1

Page 2

SCSS BookshelF 09 NOV 91

JOURNAL DEFINITIONS (cont'd)

12) Editor ....13) Class no. ....

14) Publication pattern ....15) Frequency ....
16) Publication desc. .... 17) Issue desc. 1 ....
2 ....

18) Notes
1 ....
2 ....

19) Index 1 ....
details 2 ....

20) Keywords 21) Copy nos 22) File no ....
1 .... 1 ....
2 .... 2 ....23) Holdings rept ....
3 .... 3 ....
4 .... 4 ....Entry date ....

Modifications, FI(le), CL(ear), DE(lete) –

Figure 8.6 Serials definition

10. *Issuing body.* This is the code for the issuing body.

11. *Publisher.* This is the code for the publisher.

12. *Editor.* The editor's name may be included if the name might be a means of identifying the serial.

13. *Class number.*

14. *Publication pattern* (see below).

15. *Publication description.* Number of issues published within a subscription period (e.g. 12 per year, 2 per month) (see below).

16. *Issuing frequency.* How frequently issues are published e.g. monthly, weekly (see below).

17. *Description.* The description of a particular issue as it appears on the publication, e.g. 19th June 1991, Autumn 1991, or Vol 4, Number 6 (see below).

More on Publication Description and Issuing frequency

These are the tricky fields! They reflect the complexities of serials publishing. The purpose of all of the data in these fields is to generate expected issues for registration purposes and to support automatic generation of claims for issues that have not been received.

There are two main types of publication pattern. The pattern may be based on:

(a) number of issues per volume – prefix V
(b) number of issues per year – prefix Y

If the Publication Description is to include a volume and part number e.g. vol. 4, no. 2, then the Publication Pattern code entered must include the number of issues that make up each volume. This is then also followed by a code that indicates whether or not the part numbers are reset to 1 for the first issue of each volume number.

Publishers often change publication patterns. The system accommodates such changes by a modified code for the publication pattern.

There are a number of Frequency codes available. These are:

A	Annually
AA	Biannual (twice a year)
AAA	Three times a year
BIE	Biennial (every two years)

BTM	Bi-monthly (6 issues a year)
D	Daily (6 issues a week)
ET	Eight times a year
F	Fortnightly
I	Irregular
M	Monthly
MM	Twice monthly (half-monthly)
MMM	Three times a month
MT	Ten times a year
MXA	Monthly except August
Q	Quarterly
W	Weekly
WW	Twice weekly

There is an obvious relationship between frequency and publication pattern, and so only certain publication codes may be used with certain publication pattern codes. Mandatory frequency codes for specific publication patterns are as follows:

Publication Pattern	*Valid frequency codes*
M	A AA AAA BIE BIM M MXA Q
Q	Q
B	AA
T	AAA

Journal codes may be validated.

Publication description is represented by a code, chosen from the following table:

Code	*Description*
D	Date
Y	Year
M	Month (and year)
X	Tenth (and year)
E	Eighth (and year)
S	Sixth (and year)
Q	Quarter (and year)
T	Third (and year)
B	Half year (and year)

The entry of one of the above codes causes the system to supply a textual description for each issue as it is registered. This description may be amended by the user at registration.

18. *Notes.* Any notes relating to the title such as frequency, source of title, variations in title, parallel titles and relationships with other serials not already noted.

19. *Index details.* Any details concerning the publication of indexes, such as the presence of cumulative indexes, kind of index, volumes and dates of serials included in the various indexes and the location of the index in the serial.

20. *Keywords.* Any keywords indicating the subject content of the journal.

21. *Copy numbers.* This field is available, but is not for input. The data that is later displayed in this field is derived from Copy Definition.

22. *Manual File Reference Number*, may be entered.

23. *Inclusion in Serials Holdings reports.*

Copy definition

Once specific serials titles have been defined, it is necessary to proceed to record certain data that is specific to individual copies of a serial, as they are stored and used in a given library. Journal copy definition involves recording the following data:

Code – The code for individual copies of journals comprises the ISSN (or in-house number), the location code and the copy number e.g.

A10/MP/1,
where A10 is the in-house number
MP is the location code, and
1 is the copy number.

Copy codes must be defined before an item can be ordered. Copy codes may be defined through this avenue, i.e. journal copy definition, or via Serials Holdings.

1. *Shelf* – the shelfmark for a particular copy may optionally be entered.

2. *Circ* – takes the value Y or N depending upon whether a copy is made available for circulation or routing. The default is N.

3. *Budget code* – budget or charge codes may be entered for specific copies or a subscription may be ordered on separately funded accounts.

4. *Registration notes* – any notes that should appear on screen when registering issues can be recorded.

SCSS Bookshelf 09 NOV 91

JOURNAL COPY DEFINITIONS

Code ------------- Title
1 ....
2 ....

Location description Copy no. 1) Shelf 2) Circ Date defined
.... -------- ------ ....

Order details

Order number Supplier name Order date
....

Subscription period Price 3) Bgt code Completed Cont. order
.... to .... -- ....

4) Registration notes
1 --
2 --

5) Other notes
1 --
2 --

Modifications, FI(le), CL(ear), DE(lete) –

Page 1

Page 2

SCSS Bookshelf 09 NOV 91

JOURNAL COPY DEFINITIONS (cont'd)

6) Instructions
1 --
2 --

7) Reader Name 8) Requirements
1 ------------ .... ------------
2 ------------ .... ------------

Routing List

9) Routing form 10) Reader Name 11) Loan days
-- 1 -------- .... ---------
2 -------- .... ---------
3 -------- .... ---------

12) Bound --

Modifications, FI(le), CL(ear), DE(lete)

Figure 8.7 Serials copy definition

5. *Other notes* – is an opportunity to store notes pertaining to a specific copy of a journal.

6. *Instructions* – information relating to specific processing activities, such as scanning of articles, or indexing.

7. *Reader* – the code of a reader may be entered if photocopies are required for a specific reader.

8. *Requirements* – details of the photocopies required by this reader, such as contents page, news, publications.

9. *Routing form* – the routing can be specified by an appropriate code.

Routing can take various forms:

Closed loop – where the journal issue is passed from reader to reader. The issue is returned to the library after the last reader.

Open loop – where the journal issue is passed from reader to reader, and the last reader on the routing list keeps the issue. The issue is not returned to the library.

Closed star – where the journal issue is returned to the library by each reader on the routing list.

Open star – where the journal circulates in essentially the same way as in the closed star, except that it is not returned to the library when the final reader has finished with it.

These routing forms are signified by the codes CL, CS, OL, OS, respectively.

10. *Routing list* – a list of the codes of the readers to whom the copy is to be circulated.

11. *Loan days* – the number of days that this copy can be on loan to this reader.

12. *Bound* – the value Y or N is assigned, according to whether a particular copy will be bound.

Order processing

Once a title has been defined and the details pertaining to copies of that title recorded, it is possible to proceed to create orders in respect of that title. The Order Processing menu has many features in common with the Ordering part of the Acquisitions module. The options on the Order Processing menu are concerned with creating, processing and printing orders and claims. Preliminary to creating individual orders is Supplier Definition wherein the details of the supplier to whom orders are to be sent are recorded. The following details are recorded:

1. *Code* – a code for the supplier. This is an alphabetic code of up to five digits.

2. *Name of supplier.*

3. *Address of supplier.*

4. *Claim delay* – the claim delay period that is acceptable for goods from this supplier.

5. *Telephone.*

6. *Telex.*

7. *Currency* – the code for the currency in which the supplier is to be paid, which will have been defined in Systems Reference Data, acquisitions reference data.

8. *Their ref* – the library's account number with the supplier.

9. *Notes* – any notes on this supplier.

Serials order entry

Serials order entry creates the order record on the order file. First an order number must be generated. This can be locally assigned by the library, or, alternatively the number generated by the system may be accepted.

Other data that must or may be entered in respect of an order includes:

1. *Supplier code* – the code for the supplier as defined in Suppliers Definition.

2. *Order date* – the current date is available as default, or an alternative date may be entered.

3. *Status* – of the order. The value taken by the field will alter as the order passes through the various processing stages. The values that it may take are:

S	Sent	C	Completed
E	Existing	CA	Cancelled
ES	Existing Sent	H	Hold

4. *ISSN.*

5. *Copy codes* – as defined in Copy Definition.

6. *Suppliers ref* – the supplier's catalogue number for this journal if there is one.

7. *Renewal* – takes the value Y or N, depending on whether the order is to be automatically renewed. If the order is set to be automatically renewed, the system will generate renewal orders

when all of the issue descriptions for the original order have been created. As a general rule these issue descriptions should be generated automatically in order to reduce the possibility of inconsistencies in issues' descriptions. Either Y or N may be entered.

8. *Subscription period* – is entered in terms of from and to.

9. *Unit price* – the unit price for the subscription.

10. *Discount* – percentage discount on the unit price, if any. The actual unit cost, after discount has been deducted, and the total cost of the order will be calculated and displayed.

11. *Issues/subs* – the number of issues expected per subscription.

12. *Issues received* – the number of issues received to date.

13. *Claim delay* – the claim delay that is acceptable for this title coming from the specified supplier. The default delay for the supplier may be accepted, or a different delay may be entered.

14. *Re-order date* – the re-order date; when a new order must be sent.

15. *Adjustments* – Amount – any adjustments to the unit price. Refunds are entered as negative amounts.

16. *Number of copies* – the number of copies to which the adjustment relates.

17. *Discount* – takes the value Y or N, according to whether any adjustment made is subject to the subscription discount.

18. *Explanation* – any explanation of the adjustment to the unit price.

19. *Notes* – any notes relating to this subscription.

Once the basic order has been created printed orders can be generated by:

Prepare order forms

This option initiates the input of data into the standard order form. Once the forms have been set up, they can be printed through the next option.

Print order forms

The selection of this option will merely call up a help screen with the instructions for the printing of order forms. These instructions advise that the forms should be printed using the

RUNOFF text processor for Prime systems and subsequently printed through the SPOOL command.

Issue registration

One of the main activities associated with serials control is the registration of issues of copies of serials as they arrive. There must be a quick and effective means of recording which issues have arrived.

Issues registration proceeds slightly differently for the first issue of a journal to arrive, than for subsequent copies. The process that generates expected issues, and therefore allows checking against a list of expected issues, cannot be triggered until the details of the first issue have been entered. The procedure for all but the first issue, for which details of the issue must be entered is as follows: A journal title is first retrieved via the ISSN, the CODEN, abbreviation or title. Once the record for the journal title has been retrieved, if issues are expected, details of these will be displayed, e.g.

Line	*Issue id*	*Comb id*	*Description*	*Ord*	*Exp*	*Rec*	*Orde*
1	Vol 1 No2		February 1991	1	1		283
2	Vol 1 No3		March 1991	1	1		283

The prompts that appear at the bottom of the screen support the editing of the description of expected issues, the identification of a specific line number so that the appropriate item can be registered, and the entering of additional issues other than those already expected. Where a new issue or the first issue of a serial is received, the user is prompted to provide the same data as would normally by supplied for expected issues.

When using the multi-site Serials Control software, a check is performed by the system to confirm that the location code is a valid code for that site when an item is received. For example, if a library operated a decentralized ordering system, then the receipts program would only accept items to which valid location codes for the 'home' library, or home site, were attached. 'Sites can be two or more libraries which are grouped for budgeting or staffing etc. purposes. An explanation of codes for defining areas and sites is given in Chapter 4.

Hidden under the Help Command are prompts to perform a range of more complex functions of the kind that every serials librarian wishes to encounter as infrequently as possible. These include:

(C)ombine – for the registration of combined issues, when journals combine issue numbers in one publication.

(O)rders – allows the user to examine the status of the order for journal titles.

(P)art – allows for the registration of issue numbers that have been split into more than one part.

(S)upplement – allows for the registration of supplements to journal titles, such as indexes.

W(indow) – an opportunity to modify the number of lines that are displayed on the registration screen.

(D)elete – deletes individual issues through the use of the line number.

Generate expected issues

As indicated in the last section, once the first issue of a title has been entered, a list of the expected issues can be generated by invoking this option. To re-iterate, before expected issues can be generated it is necessary that the following processes have been conducted for each copy of a title:

1. Journal definition
2. Copy definition
3. Serials order entry
4. Process order
5. Registration of first item
6. Generate expected issues.

When the option has been executed the full list of expected issues, together with the number of copies appears on the Issue Registration screen.

Review expected issues

This option offers the occasion to examine the status of expected serials. The information has been generated from the proceeding ordering and registration. The data displayed is:

1. *Status* – which will be denoted by one of the following codes:

CR – completed but needs renewal
C – completed
T – incorporate
R – required
M – manual i.e. create IDS manually.

2. *Generated issue id* – last issue description generated.

3. *Generated description* – expected date – i.e. date of the last issue expected.

4. *Generated issues description count* – the number of issue descriptions generated in the system for a copy of a title.

Issue label prints

Once an issue has been registered it may be appropriate to generate labels for that issue. There are a number of programs which generate various labels. The labels generated are:

1. Journal issue labels
2. Processing slips
3. Photocopying slips
4. Routing slips
5. All options

Readers

Reader details may be registered or reviewed by selecting this option. If the Circulation Control module has already been implemented, the reader files are integrated, so that details can be recalled in this module. If Serials Control has been implemented alone, or it is deemed desirable to enter reader details in this context, then modifications may be made through this option. It is necessary that any reader codes that are used in Copy Definition when recording circulation patterns or photocopying requests have already been defined.

The data that is held for readers is consistent with that held in the Circulation Control module, viz.:

reader code
initials

surname
status code
expiry
date
address
telephone number
notes
photocopies, and routing.

Further discussion of most of these fields is available in the Circulation Control module.

The details concerning photocopying and routing are not created via this screen, but are transferred automatically from the information attached to each copy in Copy Definition.

Serials holdings

Serials Holdings Maintenance allows records of serials holdings to be maintained. Entry is via the Holdings code in the form ISSN/location code/copy number, and this must previously have been defined on the location file. Records include:

Title
Location
Copy number
Previous code
Continuation code

all of which are held in the Serials Bibliographic File. In addition the following are entered via the Serials Holdings Maintenance Screen:

First issue
Its description
Last issue
Its description
Missing issues
Their descriptions
Shelved at:

All of these last fields are multi-valued fields.

Claims

There are four options that are associated with claims in the Order Processing menu: check for claims, review claims file, prepare claims letters, and print claims letters. Together these support the checking of the status of claims and the generation of claims at appropriate moments.

Check for claims

This option invokes the preparation of claims letters for expected serials and first orders which are overdue.

Review claims file

This option allows users to examine the status of orders for which claims have been sent. Once the option has been selected, entry of the Journal Copy code will display the following information:

1. *Order supplier* – if necessary this may be modified at this time to correct any errors in recording of suppliers.
2. *Number of claims* – the number of claims already sent for copies of a particular issue.
3. *Date of next claim*.
4. *Date sent* – the date that the most recent claim was sent to the supplier.
5. *Claim flag* – can be placed on each line of the order to indicate whether or not that line should trigger claim production, as signified by Y or N.
6. *Notes* – any information from the supplier about the corresponding claim line.

Prepare claim letters

This option initiates the input of data into the standard claim letter format. Once this has been achieved, claim letters can be printed using the instructions under:

Print claim letters

The Help screen which is displayed when this option is selected recommends the use of the RUNOFF text processor at the PRIMOS level, which is a manner that is consistent with the procedure for printing order forms in Prime systems.

Reports

A relatively large number of reports are available in the Serials Control module. These can be selected via the Listings and Reports menu, or by entering the appropriate command in INFORMATION. Reports are printed, but not displayed on the screen. The reports that are available are:

All Serials Holdings
Serials Holdings (concise)
Titles with ISSNs, CODENs and abbreviations
Titles ordered under a given budget code.
Titles on order from a given supplier.
New and overdue claims
All outstanding claims
Titles routed to a given reader
Photocopying requests of a reader.

9 Management information

Introduction

Information, be it qualitative or quantitative, which is used in the decision-making process may be termed 'management information'. The automation of library housekeeping routines has provided library managers with raw data which can be used to support decisions. Such data is a by-product of computerization in libraries. Fundamental information concerning for example the number of transactions being carried out on a particular day in a library, or the number of registered readers, or the number of overdues being sent is readily available from most automated systems. However, library managers often discover that the format in which the data is presented is not always the most useful or meaningful.

For example, in addition to knowing the number of loans a service point is making each day/week/month, a librarian may find it more useful to have information about which categories of readers (e.g. students, OAPs, teenagers, adults) are making most/least use of the library. This kind of information, which demands more complex correlations of variables, is **not** always readily available from computerized library systems. But library managers' expectations of systems with respect to the generation of management information are becoming more clearly defined.

The suppliers of BookshelF would not claim to have provided the ultimate solution to the problems of identifying management information requirements and presenting reports which are appropriate in every conceivable library situation. Nevertheless, a considerable number of reports can currently be produced by simply selecting a menu option in the appropriate BookshelF module. These are listed in Figure 9.1. It is the

This chapter is based substantially on research undertaken by Robert Kiley, with his kind permission. A full account of his investigations are available in Kiley, R. (1988). *Generating management information from BookshelF using the PICK operating system*. MSc. Thesis; Loughborough University.

CIRCULATION

1. Issue statistics

- daily, weekly, monthly, quarterly, annually.
- and/or — by selected sites/ for all sites
- and/or — with specified selection criteria e.g. date, location, class, media-type, reader category etc.
- by time period within the day/ by half hour or combination of half hour periods (for Short Loan statistics)
- with retrospective comparisons

2. Reservation statistics

- reservations received
- reservations supplied
- reservations cancelled
- reservations uncollected

3. Number of current loans
4. Number of readers
5. Number of overdue letters

SERIALS

- all serials holdings
- serials holdings (concise)
- titles with ISSNs, CODENs and abbreviations
- titles on order
- titles ordered under a given budget
- titles on order from a given supplier
- new and overdue claims
- all outstanding claims
- titles routed to a given reader
- photocopying requests of a specified reader

Figure 9.1 BookshelF Management Information – menu-generated reports

intention in this chapter to examine the real potential which BookshelF offers for generating very sophisticated reports. Indeed, one of the strong attractions of the BookshelF system to intending purchasers is the facility to generate reports for management information purposes which far exceeds initial expectations. The reason for this lies in the flexibility inherent in the operating system i.e. PICK, or INFORMATION (Prime) which allows any data element to be correlated with any other data element.

In simple terms, any data which is entered into BookshelF can be output in a form which is appropriate for management information purposes, through a query language which does not require an understanding of programming.

To avoid confusion, the examples and explanations given in this chapter are based on the PICK operating system. The principles and file structures are the same as those in the Prime computers INFORMATION environment, used in larger library systems, although there are some slight differences in the query language.

The following sections are intended to provide some insight into the potential for generating management information from BookshelF. To set this in context, it is appropriate to identify the types of information which library managers might wish to generate to support their planning and decision making.

Some management information requirements

Kiley (1988) in his research into generating management information using PICK, identified 15 major requirements of statistical (counting and cumulative) reports and the analyses which can be performed on them.

Counting statistics

	Statistic	*Management information*
1.	Number of loans per hour/day/month	Peaks/troughs in day/month/year. Influence staffing policy on loans desk.
2.	Number of overdues	Sending overdues is costly in terms of staff time and postage. May be more cost-effective to alter loan period.
3.	Number of loans which result in fines	If high, then policy on length of loan may need reviewing.
4.	Ratio of loans to total loanable stock	Achieve idea of proportion of stock which is live. If low and space at a premium, then transfer of stock to outside location should be considered.

5.	Number of accessions by subject, by medium and location	Shows how collection has grown and which subject areas and which media are growing/shrinking.
6.	Total expenditure at any point of the year	Help with budgeting. Should ensure that a library does not overspend or underspend.
7.	Number of registered readers classified and sorted by reader status	Gives a profile of the potential market a library has to cater for.

Cumulative statistics

1.	Number of loans by reader status	Which categories of users make most/least use of library, a factor which should influence the purchasing policy. Also by determining which groups are not using the library can try and identify reasons (e.g. part-time students unable to get to library because of opening hours).
2.	League table showing use of each title	More popular items are candidates for duplication or changing status to reference.
3.	League table showing use each title with flexible date parameter	Certain titles may be more popular at different times of the year e.g. near exams. May alter loan period.
4.	League table of titles borrowed in descending order of total number of copies	High number of loans/low number of copies. Good case for duplication etc.
5.	League table on use of each title by reader group	Target purchases to suit particular reader groups.
6.	Number of readers per title	Apparently popular items may be the result of just a few zealous readers.
7.	Number of reservations by title/subject	Identify heavy demand. Use with league tables to affect purchasing and loans policy.

8.	Proportion of items on loan after 1st, 2nd, 3rd overdue	Effectiveness of overdue policy. Should fines be introduced/increased?

These management information requirements have varying degrees of complexity. All of them can be accommodated in BookshelF. This may be by the use of an existing menu option which has been pre-programmed by the suppliers. More significantly, librarians can tailor management information to local requirements by utilizing the query language, by setting up macros (or PROCS – see p.141) and by creating menus to select information which is required on a regular basis. If we examine the file and record structures in BookshelF, and relate this to the functions of the PICK operating system and the query language we get a clearer picture of the extent and quality of the management information which can be generated.

The PICK database

All data held by PICK is stored in collection of files which reside in a number of accounts. Each file consists of two parts – (i) a data portion which holds the data and (ii) a dictionary portion which defines fields and field labels and where this data is stored and how it is to be processed. For example, in the file MAIN.CAT, which is the central Catalogue database, the dictionary section defines such fields as Author, Title, Class.no etc., whilst the data section holds the corresponding data. Figure 9.2 illustrates the BookshelF dictionary/file structure. BOOKSHELF is the program file, whilst BOOKSTALL carries the data.

The BookshelF system uses a relational database which means that any item of data can be used as an access point for further information, so that any data element can be linked to any other data element, either in the same file or in any other file. This is because in a relational database, no hierarchy of levels exists. All the data associated with the record is stored in columns and rows so that PICK can retrieve items which match selected criteria.

Every record in the database possesses a unique item identifier, referred to as the ITEM-ID, which ensures that every single record is unique. In the file MAIN.CAT, the unique part of the catalogue record is the ISBN, or in-house number (pseudo-

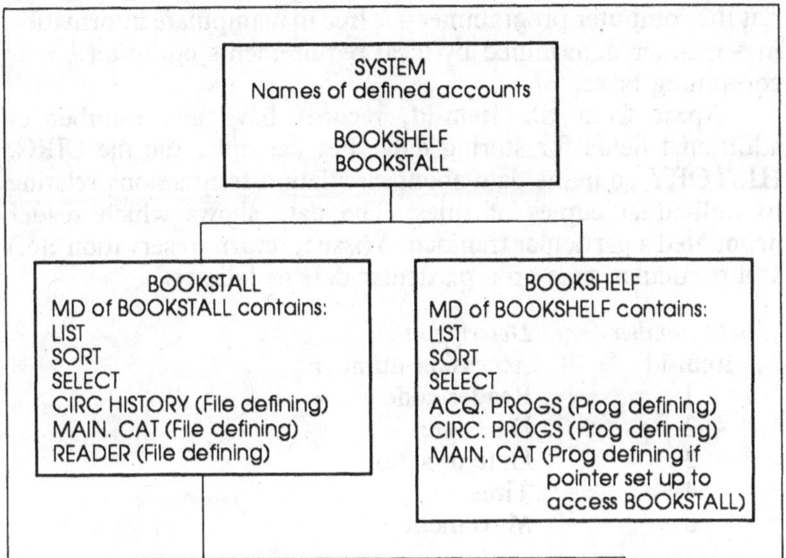

Figure 9.2 BookshelF dictionary/file structure

ISBN), whilst in the reader file, a unique number is assigned to each reader record. It is these unique identifiers which enable relationships to be formed between files. For example, to determine who (i.e. individual readers; categories of readers) is borrowing what (i.e. individual titles; subject categories; media types) from which library in the locality, it is possible to link data from the MAIN.CAT and reader files to the CIRC.HISTORY file and the location file. (see Figure 9.2). This facility to draw data from a number of independent files means that the user – and not the computer programmer – is free to manipulate information in a manner determined by local requirements on an *ad hoc* or continuing basis.

Apart from the Item-id, records have any number of additional fields for storing data. For example, the file CIRC. HISTORY contains data about circulation transactions relating to individual copies of titles. The data shows which reader negotiated a particular transaction (issue, return, reservation etc.) at a particular time on a particular date as follows:

Field number	*Description*
Item-id	Accession number
1	Reader code
2	Due date
3	Date of action
4	Time
5	Movement

Each of the fields (accession number, reader code etc.) are referred to as **attributes**, whilst data held in these fields are known as **values**. To determine which file attributes have been defined in a particular file, the dictionary of that file should be listed by entering the command SORT DICT ONLY *filename*. Thus, the command LIST DICT ONLY MAIN.CAT will provide a list of all the attributes (or fields) in the catalogue file. (see Figure 9.3). LIST is one of the verbs used in the query language, which is examined in more detail later in the following section.

The Query language

For management information which is not readily available via the BookshelF menu system, access to the database is made with the use of the enquiry language – ENGLISH or ACCESS in PICK-based systems and INFORM on INFORMATION-based Prime computer systems.

Commands are structured as sentences, the syntax of which is

<VERB> <FILENAME>
<SELECTION CRITERIA> <OUTPUTS>

Verbs

Verbs included are

sort dict main.cat

sort dict main.cat 02:01PM 11-21-91 PAGE 1

FIELD NAME	TYPE	LOCATION	CONV.	DISPLAY NAME	FORMAT
@ID	D	0		MAIN.CAT	10L
STANDARD.NO	D	0		Standard no.	10L
STD.NO	D	0		Standard no.	10L
FORENAMES	D	1		Forenames	15T
SURNAME	D	2		Surname	15T
TITLE	D	3		Title	40T
TITLE.100	D	3		Title	100T
TITLE.CATPRINT	D	3		Title	30T
GMD	D	4		GMD	1L
EDITION	D	5		Edition	15T
EDN	D	5		Edition	15T
ED.RESP	D	6		Editor	20T
EDITOR	D	6		Editor	20T
PLACE	D	7		Place	20L
PUBL	D	8		Publisher	37L
PUBLISHER	D	8		Publisher	37L
PUBL.YEAR	D	9		Year	10L
CLASS.NO					
SERIES	D	13		Series title	35T
ISSN	D	14		ISSN	8L
NOTES	D	15		Notes	100T
KEYWORDS	D	16		Keywords	45T
KWD	D	16		Keywords	20T
ACC.NO	D	17		Accession	11L
ACCESSION.NO	D	17		Accession	10L
ACCN.NO	D	17		Accession	10L
DISCIPLINE	D	18		Disciplines	20L
SUBJ	D	18		Subjects	20L
SUBJECT	D	18		Subjects	20L
ENTRY.DATE	D	19	D2	Entry date	9R
INPUT.DATE	D	19	D2	Input date	9R
RES.LIST	D	20		Res. Readers	10L
RESERVER.CODES	D	20		Reservers	10L

Figure 9.3 Dictionary of Catalogue attributes

LIST e.g. LIST MAIN.CAT will sort the catalogue and display the data in random order

SORT e.g. SORT MAIN.CAT will sort the catalogue into standard number order (i.e. ISBN)

e.g. SORT MAIN.CAT BY AUTHOR will sort the catalogue into author order

COUNT	e.g.	COUNT MAIN.CAT will count the number of bibliographic records in the database
	e.g.	COUNT MAIN.CAT WITH GMD = 'J' will count the number of records for journal articles
SELECT	e.g.	SELECT MAIN.CAT WITH GMD = 'J' will create a temporary file of records for journal articles. Any immediately subsequent commands will act upon this file.
STAT	e.g.	STAT MAIN.CAT PRICE with GMD = 'V' will give the average price of videocassettes. The STAT verb also enables more sophisticated statistical analyses of numeric values in the database, giving means, standard deviations and correlation coefficients.
SREFORMAT		enables the re-grouping of data under attributes other than the Item Identifier.
	e.g.	SREFORMAT MAIN.CAT AUTHOR TITLE would regroup the catalogue data so that author replaces ISBN as Item Identifier and title becomes the first attribute. The use of this verb is illustrated on p.137.

Filenames

Examples of filenames in BookshelF include MAIN.CAT (the Catalogue database), ACCESSION (the accessions file of individual copy numbers), READER (details about library membership), CIRC.HISTORY (transaction information), ORDER (items which are on order) etc.

Selection criteria

The use of selection criteria demonstrates the flexibility of the query language. For example, the simple sentence

SORT MAIN.CAT BY AUTHOR BY TITLE BY YEAR

will first sort the catalogue into author order. If the system finds two items by the same author, it will sub-sort this section into title order, and in the case when an author has published a new edition of a text (thereby acquiring a new ISBN and therefore a unique record on the database) this will be sorted by year of publication.

Similarly, if a report is required which shows the number of transactions for a particular month, the CIRC.HISTORY file can be sorted in date order. However, because the date attribute is multi-valued (i.e. may have more than one transaction date) it is necessary to 'explode' each item in this attribute with the sort qualifier BY-EXP so that each item (or date) in this attribute can be accessed in its own right. Thus the sentence

SORT CIRC.HISTORY BY-EXP DATE >= "1–1–90"
BY-EXP DATE <= "31–1–90"

will output (to screen or printer) a list of transactions in date order, including entries which refer to the same copy.

e.g.	ACCESSION NO.	DATE	DUE DATE	TIME	MOVEMENT
	C15406	1–1–90	8–1–90	9.35	I
	C16423	1–1–90	8–1–90	9.12	I
	C12321	2–1–90	9–1–90	14.05	I
	C16423	2–1–90	8–1–90	10.55	R

Relational operators

Relational operators <,>, =>, <= are acceptable components in the query language. In INFORM (using Prime INFORMATION,) 'greater than', 'less than', 'equal to' etc. are indicated by GT, LT, EQ, GE, LE. When used in conjunction with the Boolean operators AND, OR and NOT the database can be interrogated so as to yield precise and specific data.

Output

The output resulting from these sentences or commands may be directed to a printer or screen in a user-defined format. For example, the sentence

SORT MAIN.CAT WITH GMD = "V"

will list all videocassettes to the screen, in ISBN or pseudo-ISBN order showing a default format of ISBN, Author and title. However, the sentence

SORT MAIN.CAT WITH GMD = "V" BY-EXP SUBJECT TITLE AUTHOR LOCATION CLASS.NO ID-SUPP LPTR

will provide a list showing

SORT MAIN.CAT WITH GMD = "V"	–	all the videocassettes which have been entered into the catalogue
BY-EXP SUBJECT	–	listed in subject order (if the item covers more than one subject then a separate entry will be made)
TITLE AUTHOR LOCATION CLASS.NO	–	listing selected data in a specified order
ID-SUPP	–	not displaying the ISBN (it takes up too much space!)
LPTR	–	and will be printed out in hard copy format. (Select listings on paper are always useful – and the readers like them. They can also be published as select bibliographies or holdings lists.)

So far, this chapter has highlighted the fundamental 'tools' in the BookshelF query language which can be used to manipulate the data for management information purposes. The flexibility arising from the relational nature of the database and the easily memorable commands is evident. Some management information requirements are rather more complex than the ones already outlined in this section, which is intended to provide the reader with a 'flavour' of the potential for manipulating and correlating data to the system user's requirements. Techniques available for more complex reports are detailed in the following section. The examples are a selection of the general management information requirements which were outlined at the beginning of this chapter.

It should be noted here that PICK is case-sensitive, and therefore any attributes or criteria used in a SORT command should either

i) be entered exactly as they appear in the database OR
ii) attributes should be prefixed by the letter U to render the system case-blind. Thus, the command

SORT MAIN.CAT BY UAUTHOR

will not differentiate between authors which begin with upper or lower case letters.

Examples

Example 1. Loans by reader category

If a library manager is able to determine which reader groups are using the library most/least, an effective purchasing policy can be implemented. Similarly, if it becomes apparent that one reader group is making little use of the library – in terms of borrowing – then this situation can be investigated and, where possible, changes made to remedy the situation. The effectiveness of such changes can subsequently be seen in the following years' reports.

In order to determine how many books each reader group has borrowed, it is necessary to **reference the data** relating to reader status (stored in the Reader file) and reader description (stored in the READER.STATUS file) from the CIRC.HISTORY file. This is achieved by the creation of dictionary synonyms for these two items in CIRC.HISTORY.

It is now possible to enquire on the CIRC.HISTORY file how many items each group has borrowed. (Reader groups represent those which might be found using a medical library.) The following sentence will produce a report of the kind illustrated in Figure 9.4.

SORT CIRC.HISTORY BY-EXP READER.STATUS BY-EXP DATE >= "1–1–90" BREAK-ON READER. STATUS BREAK-ON READER.DESC TOTAL ISSUES DET-SUPP

This report is generated as follows:

Reader Status	Reader Description	Issues
00	Registrar	146
01	Medical student	61
03	Nurses – RGN	22
04	Clinical lecturer	0
05	Charge nurse	48

Figure 9.4 Report showing the number of items borrowed by specified reader categories

SORT CIRC.HISTORY	–	will search the transactions file and SORT the output into a logical order
BY-EXP READER.STATUS	–	i.e. in order of the reader status code
BY-EXP DATE >= "1–1–90"	–	selecting all items which were actioned on or after 1/1/90
BREAK-ON READER.STATUS	–	BREAK-ON is used to split the data
BREAK-ON READER.DESC	–	into sections, for presentation. For every time the value of the named attribute changes, a break in the listing occurs.
TOTAL ISSUES	–	The number of issues for each category is added up
DET-SUPP	–	and the details of individual issues are suppressed to save wading through numerous pages of print-out.

Although information about how many items the different reader categories borrow is useful, it is possible to take this investigation further and see how many readers were actually responsible for the loans.

Example 2. Number of readers responsible for loans

Being able to determine how many readers are responsible for a number of loans provides additional information which can be used to support or contradict trends highlighted. For instance, in the previous example, in Figure 9.4 there might be an argument for ensuring that more of the library's resources went on material for registrars than for charge nurses. (Another argument would of course be that material which charge nurses require is not available or inadequate.) However, if it were found that all 146 loans attributed to the registrars were caused by just 10 zealous readers, the first argument would need rethinking.

To determine the number of readers who cause issues, it is necessary to employ the SREFORMAT verb. This permits a user to direct the output of an ENGLISH enquiry to another file, and in so doing to create a new ITEM-ID for the data in this new file.

When the SREFORMAT verb is invoked, each display field specified is treated as a sequential description of the record structure of the destination file. Thus, at the most basic level, the instruction SREFORMAT MAIN.CAT AUTHOR TITLE would make Author the Item-id in the new file, and Attribute 1 would be Title. In the current example, it is necessary to create a new file which can draw data from CIRC.HISTORY, but in so doing, change the Item-id from the accession number to the reader code. This enables Attribute 1 of the new file to hold the total number of issues to each reader. With data in this format, the READER file can be accessed, and a report which details the number of readers per reader group who are responsible for issues generated.

The final stage of this enquiry is to set up two dictionary items in the file READER. One (COUNTER) provides a total number of readers it encounters during an enquiry. The second (ISSUES) references the new reformatted file to access the total number of loans made by each reader. The following enquiry is made on the new reformatted file (ANYNAME) and the subsequent report illustrated in Figure 9.5.

In addition to providing a context for the loan figures, the report shown in Figure 9.5 can be used to determine the percentage of active readers the library has to cater for. This latter objective can be met by comparing the number generated (using the enquiry COUNT READER WITH STATUS "00" etc.) with the total in the No. Readers column.

As this example demonstrates, reformatting data is a relatively complicated process, but one which gives the user the facility to perform detailed analyses on **any** aspect of **any** data. The next example demonstrates how SREFORMAT can be used

```
>SELECT ANYNAME

>SORT READER BY STATUS BREAK-ON STATUS BREAK-ON STATUS.DESC TOTAL
ISSUES TOTAL COUNTER HEADING "Readers who cause issues" DET-SUPP
```

Readers who cause issues

Reader Status	Reader Description	Issues	No.Readers
00	Registrar	146	5
01	Medical student	61	49
03	Nurses – RGN	22	10
04	Clinical lecturer	0	0
05	Charge nurse	48	30

Figure 9.5 Report showing the number of readers in each category who generate issues

to generate 'league tables to determine the library's most popular items and the most popular items as defined by specific groups.

Example 3 Determining popular items

In order to generate a 'league table', loans must be grouped by title rather than by accession number, which is the way in which CIRC.HISTORY stores transactions. The simplest way to achieve this is to use the ISBN as a tag for grouping like titles together. If the ISBN is an invalid identifier – for example, different editions of Jane Austen's *Emma* will have different ISBNs – then the group number (see p.54) can be employed. This example assumes that the ISBN is an appropriate identifier.

To determine the most popular titles it is necessary to SREFORMAT CIRC.HISTORY so that the Item-id becomes the ISBN and Attribute 1 holds the total number of loans assigned to that title. (We will call this new file LOANS.) Thus irrespective of how many copies of a book a library may hold, all loans related to these copies will be totalled and stored as one item in the

```
>SELECT LOANS

>SORT MAIN.CAT BY-EXP-DSND ISSUES ISSUES AUTHOR TITLE EDITION
HEADING "Popular items"

                              Popular items

Issues    187
Author    Cookson, C
Title     Our Kate

Issues    156
Author    Herbert, F
Title     Dune
Issues    144
Author    King, S
Title     Misery
```

Figure 9.6 Report showing most popular items

LOANS file. The final stage to this enquiry is the creation of a dictionary item called issues in the file MAIN.CAT. This dictionary will be used to access the total number of issues per ISBN from the file LOANS. Thus the following commands will generate a report (illustrated in Figure 9.6) showing the most popular items.

To determine which items a specific reader group defines as popular, further selection criteria can be added to the SREFORMAT routine. For example, to ascertain which books are most popular with children – BY-EXP READER.STATUS = "99" (here the status code for junior) would be included in the loans PROC.

A further element can be included to show how many copies of an item the library holds in any particular location. Thus the following sentence would generate a report (illustrated in Figure 9.7) showing a title, the number of issues which have been

```
>SELECT LOANS

SORT MAIN.CAT BY-EXP-DSND ISSUES ISSUES AUTHOR TITLE COPIES
HEADING "Most popular children's books"

                    Most popular children's books

     Issues         536
     Author         Dahl, Roald
     Title          Charlie and the chocolate factory

     Issues         422
     Author         Blume, Judy
     Title          Forever

     Issues         369
     Author         Danziger, Paula
     Title          The cat ate my gymsuit

     Issues         356
     Author         Dahl, Roald
                    The BFG

etc.
```

Figure 9.7 Report showing the most popular children's books

generated from a specified reader group and how many copies of that item are available.

These examples are intended to provide some insight into the depth and range of possibilities for generating management information which are inherent in BookshelF. The query language (ENGLISH, ACCESS, INFORM etc.) is a very powerful tool which allows the library manager to generate an almost infinite number of reports providing management information.

Some of the sentences may appear lengthy and complex, but they do not have to be created each time a specific report is required. Once the procedure for generating a particular report is set up, it can be saved for future use. Users also have the facility to design a menu system to access and generate these reports. This will be discussed in the following section.

PROCS

PROC is the procedure language of the PICK operating systems. With it a user can store a sequence of operations which can subsequently be called upon by a single word command. For this reason, they are particularly useful for storing long and complicated, or frequently used ENGLISH (or ACCESS or INFORM) commands. PROCs can be set up so as to accept inputs from a terminal, so this can be exploited by the system manager. PROCs do not however replace systems programming, which can only be carried out by the supplier who has access to the source code.

One of the major drawbacks in using ENGLISH, ACCESS or INFORM is that the time taken processing the query can be lengthy, and may slow the response time for other functions. When this disadvantage is weighed against the benefits of generating management information which is tailored to local requirements, the drawbacks are minor. SCSS are currently developing the management information capabilities of BookshelF for menu driven access, which will speed up the processing time considerably. Library managers, however, will no doubt continue to appreciate the facility to control the format of MI reports, particularly those which are required on an *ad hoc* basis.

PROCs, in common with other elements in the operating system, are held as items in files, and as such, must be stored in an account's Master Dictionary. All that is required is a pointer in the Master Dictionary to where the file containing the PROC is stored. The following example illustrates the procedure for creating a pointer to a PROC:

```
ED MD PROC1                 (PROC1 is the name by which
                            the PROC will be accessed)
NEW
I
001  PQ                     (Defines this as a PROC)
002  (MANINFO PROC1)        (Points to PROC1 in the file
                            MANINFO)FI
FI
'PROC1 FILED'
```

```
ED MANINFO PROC1

NEW

I

001     PQ

002     HSORT ACCESSION

003     H WITH STATUS = "O"

004     H TITLE DATE SUPPLIER

005     H HEADING "Items currently on order"

006     P

FI

'PROC1 FILED'
```

The H command stores the subsequent text string in an output buffer, whilst the P command executes the content of this buffer. The report can now be generated using the simple command PROC1 as follows

```
>PROC1
                         Items currently on order

ACCESSION    TITLE                  DATE ORDERED    SUPPLIER

o/1234/3     Jane Eyre              2/8/91          Blackwells

o/1365/4     Misery                 10/8/91         Blackwells

o/1367/1     Polo                   2/9/91          Askews

o/1377/2     The Tommyknockers      10/9/91         Askews
```

Figure 9.8 Report showing orders currently outstanding

Using the name 'PROC1' the actual record which will hold the procedure can now be written. In the following example, PROC1 is used to generate a report which shows items which are currently on order, when they were ordered, and from which supplier.

A further step would be to create a menu screen which would allow the operator to select the appropriate PROC to generate a desired report using a single keystroke. The facility to create menus is available in systems using either PICK or INFORMATION.

10 BookshelF user group

Karen Senior

The first BookshelF User Group meeting was held in September 1987 at Loughborough University of Technology, when the user base numbered just over 20 sites. The impetus for its set up lay initially with SCSS BookshelF staff, but it was stressed at that meeting that the Group should be run by the users, with invitations to meetings extended to the vendors when appropriate. The constitution of the Group states that 'the group shall be independent of the vendor' and that 'representatives of the vendor may attend meetings by invitation'. In practice, the relationship between the Group and the vendors has flourished to the extent that they are now invited to every meeting, and a senior member of their staff sits on the Group's Development Sub-Committee. Their contribution to the Group has been both extensive and welcome, without compromising the independence of the group.

The BookshelF User Group was formed to provide a forum for all users on matters relating to the use of the system. Its aims are:

- The exchange of information
- The identification of areas of development
- Discussion of problem areas
- Liaison with the vendor

In order to achieve these aims the Group holds regular meetings, usually three per year, and produces a twice yearly newsletter.

Corporate membership is open to all users of BookshelF, and to all those who have placed firm orders, on payment of a subscription fee. Each member institution has one vote.

The officers of the Group are the Chairman, Secretary and Treasurer. These officers are elected at the first general meeting of the Group of a calendar year. In the event of there being more than one nominee for a post, a vote is taken by those present. Proxy voting is allowed, and if a tie occurs, lots are drawn.

The Chairman is elected for one year and may be re-elected for a second. The Chairman chairs all the ordinary meetings of the Group, and is an ex-officio member of the Development Sub-Committee. Together with the other officers, the Chairman is also a member of the Executive Committee which manages the Group between meetings. The Secretary who is elected for two years and may be re-elected, convenes all meetings, prepares papers, agendas and minutes, and undertakes correspondence on behalf of the group.

When the Group was set up, the post of Secretary and Treasurer were combined but pressure of work resulting from the rapid growth of the user base necessitated a separate post of Treasurer being created. The Treasurer, who is also elected for two years and who may be re-elected, undertakes all financial transactions of the Group. In accordance with the Constitution, other officers may be elected as required.

The Group has two committee, namely the Development Sub-Committee, formed in 1988, and the Executive Committee, formed in 1991 to run the Group between meetings. The latter committee is composed of the three officers of the Group, the Developments Sub-Committee chairman and one other member of the Group. The executive, which meets roughly eight weeks prior to each User Group meeting, discusses the current finances and correspondence. One of its tasks is to evaluate the previous full User Group meeting, while another is to plan the next one in detail, covering topics such as venue, content and catering.

Most meetings are hosted by a BookshelF user. This arrangement enables members to view the idiosyncrasies of another BookshelF site and avoids or reduces the cost of room hire. As the Group gets bigger, user sites with accommodation of sufficient size (now 120+ users) in convenient locations is becoming scarcer. However, a venue pattern is emerging which comprises meetings being held once a year in London and Manchester, and one at another venue around the country. Successful meetings have been held at the Royal College of Nursing, the Institute of Personnel Management, and the Museum of Mankind, all in London; Manchester Polytechnic Department of Library and Information Studies, Suffolk College of Further and Higher Education at Ipswich, the Cairns Library Oxford, and Farnborough College of Technology.

The Group has considered and rejected plans to hold meetings by region, or by type of library, the consensus being that this would inevitably weaken it and that much of its coherence would be lost. It is intended, however, that smaller specialist meetings will be held if the need arises; one is being planned for the experienced users of the Serials module, with the intention of evaluating the major revision that module is now undergoing.

A compromise has been reached regarding the needs of the large number of BookshelF users attending meetings.

The meetings follow a recognizable pattern of four main elements:

1. Business This section includes Minutes of the last meeting and Matters arising, and reports from the Chairman, the Treasurer and the Developments Sub-Committee Convenor.
2. News from SCSS The BookshelF manager usually attends, together with at least one member of the BookshelF team. News can be of a general nature, regarding staffing or structure, or more specific, such as the detailed explanation of a major software release.
3. BUG reporting session This extremely valuable section allows users to voice their concerns about faults and problems, or indeed about any area of BookshelF which they wish to bring to the attention of the Group. Here, it has proved helpful to split the users into smaller groups by either operating system (PICK/PRIMES/UNIX), or by type of library (public, special, academic, school). These sessions promote lively and informative discussion of user problems, and members who would otherwise not speak up before a large audience are happy to do so in a smaller forum in less formal circumstances.

   Formal methods of reporting faults already exist in the form of the SCSS HELP desk and the A4 Fault Log form, but the BUG Reporting Sessions provide a useful informal way of sharing problems or worries. They promote discussion of areas which seem too trivial to mention on a formal basis, or which are not strictly in a 'fault' category. They also serve to identify the occasional longstanding 'bug' which has not been resolved.

They also provide answers to minor problems, simply by the sharing of expertise and experience. For instance, someone else may have discovered a way round a particular problem, or constructed a difficult and involved ENGLISH/INFORM sentence which can be used by other members.

Each group's discussion is lead by a committee member and notes are taken. When the meeting reconvenes as a whole, the main points emerging from them are discussed.

4. Presentations Each meeting concentrates on a particular module or on a discrete area of BookshelF such as Systems Management, multisite software, user education and developing the menu-driven OPAC. An experienced user will give a presentation on the chosen topic, and this is followed by questions and discussion. SCSS have been helpful in providing their own personnel for particular presentations, such as systems management. They have also secured the services of outside speakers who have addressed the group about other areas such as database management systems and inter-library loan packages. These outside speakers were part of SCSS's 75th Customer Celebrations in March 1990, which were held at a splendid London hotel. The entire user base gathered together, at SCSS's expense, and during the day, an extremely short User Group business meeting was held! In future, the Group intends to invite outside speakers to give presentations or demonstrations when the context of a particular meeting demands it. The notes from the presentations are edited and reproduced in the next BookshelF User Group newsletter.

User Group meetings allow plenty of time for informal discussion, either in the coffee or tea sessions which start and end the meetings, or during the lunch interval, where a buffet is usually provided. These informal gatherings benefit everyone from the big users to the one-man bands, and they can be more useful and informative than the formal proceedings themselves.

Users are given the opportunity to view the host's library BookshelF system and other facilities during the lunch break, and again this often provides valuable and useful sources of information. One user forgot to return to a main meeting for the afternoon session because he had become totally engrossed in the host library's BBC Domesday interactive video system, which, at the time, was state of the art technology!

The Development Sub-Committee is responsible for providing the vendor with a coordinated view of user requirements, an essential role of a user group. Membership of the Sub-Committee comprises the Convenor, the Chairman and Secretary and four other experienced users. It meets three times a year.

Its first task, when formed in 1988 was to undertake an overview of all aspects of the system in order to identify functional deficiencies. More recently it has selected more specific areas for consideration, e.g. the future direction of library housekeeping systems, indexing techniques, interfacing with CD-ROM, communications, and additional modules that may need to be added such as inter-library loans and management information.

The committee is pro-active in soliciting member's views, formally by questionnaires, or informally at User Group meetings, or by correspondence. It responds to member's needs, complaints and concerns; some of this work being done on an *ad hoc* basis by individual members and some more formally through meetings.

It is interesting to note the influence that the User Group has had on the development of the BookshelF software.

In early 1988, prior to the formation of a Development Committee, the Chairman circulated a list of possible developments of BookshelF, which provided a starting point for the Developments Sub-Committee. Users were asked to add their own suggestions to the list, which contained proposals for an on-line public access catalogue (OPAC), user-defined catalogue prints, full AACR2/MARC compatibility, a database creation/information retrieval module, on-line ordering, and menu-controlled management information. A description of outcomes in each of these areas illustrates the functioning of the Development Sub-Committee.

An OPAC was already under development when the Sub-Committee was formed and a command driven OPAC was released in March 1988, followed by a menu-driven version in the April/May 1989 software release. Though the arrival of the OPAC was welcomed, many users found implementation difficult and the Development Committee considered suggestions for greater ease of use. As a result SCSS have run several courses for menu-driven implementation, in addition to producing a screen designer manual. The framework of the OPAC is flexible, allowing users to adapt it to their own libraries, but this task is proving difficult for sites needing many access points, and media sub-searches. A major rewrite of OPAC and a media sub-selection facility are promised in SCSS's new development plan.

With the exception of one or two fields BookshelF is now fully AACR2/MARC compatible. User-defined catalogue prints are still not possible from the print option on the Catalogue menu, but some user definition is possible on prints from ENQUIRE. Once a search has been done on ENQUIRE, users can now define specific fields for display/print rather than choosing one of the seven pre-defined display/print formats. Of these original early suggestions, database creation is still being debated within the Group whilst a Management Information module has been implemented recently. This will be menu-driven, and designed to substitute for the *ad hoc* reporting facility provided by ENGLISH/INFORM. The Development Committee has assisted SCSS in providing user's views for this module. In addition to this, the extremely welcome and much sought after statistics package has been completed. This package caters for SCONUL, PLR and other statistics. Throughout the whole of the Development Committee's work, these facilities have been quoted as a priority need from many users; they have appeared on every questionnaire, and they have been mentioned at every User Group meeting. In an era of accountability, justification, and performance indicators, it is essential that BookshelF should provide its users with ease of access to management information statistics.

Management information has long been a key area for development within the BookshelF system. The development of the statistics package, referred to earlier, was preceded by a survey conducted by the User Group via the BookshelF User Group Newsletter. Priorities on specific statistics were asked for. SCSS stressed the urgency for obtaining user views for statistics on circulation, the first section of their package to be written.

All but two of the 19 respondents to the survey asked for a breakdown of loans per hour/day/month. The next highest priority was for details of the number of overdues generated, followed by the number of loans by reader status, and the number of readers per title. A league table showing use of each title, and the proportion of items on loan after first, second and third overdues were also priorities. The results of this detailed survey have hopefully been taken into account in the design of the new statistics package, together with statistics which need to be generated in a specific way for outside bodies.

The User Group will monitor the statistics package, to ensure that it provides the basic statistics that all users require. The addition of similar statistics for other modules is a continuing development. In the latest draft development plan issued by SCSS, a software link to allow download to records from CD-ROM into the BookshelF ordering format is under development, while further research into on-line ordering of items is to be undertaken.

At the Development Committee's first meeting, held in September 1988, two agendas were discussed. One of these was provided by the users, and one by SCSS. The Committee decided to amalgamate these two development programmes and to circulate the result to the users, asking for their priorities. Twenty-eight users replied to the questionnaire, and the results were summarized and made available at the March 1989 meeting. When the results had been circulated and analysed, a second questionnaire was drawn up by the Committee. Users were asked for further details in the highest priority areas, in order to assist SCSS, and to provide a rationale for developments.

The development options which attracted the most preferences concerned the Catalogue module, not surprising since this is the core module and it was the one with which most users were familiar. The ability to enter ENQUIRY from the Catalogue Maintenance screen, and return to where you were before, achieved the highest number of votes in all the modules. This facility became available via CMND key access on the 1990 software release together with CMND key access to ENQUIRY from Order Request and Receipt screens, the highest preference on the Acquisitions module.

The second highest preference on the Catalogue module was for user defined options for ENQUIRE display. Items retrieved by ENQUIRE are displayed in standard number order, but users wanted the facility to display the results of a search in their own preferred order, usually by class or by author. When the Committee investigated the position *vis a vis* other systems, they discovered that very few systems worldwide had this facility, and certainly no commercial integrated systems offered it. However, SCSS were made aware of the requirement, which at long last appears as part of their 1991 development plan as a 'sorting the results from OPAC enquiry' facility.

Further Thesaurus development attracted the third highest total of preferences, receiving the same total as Management Information, which was the top requirement on the Circulation module. Particular Thesaurus developments requested were access from the Catalogue, and links with other modules. The new SCSS development plan includes three enhancements: the ability to access the Thesaurus from the keywords field in the Cataloguing screen (CAT 1); the system automatically searching on a synonym by transferring the search to the preferred term; and the means to globally change all keywords affected on the Thesaurus entry screen.

From the Catalogue module, the survey also highlighted the need for a withdrawn items file, and the provision of more accession status codes (In transit, Missing). These enhancements have been programmed by SCSS, and all are now functional.

Many other developments highlighted in the User Group survey have already been implemented by SCSS. These include automatic archiving, display of incremental total of issues on the Accession file, downloading MARC records from external databases, multi-value corporate author field, display of personal before corporate authors, the ability to search for a standard number in OPAC, stock transfer, location history, enhancements to budget control, a short loan circulation function, and the option to display author and title when a book is returned.

Some of the requirements are still at the development, or under consideration, stage. These include the provision of recall letters for items on reserve (under development), and calendar enhancements for inputting a range of dates enabling long loan periods to be used on normal Circulation files during times when the library is open e.g. summer vacation for academic libraries. The ability to specify reader code and class number on letters is not being considered, although accession numbers are now included on them.

The original survey identified several new modules for development; the most frequently requested module being for an inter-library loans facility which would integrate with BookshelF software. The Developments Committee and SCSS have discussed various options, and users' views have been sought regarding the type and level of integration needed. The group identified over 20 users who were keen to purchase such a module as soon as it became available, and as the number of users has grown, no doubt this figure has increased. The Developments Committee investigated the PICK-based system developed at

Lancaster University, and a report produced for the Group and SCSS also appeared in the BookshelF User Group Newsletter. SCSS arranged for this system to be demonstrated at their customer celebration event in London, together with other PICK products. Other systems are being investigated, and SCSS are fully committed to purchasing and enhancing an existing inter-library loans package.

Two more modules were suggested for development by users: a database creation facility, and a training module. The former had been brought to the attention of users by the Chairman's original list of possible developments. The Developments Committee began to seriously explore database creation at the beginning of 1990, together with word processing and spreadsheet facilities. SCSS's view was that this area had to be user-led, and that it was up to the users to identify what they wanted. Questionnaires and background information prepared by the Developments Committee were distributed to the User Group. Unfortunately, the results were not conclusive. Fifteen replies were received, and of these, 13 respondents required software for creation of address labels, nine for equipment inventories, one for a diary and one for creation of staff manuals.

Possible solutions to some of the needs are to buy existing products, or to utilize ENGLISH to use existing files and statistics. Some of the requirements will be accommodated by SCSS's hardware and third party development plans. These plans include links to office automation (UNIPLEX), links to word processing (PRIMEWORD-WORDMARC), viewbase (under development) and an on-line link menu to on-line databases.

By late 1990 SCSS had satisfied the majority of the priorities identified by the Developments Committee. The full User Group, containing many new members, is being asked what features they would like to see in a new plan. Once again, the committee will coordinate the response. In parallel, SCSS have been formulating their own new developments plan, and the Committee has undertaken to help them clarify certain areas and to inform them of user reaction. The development process has hitherto been one of mutual cooperation between the Group and SCSS, and it is hoped that this will continue to be the case.

In addition to coordinating user's views on software development, the User Group undertakes other tasks which provide a useful service to its members.

For instance, it monitors software upgrades which have long been recognized as a source of problems in spite of the benefits that they obviously bring. Much of the 1991 full User Group March meeting was devoted to discussion of the 1990 major software release, which preceded the meeting by a few weeks. The group was critical of SCSS's method of upgrading software. Upgrading all modules at once in a complex system is unsatisfactory. SCSS are now re-evaluating the process and changes are promised for the future. The User Group also monitors the fault log sheets which are sent to SCSS to officially report software faults. One copy is sent to the Secretary, and one to the Editor for inclusion in the User Group Newsletter. In this way, members are able to see what is happening in other systems.

Librarians cannot afford to operate in a vacuum; learning alone can be time-consuming, and duplication of effort a waste of resources. Training and ongoing education needs are being examined by the Group; one member of the executive committee having recently been made responsible for this area. The Group has already identified the need for more detailed and useful user manuals and documentation. The experiences and knowledge of the members of the Group will be coordinated to provide a picture of the type and level of training needed at various stages of implementation and use of BookshelF.

Another extremely vital and useful function of the User Group is the provision of an awareness medium via a newsletter. The BookshelF User Group Newsletter, edited since its inauguration by Hilary Dyer at Loughborough University, provides a forum for the exchange of ideas within the Group. It has recently undergone a major change in format, and for the first time, the Spring/Summer 1991 issue is being sent for production to outside printers. There is currently a lively and so far inconclusive debate concerning a suitable logo for the newsletter.

The contents include an editorial; news from the supplier, which includes details of new sites and the latest developments; news from the users, covering new ways of looking at BookshelF, new sites and their plans, and new plans of existing sites; a problem page which incorporates the fault log sheets; reports or requests for information from the Developments Committee; and finally, letters to the editor. Summaries of presentations given at User Group meetings are printed in the newsletter; this being thought a more appropriate place for them than the User Group Minutes.

Recent issues of the newsletter have contained a comprehensive PICK bibliography, an article on a PICK environment word processing package called INFOLEX, and a presentation feature on BookshelF and local area networks. In common with colleagues in similar circumstances, the editor works extremely hard in gathering copy for the newsletter.

Information is circulated around the Group in another way. Because many people are unable to attend BUG meetings, detailed minutes are prepared and circulated to every member of the Group. These provide users with useful information and contacts, in addition to keeping them up to date with User Group activity.

Many user groups are set up solely to exert pressure on the vendor. While this is an acknowledged function of the BUG, it is only one of several functions.

Nevertheless, the user base has grown rapidly, and there is increased activity in the potential user base. Vendors have to think innovatively about their product: being the first to introduce new developments, or to promise bespoke contractual work will give the company an edge over competitors and produce a sale. Research and development should obviously be part of a vendor's business strategy, but at the same time, a vendor's current customers also need constant development, improvement, and support in their software/hardware options. A fine balance has to be maintained between the two and BookshelF User Group activity tries to ensure that this balance is maintained.

The group has had substantial input in many areas of the BookshelF operation. It has addressed the wider issues of integration, windowing, networking, indexing, and new modules, in addition to being concerned about the nitty gritty issues which confront users every day, and which are therefore equally important. It provides the means whereby users can help to direct and influence their own future. What else could be more challenging or rewarding?

BookshelF's Scottish user group

BookshelF's Scottish User Group came into being following informal discussions between several users as to the desirability of a more localized supplement to the BookshelF User Group based in the South. An invitation was issued to all BookshelF customers in Scotland to attend a meeting in Paisley College of Technology on 1 August 1989. It was agreed at the inaugural meeting that, at least initially, there would be no formal constitution and no office bearers – the objective was to allow users to meet together to discuss matters of mutual interest and to provide localized mutual support. Biannual meetings were to provide an opportunity to discuss product development and to offer the opportunity of a coordinated interface between users and SCSS. It was considered by all present that tangible benefits could thus accrue to individual users, large and small, by participating in such a forum. It was also agreed that meeting venues were to be by rotation amongst users and to be organized and minuted by the host user. A geographic spread of meeting locations was thus assured. The second meeting was held in Edinburgh, hosted by the Scottish Office Library (October 1989) followed by Dumfries (May 1990), East Kilbride (October 1990) and Old Meldrum (March 1991) hosted by North East Scotland Library Services. Due to the ever-increasing numbers of large BookshelF users based in Scotland there is no doubt that the Scottish User Group has developed, however unwittingly, into an extremely influential pressure group for product development. The results of the early group meetings are now showing in the BookshelF software and in its product upgrade and development plan. Another of the positive outcomes from group meetings has been the opportunity to view BookshelF in action in different library environments. Librarians from the academic and special sectors have been impressed by the scale and amazed at the simplicity of public library systems whilst their public library colleagues have both admired and been overawed by the complexities of cataloguing and classification in special and academic libraries. There is no doubt that the status of BookshelF User has added a very welcome level of communication to the library profession in Scotland.

11 Support services

Introduction

Most librarians would agree that amongst the primary criteria for selecting a library system is the degree of support offered by the system supplier. 'Support' involves basic help with program functions in the initial stages of setting up a system, training courses, adequate manuals, dedicated programmers involved in software development, dedicated engineers who are *au fait* with the computers and peripherals in use by customers, fast response times for requests for assistance, an established user group which enjoys a good, interactive relationship with the supplier, and a 'Help desk', easily contactable by telephone. Specialist Computer Systems and Software Ltd. (SCSS) have, since their inception , adhered to a 'total system' philosophy, the principal tenet being that they provide a 'total solution' to system requirements. This 'solution' covers software, hardware, maintenance, support and training.

SCSS acquired the distribution and development rights to the BookshelF software in 1985. The first significant development was the conversion of the software to a multi-user environment. A further development was the porting of the software to a Prime INFORMATION environment, thereby utilising a platform which used extremely powerful processors.

The Company, the software and the support offered have gone from strength to strength since those early days, and the 'total solution' philosophy has become a reality. This chapter describes the ways in which SCSS supports its BookshelF users, in terms of advice, software and hardware maintenance and documentation.

The Help desk

Two qualified librarians are currently assigned to the Help Desk, based in Stoke-on-Trent. They provide telephone support for all customers i.e. those who pay an annual maintenance fee. SCSS respond to all requests for help – major or minor – from queries about basic functions in specific modules, to complex systems problems or hardware faults.

On receipt of a request for assistance from a user, with either software or hardware problems, the call is logged to a computerized system, detailing the name of the caller, organisation, problem details, who took the call, who is to deal with it if immediate assistance is not possible from the duty Help librarian. A daily report of requests for help is produced and outstanding calls are 'chased' and remedied, or actioned at the earliest possible convenience. Calls are coded for quick reference and to provide a management information facility for SCSS. The calls are coded as (W)aiting, (B)ug, (D)evelopment (i.e. bespoke programming required, (U)rgent, and (C)ustomer will phone back. In the last category, the user is asked to repeat a procedure, to ensure that human error is not the cause of the problem.

In the case of hardware problems, the Help librarian runs through a series of diagnostic checks with the customer, over the telephone, before the problem is passed to the engineers. If equipment has malfunctioned, or broken down, and requires an engineer on site, an 8-hour response time is guaranteed. Replacement parts are supplied for faulty computers and peripherals.

If programming assistance is required, the response time for help will vary according to whether the problem is at a system-wide level, whether it is due to a software 'bug', or whether the system needs additional programming to allow a user to execute a non-standard function. There is no doubt that software assistance is more expeditious for customers who have modem support. In these instances, programmers are able to login to a particular library's system, from Headquarters, and diagnose and/or rectify the problem either immediately or only hours from the receipt of the request for help. Timescales and costs for **bespoke** programming, however, are agreed by negotiation with the customer.

Seventy-five per cent of BookshelF customers currently have modem support. All new installations are encouraged to acquire this facility to obviate the need for BookshelF programmers to go on-site – a costly and time-consuming exercise.

Support costs

At present, BookshelF customers pay an annual maintenance fee of 12½ per cent to 15 per cent of the initial purchase price of the system to SCSS in return for support. This is an approximate figure as some libraries' systems are developed over time, additional modules are added, new equipment is acquired etc. and this may affect the maintenance charges. Sites which have not incorporated a modem facility into the system pay an additional charge.

Training

When a library organization acquires a BookshelF library system SCSS expects the customer to purchase a minimum of two days training for each module acquired. This training is normally carried out on site and is essential in familiarizing the new customer with the functions of the system. By arrangement with the customer training on the BookshelF system may be for a single person (i.e. training an on-site [in-house] trainer) or for a number of people who will be using a particular module. The training course will take account of the local situation and needs and will be tailored to the local hardware configuration. Further training days may be purchased from the company as and when the need is identified. The current (approximate) cost of one day's training (as a one-off) is £350 per day for the BookshelF training staff to go 'on-site' to a library in response to specified training requirements.

For larger systems, e.g. public libraries and some colleges, it is usual for the organization to purchase a set of days. The BookshelF approach is to focus concentrated attention on a purchasing site for a considerable period of time when the system is installed, until it has reached a stable state. This stabilising period is agreed with SCSS and during this time the bulk of basic skills training on the functions of specific modules takes place. Public library systems, for example, which are multi-site have purchased between 20 and 40 days training in the installation period. This has its advantages – i.e. the cost per day for such bulk purchases is considerably discounted! Such concentrated training periods, however, allow SCSS, and the purchasing library to tailor the programme to local needs and circumstances.

Training courses

SCSS mounts courses which include more advanced features of the BookshelF software, addressed particularly to users concerned with system's administration. These courses are usually held off-site, at various locations throughout the UK, for BookshelF users from a number of different library organizations. Courses have been held at BookshelF HQ (Stoke-on-Trent), Prime Computers London and regional offices, and occasionally sites which have established systems running will host courses on specific topics. Once a library has successfully progressed through a settling-in period, courses on 'How to live with your system' are the next stage in skills acquisition.

The advantage of being trained off-site for one or two days are twofold. Firstly, users are free from the usual (and inevitable) day to day interruptions in the workplace, and secondly, users can share experience, common knowledge, problems and solutions by working together at the training location. SCSS mounts such courses in response to expressed needs from customers, which come either via the User Group or from individual users direct to BookshelF.

The training courses so far offered and run by BookshelF have included the following.

1. *OPAC design*

The nature of the BookshelF OPAC (On-line Public Access Catalogue) is such that a set of default screens exists which act as a template for a menu-driven OPAC. SCSS decided on this approach to OPAC design in order to cater for the wide variations in requirements of different library organizations. Thus, although the default OPAC is serviceable it can be customized by the user, to suit local requirements. Customization necessitates using the PICK or Information Editor facility to rewrite the screens, and to select the wording and layout appropriate to their particular catalogue database. Thus users can accommodate their own particular style of classification scheme, thesaurus descriptors, keywords, title words, author headings and so on.

2. *Query or control languages*

ENGLISH, ACCESS, INFORMATION etc. are the languages which users need to familiarize themselves with in order to exploit the data held in the relational files as management information. Specific courses are held on each of these languages to introduce systems users to the use of verbs (e.g. SORT, LIST, COUNT, STAT, SELECT etc.), syntax, simple sentence structures and finally straker manipulation, a facility which allows queries or instructions to be saved.

3. *Advanced techniques in PICK, INFORMATION, and UNIX environments*

At this level, system users learn details about file structures, how to create dictionary items, how to display data to show different correlations for management information purposes, e.g. in the Prime INFORMATION environment. Users learn how to create their own menu systems for stored executable commands, and provide on-line documentation for the menus which they create.

4. *PRIMOS courses*

PRIMOS is the operating system of Prime computers and is the platform on which INFORMATION resides. The PRIMOS courses are aimed specifically at systems administrators. These may be conducted by BookshelF systems staff or by Prime computer trainers.

Project and account management

In addition to basic module training and advanced courses for BookshelF users, SCSS assign a project manager to all new large installations. The project manager acts as the main coordinator of software and hardware procedures at installation set-up and 'going live'. The project manager functions as a primary point of contact between the user and the Company, and he/she attends preliminary meetings and review sessions held on site, enabling SCSS, as the supplier, to keep abreast of developments and progress. This interface is regarded as an important activity, particularly in the early stages of implementing a system in a library organization and is carried through to the installation's establishment and maturity when an account manager adds the site to his/her caseload. All sites are overseen by dedicated BookshelF managers with regional responsibilities throughout the UK, ensuring continuity of support and a point of contact.

Newsletters

The Help Desk produces an occasional newsletter – 'Off-the-Shelf – with the aim of keeping customers up-to-date with developments at BookshelF and SCSS. It includes items on general news and views, staff changes at BookshelF, new services, developments in technology and new equipment, software developments, technical tips and advice, new customers, and notices of forthcoming meetings and seminars. 'Off-the-Shelf' also includes special features which take the form of customer profiles written by users of the BookshelF system. These give a brief library history, equipment used, software, staff, advantages and disadvantages of the BookshelF system, future plans and photographs.

'Off-the-Shelf' is intended to complement the BookshelF User Group Newsletter which is produced independently by an editorial team of BookshelF system users.

Documentation

A range of manuals are available for librarians and systems managers. These are issued in versions appropriate to PICK or Prime (INFORMATION) users as follows:

1. Acquisitions Module
2. Back-up System
3. Catalogue Module
4. Circulation – PICK sites
5. Circulation – PRIME sites – Multi-Site
6. Circulation – PRIME sites – Single Site
7. Editor – PICK
8. Editor - PRIME
9. Logbook – Circulation Transaction Logging System manual
10. OPAC Module
11. OPAC Screens Manual
12. Preparing for BookshelF
13. PRIME Systems Manual
14. PRIMOS Manual
15. Screen Designer Manual
16. Serials Control Module
17. Software Releases
18. Systems Definition Manual
19. Thesaurus Module

Part 3 BookshelF in context: case studies

12 BookshelF in the academic library: Paisley College of Technology

Stuart James

Introduction

Paisley College is a Scottish Central Institution originally founded in 1897; all its courses are now to either first degree or higher degree level. The College's degree and postgraduate courses are validated by the Council for National Academic Awards (CNAA), and the College is a CNAA self-validating institution. In 1987 (when the BookshelF system was acquired) the College had 3,000 full-time equivalent (FTE) students and a teaching staff of 296. In the intervening years it has grown further to some 3,500 FTE although the teaching staff numbers have slightly declined. From 1990 the College has been pursuing a closer association with Glasgow University.

The courses at Paisley College are largely technical and vocational: engineering (civil, electrical and electronic, mechanical and production); natural sciences (physics, mathematics and statistics, chemistry including industrial chemistry, and biology); and social/business etc. studies (applied social studies, economics and management, land economics). The College also houses a number of specialist units (for example, the Paisley College Quality Centre).

The task of the Library is to serve all the College's needs: primarily undergraduate and postgraduate teaching but also research and development and consultancy. In 1987 the Library had a stock of 102,000 volumes and a total library staff of 23 FTE (of which seven were professional graduate librarians). In 1987 the College Library subscribed to some 1,500 journals, but these have been subsequently cut to approximately 1,200. The Library has always been heavily-used and a short loan collection has been especially popular with students. The pattern of student residence, with only a limited amount of residential accommodation available at the College, put the emphasis on study use of the Library during the day and overnight borrowing from the short loan collection in the late afternoon, supplementing standard lending services.

Adoption of the BookshelF system

Immediately prior to its acquisition of BookshelF in 1987 Paisley College Library had operated with an automated catalogue and a manual issue system. The need for automation had become urgent with the prospect of the manual issue system, which had long outlived its planned lifespan, about to break down irretrievably and the likely ending of the SCOLCAP/LOCAS Cataloguing Service; replacement by manual alternatives was not considered given the availability of efficient automated systems.

If this gave some urgency to the situation, there were also considerable positive reasons for wishing to automate the Library fully. In a period of rapidly expanding student numbers (and with student numbers predicted to continue expanding for the foreseeable future) but at the same time with a more-or-less static library staff complement, the advantages of the greater efficiency of an automated system were of course attractive. Furthermore it was recognized that an efficient automated system could provide a vastly improved level of service to all Library users; the labour-intensive manual issue system resulted in issue of books for a longer period than was desirable. Increased turnover of the Library stock, and consequent higher probability of availability of books to all users, were seen as advantages likely to be gained from an automated circulation system. At the same time, looking even further into the future, it was recognized that the further potential for improvement in the Library service through an automated circulation control and sophisticated database system offered very considerable longer term benefits.

One of the first stages undertaken was the preparation in 1986 of a highly detailed specification for a potential system specifically suited to the requirements of Paisley College Library. This specification was issued widely to suppliers of library automated systems and their responses and tenders were invited.

By early 1987 the Library's choice had been narrowed to two systems, one of which was BookshelF.

In 1987 Paisley College was one of the largest users of Prime computing equipment in the United Kingdom. The compatibility of BookshelF with Prime was, therefore, a distinct attraction. Considerable benefits in adopting hardware which was compatible with other College systems were foreseen, and in the event have proved to be as valuable as anticipated: expert support has been provided by the College's Computer Centre staff, and having a system which is compatible with the College's administration system, the download of student records into the BookshelF system has been achieved following some initial teething problems (mainly relating to the College's database format).

While the hardware benefits were considerable, BookshelF had already been shortlisted for its intrinsic merits. With two exceptions it matched the highly detailed specification as well as any other system available. These two exceptions were: the non-availability of MARC tags which the College Library had been using through the SCOLCAP and LOCAS Services; and the non-availability at the time of purchase of a short-loan system. The College Library was prepared to accept the loss of the MARC tags, given all the other benefits which would accrue from the BookshelF system; the second lack was, however, critical. The promise of such a short-loan system being written to the College's specification was a condition of purchase. In the event a system was supplied on time and has proved satisfactory; more details of this are given below. The fact that BookshelF had been developed and was being marketed as a British system also aided the decision: the ready availability of software support from SCSS has proved a particularly useful feature of BookshelF and allowed its flexible development within Paisley College Library.

The BookshelF system was therefore purchased in 1987 for Paisley College Library as a fully integrated library administration system. The only exception to this was that the Serials module was not purchased; in-house microcomputer programs had been developed which were running perfectly satisfactorily (although not dealing with ordering and receipting). Details of bound serials holdings are, however, now entered on the main Library catalogue database.

The initial processor used was a Prime 250, a piece of hardware already within the College and which had an estimated life for the Library system of only some two or three years.

Application was made almost immediately for a replacement processor and a Prime 4050 was acquired in 1988. The hardware is located in the College's Computer Centre and, although entirely dedicated to the Library system, is fully integrated with other College processors. Full hardware support is provided initially by the College's Computer Centre staff. Since the BookshelF system in Paisley College Library is written in Prime Information and this is a language which is used elsewhere in the College, additional programming support had also been made available within the College for a number of purposes (for example, different levels of password control were established by College staff). In addition, members of the College Library staff have also been taught Prime Information to enable them to use the system to its maximum benefit.

Acquisitions module

Prior to the acquisition of BookshelF Paisley College Library had tested the SCOLCAP acquisitions system for a full financial year. This had proved a generally satisfactory system although some financial operations had to be carried out manually by SCOLCAP staff in Edinburgh. The Library reverted to a manual system for one financial year (April 1987 to March 1988) before changing to the BookshelF module. Some initial software problems were experienced in allocating and totalling budgeted amounts, but following an upgrade of the accounts system as supplied, the College Library staff became accustomed to the method of accounting using the BookshelF system. A number of changes to procedures have proved necessary, such as: bar-coding on receipt; dealing with initial cataloguing problems at the acquisitions stage; allocating control numbers; and setting up budget and suppliers files. Once these procedures were settled the system has worked well.

Estimated prices are entered at the time of acquisition and these are automatically updated by the system once the book is delivered and the real price is known. Thus accurate bookfund commitment and expenditure figures may be made available at any time without notice, and without clerical effort. While this is monitored regularly, it becomes particularly important in October of each year when unspent funds from departmental bookfund allocations and from the reserve fund are re-allocated for book purchase for the remainder of the financial year, and

	Additions	Total Stock
1987–88	4457	102,000
1988–89	4013	105,500
1989–90	7535	112,000
1990–91	5438	114,000

Figure 12.1 Bookstock and additions to stock

towards the end of the financial year when constant checks are made to ensure that funds are being spent as fully as possible.

The high average cost of academic titles, particularly in the light of the College's concentration on scientific and technical subjects, means that Paisley College Library has a lower throughput of numbers of titles per year for the amount of money actually spent than many libraries. Inflation in periodical subscription prices also affects this trend. Since the main role of the College remains undergraduate teaching, greater emphasis is currently being placed on the acquisition of further books for student use.

Orders are printed out in the standard BookshelF format on standard paper (special stationery was considered unnecessarily expensive) and sent by post to suppliers. For many years the College's major book supplier has been John Smith & Son (Glasgow) Ltd. In October 1990 the College Library agreed with Smiths to an experiment of transmitting orders electronically. A sub-program was written by a member of the College staff in Prime Information to format the BookshelF order record into the new BEDIS format which Smiths were adopting. The experiment proved a great success and all orders now are transmitted electronically to Smiths, with paper copies produced only to check catalogue records for the OPAC. While this system has obvious immediate advantages, it is in its future possibilities that it is most exciting. The College Library expects to have access to Smith's own database; electronic invoicing is a further probability. In the longer term the possible downloading of records from Smiths back into the College's BookshelF system becomes a possibility. One attraction of this is the possible purchase of full catalogue records (ultimately including enhancements such as contents lists etc.) at the time of ordering a particular title.

Cataloguing module

The overall effect of using the BookshelF integrated system has been to move the cataloguing process back to the acquisitions stage (and staff). This has proved a natural and simple process in a smaller/medium size academic library. On receipt of copies order records can be identified with a separate stream of control numbers for upgrading where necessary. Although the decision hitherto not to download records was taken for other reasons, this process has made the decision easier to implement and the system has proved cheaper and simpler than downloading.

Prior to its acquisition of the BookshelF system Paisley College Library had been a member of the Scottish Libraries Co-operative Automation Project (SCOLCAP) for a number of years. As a result of this the College Library had immediately available a standard MARC tape containing 25,000 of its most recent and most heavily-used records out of a total potential database at that time of 70,000 records. This tape was immediately and successfully downloaded into the BookshelF system and indexed to provide an initial database. As indicated above the College Library had accepted the decision to lose MARC tags and a few MARC fields from its catalogue records; it was, however, felt that should the need arise the re-introduction of tags on a global basis would not present an insuperable programming problem. Various methods of adding the remaining records to the BookshelF database were considered: among these were download of records from a proprietary database system (such as the British Library or OCLC) or the employment of a contractor to generate records. In the event funds for such an exercise were not available, and so conversion began immediately by manual keyboarding using existing staff in the Library. This exercise is described in some more detail below, but suffice to say that it was effectively completed in 1990 by which time the database stood at 90,000 titles.

In practice a number of local modifications to the standard BookshelF system have been found necessary. The edition field is not used, but edition statements are placed immediately after the title. This enables edition data to be displayed in the standard default display format on the OPAC screens. Similarly, it was decided to simplify headings by entering authors, compilers, editors etc. in the same author field. Where differentiation is required the term 'editor' etc. is inserted in the heading. The series field presented some problems due to the difficulty of

1987	26,000*
1988	56,000
1989	78,446
1990	92,000
1991	105,189

* Records transferred from SCOLCAP file.

Figure 12.2 Records on the BookshelF database

searching on a combination of series title and series number; in some instances in Paisley College Library, where series numbering several hundred items might require to be searched, this posed some particular problems. A temporary solution was produced by joining numbers to the series title with a hyphen, but eventually an upgrade of the software has allowed searching by series title and number where the two items are entered in the series title field only. The notes and keywords field have both been used quite extensively, but to date Paisley College Library has found no use for the subject field.

Prior to the introduction of BookshelF, Paisley College Library relied for subject access on a UDC card catalogue. Since conversion to BookshelF, UDC numbers in a simplified form are only used for shelfmarks. Extra classified entries are no longer made, although their use was considered in the early stages. Experience, however, has shown that alphabetical subject access is a more popular, and potentially more powerful, means of subject access for users of the OPAC. Searching on UDC numbers is, however, possible.

OPAC

An OPAC system was seen as one of the major requirements of the College Library in the original specification. From the experience of other libraries, and from practice which developed within Paisley College Library itself, it was recognized that the College Library would be committed to a wide-scale programme of user education. It was therefore decided early on to offer the standard BookshelF command-driven system as an OPAC. This was made publicly available in 1988, before BookshelF had produced its own menu-driven OPAC system. Simple instructions were provided in notices beside each terminal with more detailed instructions available in leaflets. Library staff were also available to give assistance where necessary. The system was tested briefly on a small number of public terminals and worked satisfactorily; it was then quickly expanded to provide up to 18 OPAC terminals for student and staff use.

The introduction of a fully automated system has given a greater impetus to library education programmes. This instruction coupled with a printed handbook and instructions displayed beside each terminal have generally proved adequate for student use of the command-driven system.

The initial OPAC menu-driven system provided by BookshelF was not considered suitable for use in Paisley College Library. It was found to be too slow and to have unsuitable examples. In the Summer of 1990, however, the menu-driven system was re-written by Library staff to their own specification. This is now offered as an alternative for students who have not been given instruction in the command-driven system or who do not feel confident enough to use it.

The OPAC thus described has worked satisfactorily since its introduction. The main problem with it is related to its success with users in the amount of processor time absorbed by searches. It does, of course, have considerable potential for immediate improvement, as well as for long-term development. A number of these aspects are indicated below in the paragraphs on Thesaurus and future developments.

Circulation

Circulation was seen as the most urgent requirement of the new system, although of course it depended on the provision of a catalogue database. As the Library had not had any previous automated issue system it was necessary to bar-code the entire Library stock. The bar-code and transitional procedures are described in greater detail below.

One of the many attractions of an automated issue system was that it would allow the Library greater flexibility in the loan of materials. Initially it was decided to adopt a standard loan period of three weeks for most materials. The short loan system is described below, but both collections were supplemented by selected books being available for three-day loans. This pattern

BookshelF CATALOGUE ENQUIRY 13 NOV 1991

Std. no 0745600107 Medium Text Classes 32(41)
Title Introduction to British politics: analysing a capitalist democracy

Author Dearlove, John; Saunders, Peter
Edition edited by
Imprint Oxford: Polity, 1984
Series
Series no. Collation 458p
Subjects
Keywords Great Britain. Politics

Notes Includes bibliographies and index 6 COPIES IN STOCK

	Acc'n nos.	Status	Date due	Location
1.	7480003361	Available	13-06-91	Reserve collection
2.	7480003362	Available	12-06-91	Reserve collection
3.	7480005023	Available	05-11-91	Reading-room, three-day loan
4.	7480015108	On loan to 74902123	20-11-91	Reading-room, loan stock
5.	7480014638	On loan to 74905513	02-12-91	Reading-room, loan stock

P(revious), S(elect), A(ccessions), Q(uit), R(ewrite)

Figure 12.3 Record display from Catalogue Enquiry

has remained unchanged so far, but a new category of one-day loans (based on management data from the Circulation History file) is being considered to reduce even further reliance on the short loan collection.

The Circulation system was introduced fully at the start of the 1988–89 session. There have been, however, considerable delays in making the overdue and fines systems work satisfactorily to the College's specification. In the event these have only been fully operational from the start of the 1990–91 session. The two years in between did, however, allow a more gradual and slightly less traumatic (for both Library staff and users) transition from a previously very lax and liberal system to a more rigidly controlled automated system. There was considerable internal discussion at various committees concerning the method of operation of the system; the Library staff had worked out entitlements for different categories of readers based on previous experience. (See Figure 12.4 for Reader Categories.) There were, however, moves within the College to insist on the equal treatment of all users, whether staff or students. A workable solution to this has been found which gives equality to all users within what is possible in relation to their differing patterns of use of the Library. One

PCL READER CODES

Code	Description
DB	DEPARTMENTAL BORROWER
DF	DEFAULTER
EC	EXTERNAL, CORPORATE
EI	EXTERNAL, INDIVIDUAL
ET	EXTERNAL, TEMPORARY
EV	EXTERNAL, VISITOR
GC	GRADUATE COURSE
HD	HONOURS DEGREE
IS	IN-SERVICE COURSE
OD	ORDINARY DEGREE
OL	OUTGOING ILL
PG	PART-TIME GRADUATE COURSE
PU	PART-TIME UNDERGRADUATE COURSE
SE	STAFF, ESTABLISHMENT
SR	STAFF, RESEARCH
SV	STAFF, VISITING COLLEGE
TL	TEST, LIBRARY-BASED
TR	TRANSFERRED FOR REVIEW

List as of 13.11.91

Figure 12.4 Reader categories

outcome of this debate was the decision, taken at the highest level within the College, that academic staff be charged fines for overdues. After much initial discussion, and now after experience of the system, a pattern of overdue notices and fines charged has been established.

In addition to the standard loan system an immediate requirement had been for a short loan system. The short loan

Table of Fines

a) The cost is per item.

b) 'Days' refers to days when the Library is open.

RESERVE COLLECTION

5 pence per quarter-hour, up to £1.00 per day.

REST OF LIBRARY STOCK

3 days overdue	20p
4 days overdue	25p
5 days overdue	30p
6 days overdue	35p
7 days overdue	40p
8 days overdue	60p
9 days overdue	80p
10 days overdue	£1.00
11 days overdue	£1.20
12 days overdue	£1.40
13 days overdue	£1.70
14 days overdue	£2.00
Cost-recovery thereafter	

Figure 12.5 Table of fines

collection in Paisley College Library had grown to be of very considerable importance to students and so its immediately efficient operation was absolutely essential. SCSS had promised to write a short loan system to the Library's specification. This was done and worked generally satisfactorily from the start. Advantage was taken of moving to an automated system to make the operation of the collection more flexible; where, under the manual system, days had been divided into specified periods for loans, the automated system simply offered a three-hour loan period. At the same time there was written into the system the facility for overnight loans from 4.30 pm in the afternoon to 9.15 am on the following morning (although the Library remains open to 9.00 pm). This was also extended to cover weekend loans from 4.30 pm on Friday afternoons to 9.15 am on Monday mornings, even though the Library is open on Saturdays. A booking system for students for the short loan collection was written, but took over a year before the software operated satisfactorily. The fines system essential to the short loan collection was introduced from the start.

	Short loans	Standard Loans	Total	FTE
1988–89	22,000	48,000	68,000	3,037
1989–90	27,500	53,500	81,000	3,117
1990–91	34,000*	66,000*	100,000*	3,365

* Estimated projections

Figure 12.6 Loan issues and student numbers (FTE)

As indicated above one of the aims in establishing the new automated circulation system was to improve overall access to and use of the bookstock by all users. In particular one prominent intention was to move students away from over-reliance on the short loan collection into making greater use of the Library's full collections. The greater flexibility and control offered by an automated system, particularly given the pattern of three-week or three-day loans in addition to the three-hour loans from the short loan collection, has aided this process. Similarly, the more regular return of books into the lending collection is intended to increase accessibility of the bookstock for users. Additional sums of money have been made available in order to purchase extra copies of heavily-used student texts. This has all helped to achieve the aims stated above, and the benefits of the new system are now being seen more clearly.

Unless a book is requested by another reader up to two renewals of each loan are possible without the book being brought back to the Library. In fact, the more regular return of books to the Library has been a feature of the new system. This has ultimately been reinforced with the full implementation of the fines system. The system has now gained general acceptance and is working satisfactorily in all but a few cases.

Conversion to BookshelF

Paisley College Library's conversion to the BookshelF system was achieved with only the addition of two temporary members of staff for a one-year period, and with the Library open at all times during the conversion. The largest physical problem was undoubtedly that of bar-coding the bookstock. None of the stock had been bar-coded until the conversion programme began.

As with database conversion the initial concentration was on works in the short loan collection. When these had been completed and with all new books being bar-coded as they were added to stock, staff time during the first Summer vacation available was concentrated on bar-coding books for which a record was available from the SCOLCAP database. At the same time a system was established at the issue counter where any book presented for loan which had not been bar-coded could have a minimum record created (comprising its shelf number and the first letter of the first significant word in the title), be quickly accessioned in the accessions file, have a bar-code added to the book and the book thus issued through the circulation system.

Under the previous manual issue system each book had carried a plastic card containing the name of the author, a short title and accession number; two copies had been bought of every bar-code, and the second bar-code was added to the plastic card which was removed from the book and put in a box for the two temporary members of staff to take away and catalogue from the master card catalogue record. The system was intended to ensure that all books issued for loan were bar-coded and catalogued with no delay for the reader. Since records of items on loan could not be altered until their return a correct record was created from the stock card and the bar-code transferred from the minimum record on the book's return.

At the end of that session, during the following Summer vacation, it then became a simpler matter to check the shelves for those books which had not been bar-coded. Unbar-coded stock cards were matched with books on the shelves, both were bar-coded and the stock card and bar-code were keyboarded while the books remained on the shelves available for issue. Following these procedures the database, and bar-coding of the bookstock, were effectively completed for all the active stock of the Library by the end of the 1989 Summer vacation.

With no extra appointments made to the Library staff, other than the two temporary ones mentioned above, it was not possible to appoint a Systems Librarian. Thus systems responsibility fell to two then Assistant Librarians in particular (for Circulation and for Technical Services) with other members of the Library staff, both professional and non-professional, taking specific systems responsibilities related to their particular areas or tasks. This spread of expertise among a fairly wide range of the Library staff has proved beneficial in several ways: not only has it provided more than one member of staff able to respond to problems in other areas with some confidence in the absence of staff with specific responsibility, but it has also broadened general familiarity with the system.

Given the problems inherent in the previous system full automation of the College Library had been seen as a major positive development by all levels of Library staff. Motivation towards automation and the changes that it would involve did not, therefore, prove a serious problem. Inevitably, as a completely new system was introduced and some bugs were discovered by staff working directly with Library users, some annoyance and disenchantment came in. This has, however, been kept to a minimum not only by dealing with problems as they arise but in attempting to set up the system in such a way that it would cause the least amount of friction between Library counter staff and users; overdue fines, for example, do not have to be paid immediately and any complaints were to be directed to senior Library staff, supposedly bypassing the counter staff and so minimizing the amount of conflict that might arise. At the same time full training in the BookshelF system as it related to their own areas of operation was of course given to all members of the Library staff. This has been a continuing process as new areas of the system have been introduced or as it has been changed in any way. Automation led inevitably to surpluses of labour in certain areas but these have been taken up by new tasks created and by overdue re-deployment of staff time into direct services to users.

Further development of BookshelF in Paisley College

The preceding sections of this chapter should all have indicated the successful conversion to the BookshelF system in an intensively-used academic library over a four-year period. They should also indicate that the BookshelF system has for some time been fully operational within the College Library, with only final tidying up and adjustments of the system being undertaken during the last twelve months. Many benefits were foreseen for the introduction of the system, as explained above, and these benefits are now being felt within the College Library. In particular they are enabling the Library to provide a higher level of service to increasing numbers of students, with greater flexibility of response to varying student needs. All these patterns will continue, but the Library staff can see many further developments arising out of automation to equip the College Library for the 21st Century. Initially two modules of the system will take the Library some way in that direction.

Community Information

The Community Information module was introduced in 1989. At a training course in Edinburgh and immediately subsequent to the course, an outline of how the system would apply in Paisley College Library was drawn up and various sample pages were entered. Since the Community Information system is entirely menu-driven, and pages may not be directly searched by keyword, the structure of the data is of great importance. The initial division in the Paisley College system is between pages giving information about the Library and pages giving information about other departments in the College. In both cases the system will be expanded to include relevant data from outside the College (for example, details of other libraries and facilities in the area). Keeping existing information up-to-date and adding new pages have proved time-consuming tasks which have frequently been put aside to concentrate on more immediately urgent work. As a result the system is not as fully developed as had originally been planned. Although some student use is made of it, it is not as heavily used as had originally been hoped. The initial task in making full use of the Community Information system is still to add the remaining pages originally envisaged. It is also hoped that provision of colour screens, and possibly some hypertext principles, will make the system more attractive and encourage wider use of it.

Thesaurus

The potential for using the Thesaurus module to aid users in natural language searches on the database is both powerful and sophisticated. In order to achieve this, however, the Thesaurus database itself needs to be built up with great care and using the full potential of the relationships provided by the software. Paisley College Library has decided against a partial solution of entering terms with only incomplete cross references, or with some relationships not expressed. On the other hand, a trial of developing the Thesaurus in a specific area indicated clearly the complexity of the task of attempting to build a Thesaurus across wide subject fields, and of course the amount of time that would be required for such an exercise.

An alternative would be to take a commercially produced Thesaurus in machine-readable form and download it directly into the BookshelF software. While the technical difficulties of such an approach could no doubt be overcome, no suitable commercial Thesaurus has been found to be available covering the range of subjects required by Paisley College Library. Meanwhile development work continues within the College Library and means of extending this to provide ultimately full Thesaurus coverage across the whole database are being explored using existing Library staff resources. The possibility of using a machine-readable version of UDC to provide the basis for a Thesaurus will also be investigated.

Other developments

Besides the areas of the Thesaurus and Community Information, further developments are foreseen in the structure of the database, particularly with a view to back-loading records in BEDIS format from suppliers, and thus possibly offering enhanced catalogue records. At the same time the College Library is also embarking on a programme of replacing its dumb terminals with PC microcomputers; these will provide facilities for networking for screen printers, and act as intelligent front-end terminals enabling such facilities as spell-check, networking, colour screens etc. to be made available. Such networked PCs will also be able to offer access to CD-ROM programs and to databases via JANET without users having to move to dedicated terminals.

Conclusion

BookshelF originally matched the specification for Paisley College Library as closely as any other system. For reasons indicated previously it was selected and purchased for the College Library in 1987; its initial installation took place in the Autumn of that year and the system was fully operational in all respects for the start of the session 1990/91. Some inevitable teething problems, bugs and other difficulties arose during its implementation, but by and large its installation in Paisley College Library has been relatively trouble-free. The only area of the Library's operations still to be integrated is inter-library loans. The College

Library now has a system which enables it to give a higher level of service to a larger number of students than had previously been possible, and certainly much greater than would be possible without far larger numbers of staff than are available. Continuing restrictions on the number of professional staff employed in the College Library remain one of the greatest constraints in developing the system towards its full potential. The level of management information now available is considerable; this is only now being explored fully but will in the long term enable Library services to be refined and geared even more closely to the requirements of ever-changing patterns of students.

The BookshelF system as installed is now working satisfactorily and providing considerable benefits. Clearly, however, this stage is still only a beginning; the refinement of the system ever more closely to user requirements and making it ever more user-friendly will require a long-term commitment. In that sense it is unlikely that there will ever be a time when it can be said that the BookshelF system in Paisley College Library is complete, but it does provide a flexible system which will enable the Library to move towards that goal.

13 BookshelF in the public library – Dumfries and Galloway public libraries

Alastair R Johnston

The region

Dumfries and Galloway lies in the South West of Scotland and includes the most southerly point in Scotland, the Mull of Galloway. The region covers an area of 2,460 square miles and is the fifth largest of the nine mainland regions of Scotland with a population of 148,400 and a coastline of some 200 miles.

Dumfries and Galloway is an area of surprising variety. It is the region of Scotland closest to Ireland but it also shares a common border with England. It is a new region in terms of local government boundaries comprising the former counties of Wigtown, Stewartry of Kirkcudbright, and Dumfries and from whom it has inherited a long and colourful history. The landscape of the region, like its people, has a character of its own, combining the rugged scenery of the Highlands and the gentler rolling countryside of the Lowlands to give an impression of Scotland in miniature. In the past most of the employment in Dumfries and Galloway was to be found in the traditional primary industries of farming, fishing and forestry. In fact, agriculture and forestry continue to represent 95 per cent of the total land use. Major companies such as ICI Films, Wolsey Knitwear, Gates Rubber, Nestle and British Nuclear Fuels have been established in the area for many years and they have been joined by thriving new companies such as Pinney of Scotland, T C Farries and Company, Lochar Publishing, and Galloway Gourmet Foods together with a host of craft-related activities.

Dumfries and Galloway can claim to be the gateway to Scotland being located astride important road and rail links joining Scotland, England and Ireland. The road network is the main communication system in the Region with 64 per cent of households possessing at least 1 car – the highest proportion in Scotland. The strategically important A75 trunk road, an EEC Euroroute links the Irish ferries at Stanraer to the national motorway system at Gretna, and many of the areas main towns are situated along its length. These include the biggest population centre, Dumfries with 38,000 inhabitants, as well as Annan, Castle Douglas, Newton Stewart and Stanraer. Other major settlements in the region include Lockerbie, Dalbeattie and Kirkcudbright.

Regional library service

Dumfries and Galloway, together with the Borders and Highland Regions, is unusual in public library terms in that public libraries are a Regional Council responsibility – in other areas of Scotland they are either a District Council or Island Council function. In Dumfries and Galloway the opportunity was also taken to bring together both public and schools library services by administering the Library Service as a section of the Department of Education. The Regional Librarian, with a status equivalent to Assistant Director of Education, is responsible through the Director of Education to the Education Committee of the Regional Council.

The Regional Library Service provides service through 22 static public libraries, which vary in size from the Ewart Library, Dumfries with an annual issue of almost 500,000 to the very small part-time branch library at Port William which issues 11,000 items each year and opens 9 hours a week. Eight libraries are regarded as main branches and are open between 35 and 54 hours per week. Fourteen libraries are part-time with the preponderance of smaller service points being an indicator of the rural nature of the region. Five public mobile libraries provide service to smaller settlements on either a one, two or three week basis. In remote areas this amounts to a door-to-door service. These vehicles all have issues of between 80,000 and 100,000+ per annum making them busier than most of the static libraries. The schools library service also operates a mobile library service which visits all 116 primary schools at least three times each school session.

The headquarters of the Regional Library Service is based in the Ewart Library, Dumfries which also houses the largest branch library in the system. The annual issue statistics for the region peaked in the early 1980s at 2.2 million per annum from a lending stock of around 400,000 volumes with a registered readership of around 60,000 members. Since that time the annual issues have gently declined to a 1990–91 level of 1.8 million which represents 12.26 loans per head of population – still well above the Scottish average.

In staffing terms the Regional Library Service has exactly 100 permanent employees with an additional 23 trained Relief Library Assistants who are engaged on a temporary basis to provide holiday and sickness cover in small branch libraries. Eighteen posts are professional with 14 being public library based and the remainder in the schools service.

Criteria for automation

Unusually for a public library service the principal objective of automation was not circulation control of loans to members but rather stock management over a vast rural area. A particular aspect of rural library life is the number of small service points, both static and mobile, with limited shelf space. In order to allow users to see a constantly changing selection of the total stock it is necessary to move stock regularly between service points. In addition, the ability of users to read-out areas of stock which particularly interests them is an acute problem in small service points but also applies, albeit to a lesser degree, in the larger ones. In an average year over 250,000 items of stock are circulated around public libraries together with regular stock exchanges for almost 50 homes for the elderly, prisons, and other centres. By 1986 only 36 per cent of the stock had current location data available and this lack of information resulted in an inefficient request service and in unnecessary duplicate stock being purchased. A more efficient and effective means of stock management was required.

. . . And so to tender

Coincidentally with preliminary investigations into automation by the Library Service the Regional Council adopted an IT strategy based on distributed processing. Previously central mainframe processing had prevailed. The Library Services'

Specification for an integrated Library computer system (June 1986) was presented to a group of 25 computer manufacturers who had indicated interest in providing the Regional Council with super mini-computers. Each response received was carefully examined and a considerable number of demonstrations and further meetings organized. By this stage a clear preference for Pick-like operating systems had emerged within the Library Service. The result was a shortlist of five suppliers who received invitations to tender on 26 October 1987. Three tenders were returned and that of Prime Computer (UK) Ltd/Specialist Computers Systems and Software Ltd (SCSS) was accepted on 1 December 1987 with live running being required by 4 April 1988. The contract was spread over three financial years. The agreed initial configuration was for a Prime 2550 CPU with 4mb of main memory, one 287mb disk drive, one .5″ tape streamer, one laser printer, one high speed line printer and 16 Televideo 905 terminals. This allowed for all new acquisitions to be made on the system and a start to be made on retrospective stock conversion. The lead-in time to the first branch going live on circulations was 25 months.

Implementation

An implementation stategy was also agreed based on the system being totally within the care and control of the Library Service. No specialist staff were appointed and no regular out-of-hours duties were to be involved. Project management was added to the Assistant Regional Librarian's remit and took its place alongside existing duties. Both Senior Librarians based at Headquarters took responsibility for specific elements of the project including staff training and stock conversion, again concurrently with existing duties. The project was, and continues to be, closely monitored both by the library team and by SCSS's post-sales professional librarians and programmers. Specialist communications and IT advice was, and continues to be, readily available from the Regional Council's Department of Information Technology.

Hardware

System centre

The final system configuration called for Library Headquarters and eight branch libraries to be on-line to the Prime with

14 branches, five public mobile libraries and one schools mobile library to be operated in off-line mode. Library Headquarters would house the system centre – initially the Prime 2550, subsequently upgraded to a Prime 2755, and presently a Prime 5320. Headquarters would be equipped with 11 Televideo 905 terminals spread between the various departments. Four additional terminals were allocated on a temporary basis to the Stock Conversion Team for the duration of that exercise. Additional terminals have subsequently been installed to assist with data entry in connection with the Lockerbie Air Disaster archive and to allow the Request section to access the library database and Whitaker's Bookbank from the same PC. This PC also holds, for training purposes, copies of the off-line branch software and on-line emergency stand-by software. Increased computer use and reliance indicates that further terminals will be required in Headquarters over the next few years.

On-line branches

Each on-line branch is equipped with either two or three Televideo 905 terminals depending on physical size and annual issues, together with an equivalent number of SB Telepen bar-code readers and a Diconix or Dataproducts screen dump printer. An additional Televideo 905 terminal is used as an OPAC terminal. A 1mb Arche Parade 286 PC with 30mb disk drive and SB Telepen bar-code reader provides the capacity to run the on-line branches independently for extended periods should the need arise. This PC, equipped with BookshelF's Logbook software, normally acts as a dumb terminal in the on-line mode.

Off-line branches

The off-line branches are equipped with similar Arche Parade PCs and SB Telepen bar-code readers but in this situation are loaded with BookshelF's Off-Line software to operate the branch independently throughout its opening hours. Additionally a Televideo 905 terminal is provided which gives the capability for the branch to go on-line to the Prime via the public telephone network should the branch PC catastrophically fail. At the conclusion of each opening period the branch PC connects via a Case 4648 modem and the public telephone network to the central Prime. All new transactions, reader information and reservations are uploaded to the Prime and this is followed by a download from the Prime to the branch PC of all locally relevant files thus ensuring that the branch is up-to-date. All necessary re-indexing on the branch PC is automatically implemented after the file download is complete.

Mobile libraries

The Regional Library Service operates five public mobile libraries together with one schools mobile library, a stock circulation mobile and a spare vehicle. The public mobiles are configured with Tulip It 286 1mb Laptop computers with integral 20mb hard disks. The computers are powered from the vehicle's 12 or 24v DC electrics through a Powerverter which provide a constant 240volt/50hz power supply. The laptops are also capable of independent rechargeable battery operation with this option being retained as a stand-by facility. An SB Telepen bar-code reader operated through an IBM keyboard completes the installation. The hardware configuration for the schools and stock circulation vehicles have yet to be finalized but will most probably be based on similar laptops with increased disk storage capacity.

Communications

The seven remote on-line branches are connected to the central Prime via the Regional Council's ICL X.25 communications network. The network was primarily installed to handle cash receipting for the ill-fated Community Charge but much of the network development work was carried out using library data traffic. The network is based on eight nodes which offer local access to the network through Datalmux PADs (Packet Assembler and Disassembler). Having entered the network, data takes the fastest available route to the Prime which has its own built-in PAD. At least two routes are available to each node should any part of the network be busy or fail. Catastrophic network failure would result in BookshelF's Logbook software being used on the branch Arche Parade PC to record circulation data at local level. A catch-up routine is accomplished automatically when the network link is re-established. The eighth on-line branch, the Ewart Library, Dumfries is hardwired to the Prime but has similar back-up facilities to protect against central processor failure. Most of the X.25 Network operates at 9600 baud with some lines set at 7200 baud. The two most heavily used links – Library Prime to Library Node and Library Node to Regional Council HQ Node operate as kilostream links.

The fourteen off-line libraries operate as stand alone units with automatic upload and download of information to and from the Prime at the end of each opening period. This process uses Case modems over the public telephone network. At Library Headquarters four telephone lines are available to access the Prime, each line being equipped with a Case 4648 modem and with automatic line progression should the first or subsequent lines be engaged. It is envisaged that this facility will also be used to allow secondary schools direct access to the library database with the possibility of eventual direct public access to a viewdata service which will subsume existing OPAC facilities.

All mobile libraries operate from on-line branch libraries and the transfer of data to and from the mobile libraries will be accomplished on a daily basis by connecting the mobile library laptops directly to the Prime via the X.25 network where necessary. The long-term aim is to operate the mobile libraries through the Cellnet system and thus achieve on-line status in these service points.

Back-up

The fear of total data loss, however unlikely, is without doubt the number one horror scenario in any computer installation. From the very beginning it was agreed that back-up tapes would be taken daily and that mirror disking would be required before the Circulation module was implemented. As the database grew however it was recognized that mirror disking also represented an opportunity to maximize system availability within the constraints of zero out-of-hours working. Mirror disking allows back-ups to be taken whilst the system is up and running by operating two independent but linked disk drives, one as a copy or 'mirror image' of the other. Back-up tapes are produced by breaking the mirror and backing-up one disk drive whilst the other disk drive continues to operate normally recording system activity. After the back-up has been taken a process is automatically activated to allow the second disk to catch up with the original. An additional and substantial benefit of mirror disking is as a built-in insurance policy against the unlikely event of a disk crash. An advance in tape drive technology allowed the time taken to run back-up tapes to be reduced by some 80 per cent and the process to be completed on a single 2 gigabyte tape. Such an Exabyte helical scan tape drive unit was installed during early 1990. The viability of running back-up tapes as part of the automatic overnight process is currently being considered.

Software

From the very first demonstration of the BookshelF software it was obvious that the system was basically right for the Dumfries and Galloway scenario. The degree of integration between the various modules was demonstrable and impressive. The fact that BookshelFs early development was as a stock orientated and totally integrated library management system rather than as an add-on development of a pre-existing number-crunching circulation control system gave the software a fluidity and flexibility not apparent in other products. The user-friendly nature of the whole system made it immediately attractive. The degree of willingness to adapt and enhance the software to suit our specific needs was a further positive factor in the selection process.

As configured in Dumfries and Galloway the Prime 5320 uses the PRIMOS operating system and runs Prime Information software as a powerful, fourth generation, relationally-based, distributed database management package. The BookshelF application resides within the Information environment and uses its INFORM query and report generator to provide management information. INFORM uses an English-like, very flexible and user friendly enquiry language with user defined and stored procedures being capable of execution with single word commands. The off-line Arches PC's use MS-DOS as their operating system with Prime Information PC being utilized as the software platform for BookshelF. The full facilities of Information PC are therefore available at branch level to provide the INFORM query and report generator at each off-line site.

Retrospective conversion

The Dumfries and Galloway approach to automating its Library Service called for all stock orders placed with library suppliers after 1 April 1988 to be generated on the computer system. This fundamental decision ensured that there was a watershed within the Bibliographic Services section whereby the number of items of stock on the computer system would grow day-by-day whilst the number of stock items which required retrospective conversion was a finite number which actually decreased as normal withdrawals from stock were processed. In the main, retrospective conversion was accomplished by re-deploying library assistants from the various sections of Library Headquarters and the Ewart Library to form a Conversion Team. This team was led by either a librarian or a trainee librarian depending on staff availability and supervised by a senior librarian. The size of the team varied both in number and personnel but averaged 2.5 full-time equivalents over the first two years of the project. During this time over 200,000 items of stock were handled by the team. All data was input from the item of stock concerned thus no reliance was placed on pre-existing stock records. In effect this acted as a stock take and ensured that records on the database reflected actual rather than theoretical stock. To assist this process computer tapes offered by library supplier, James Askew & Son Ltd were loaded onto the database and by using a separate General Media Description (GMD) formed a discrete Potential Records File. The Askew tapes were based on their MARC database with records stripped to a Dumfries and Galloway specification. The BookshelF team then wrote loading and mapping software to convert the Askew data to BookshelF format. To ensure currency the Askew tapes are updated on a monthly basis and form a powerful bibliographic tool for the Library Service. As the on-line branches were connected to the system centre over the X.25 communications network considerable amounts of stock were locally converted and input to the central database. Despite this invaluable assistance the majority of data entry continued to be input by the central team with consignments of stock being sent to Library Headquarters for reprocessing on a continuous and branch by branch basis. After 19 months of intensive stock conversion the implementation schedule from both the Library's and BookshelF's standpoints was exactly on target and it was jointly agreed to proceed into the Circulation implementation phase. The largest branch library in the system, the Ewart Library, Dumfries was designated to lead with a projected live date six months ahead – 2 May 1990. Input of membership records was added to the remit of the Conversion Team and the necessary forms, membership cards and publicity materials were designed in-house and commerically produced. Within the six month lead-in period over 20,000 membership records were input to the system alongside a further 40,000 retrospective conversions. The 2 May target was achieved with over 1,400 issues being recorded during the first day. Lockerbie, the second on-line site to go live, followed on 3 September 1990 and was the first to go live over the X.25 network. The reliability of the whole package – hardware, software and communications – has been such that the branch staff have had little opportunity to bring the Logbook software into action in earnest. The first off-line site was the small branch library at Lochside, a suburb of Dumfries, which went live on 1 June 1990. At the time of writing additional sites are going live on the system at an average rate of one every six weeks – the current record being two sites within eight days.

Enhancements for Dumfries and Galloway

Multi-site software

The fundamental development to the BookshelF software required by Dumfries and Galloway was for a multi-site version to be developed. Although requiring an extensive rewrite of the Circulations module in particular, the implementation schedule required by the Library Service allowed for this to be accomplished well before the first library was due to go live on Circulations. Multi-siting was thought necessary for a number of reasons – firstly, the original software could handle multiple locations as independent entities but could not handle nested locations such as are found in most large library systems. Multi-site provided the answer within Systems Definition (screen XS) by tagging locations to sites and then tagging users to sites rather than locations. Secondly, there was a need to ensure that stock returned to a servicepoint other than that from which it was borrowed was recognized as such and a method evolved to ensure its return to the proper library. Arising from this, stock moving between libraries had to be identifiable as such and not showing as available for issue at either the home or away location. The facility to allow members to use any servicepoint was a mandatory requirement as was the facility to allow them to return borrowed stock to any service point. The only concession to these requirements was in the case of mobile libraries which were to have a separate Family Card type of membership.

Password control

For the multi-site version of BookshelF more extensive password programs were another mandatory requirement for Dumfries and Galloway. Security works at two levels, at login menu options can, if required, be protected thus giving users access only to permitted areas of the software. As an example, on-line service points in Dumfries and Galloway do not have access to the full Acquisitions module. In addition passwording can be implemented at screen level controlling whether users have access to the selected screen and whether that access is read-only or read and write. Additionally the PRIMOS operating system and Prime Information software have extensive security options.

Enquiry – Catalogue module

On first viewing one of the most impressive features of BookshelF is its powerful Catalogue Enquiry facility. To make it even more useful to the public library sector two enhancements were required. Firstly a display format which would show the shelfmark – particularly useful when an item has more than one classification number. Dual classification is prevalent in local studies and lending stocks and between schools stock – prefix 'E' and public children's stock – prefix 'J'. The solution was the D7 display format which also displays 'home' and 'away' locations within the multi-site software. The standard author search facility was the subject of the second enhancement. The standard search format, surname followed by christian name – e.g. BLYTON, ENID, proved unsatisfactory in the case of corporate authors e.g. JAMES ADAIR AND COMPANY LIMITED. In order to improve the hit rate with corporate authors a Boolean facility was utilized for all author searches – e.g. BLYTON & ENID which also allowed JAMES & ADAIR or ADAIR & JAMES or any other combination of the various elements in a corporate name.

Transit status – Catalogue module

Having been received by the system new stock is given a status of 'In Transit' (T) by the system to indicate that it is on its way to its home location but not yet available for issue. By putting each item through a 'Returns' screen (C2) at the home site the status changes from 'T' to 'A', available, and is then ready for issue.

Missing status – Catalogue module

A status to which an item is put when, having been at status 'A' available, it cannot be traced on the shelves. Effectively the status of 'M' missing does not allow reservations to be placed and makes it clear on OPAC that the item is temporarily not available. A missing item cannot be flagged.

Reference status – Catalogue module

Equivalent to the 'A' available status but this 'R' reference status makes clear on the OPAC that the item is part of reference stock and is not normally available for loan or reservation. This status does allow loans and reservations under exceptional circumstances.

Flagged status – Circulations module

This 'F' flagged status refers to the reserving of items within the multi-site Circulations module at on-line service points. A fuller explanation of flagging appears below.

Query status – Circulations module

A temporary holding status 'Q' query to which items can be allocated when there is any doubt about their proper status. Normally trap notes would be applied to explain the status.

Stock transfer – Catalogue module

One of the criteria for system selection was the requirement either to have, or be prepared to develop, a system for bulk transfer of stock. As has already been stated Dumfries and Galloway is a largely rural library authority and moves large amounts of stock on a regular basis between its branches, mobiles and other service points. In any one year well over 250,000 volumes are moved in regular stock exchanges. Additionally, around 60,000 items are temporarily moved between locations for re-sleeving, re-binding or conservation. A further 20–25,000 items are moved between service points to satisfy individual reader's requests. 'ACCESS.LOC' the program specifically designed to cater for this requirement, allowed stock to be transferred between locations by specifying the location to which the item or items were to be transferred followed by wanding in the relevant accession bar-codes. The subsequent multi-site enhancement of this program brought a Stock Transfer Menu which added 'site' options to the previous program.

OPAC – Catalogue module

The provision of an On-line Public Access Catalogue (OPAC) was seen as one of the greatest benefits to be gained from automating the library service – certainly from a public relations point of view. The development of the powerful BookshelF enquiry module into an OPAC was achieved by designing a split-screen version of the Enquire facility. The lower half of the terminal screen became a comprehensive help facility whilst the topmost half of the terminal screen provided the much admired enquiry screen. The help screens are written in a clear and concise manner but are also capable of being edited and completely reworded if required. The provision of a dedicated front screen for each service point i.e. 'Welcome to Annan Library etc. etc. . . .' does not present a problem. From the outset the OPAC was designed to allow the end-user to access the information provided with as little, or as much, help as was required to accomplish the task effectively. The option for users to make on-screen reservations directly from the OPAC was yet another enhancement required within the Dumfries and Galloway specification. The solution, in this instance, was to provide users with the facility to enter their membership number which then prompts for a personal identification number (PIN) which has been previously set-up and issued. The reservation can then be made. The facility is parameterized and can be disabled if not required.

Community Information module

The provision of Community Information has been recognized as a service provision growth area in public libraries for a number of years and the specification requirement to provide a Community Information module came as no surprise to SCSS. The Community Information module was developed independently of the BookshelF software by using Prime Information and is designed as a menu-driven facility. The format of screens is completely library defined and the ability to access OPAC via the Community Information screens was provided as standard. A Screen Designer utility allows screen formatting to be made as simple as possible whilst retaining the facility to provide highly complex screen designs. In the longer term it is likely that the existing facility will be upgraded, or superseded by a viewdata system with an interactive database.

Computer Output Microfiche (COM) – Catalogue module

The initial system specification saw the need for some service points to be on-line, others operating in an off-line mode. On-line branches could have direct access to the central database, off-line branches would have access to their local database together with on-line dial-up access to the central database. Limited finance precluded other than occasional or emergency use of this dial-up enquiry facility and a need was identified for a microfiche version of the main catalogue. COM output was achieved by using the INFORM report generator to process the catalogue into three files – author, title and class. The alpha-numeric classification used within the Local Studies collection required the development of additional sorting routines. The sorted files are then run to magnetic tape using the MAGSAV utility and subseqently converted to microfiche by an outside facilities house. At present 40 copies of the catalogue are produced three times each year for distribution to libraries and secondary schools.

Reservations – Circulations module

Reservations are the most complex aspect of our library operation in terms of the integration of off-line and on-line sites within the multi-site BookshelF software. The reservations programs of the single-site software required considerable alteration to take on board these complexities. Every site had to have the capability of reserving any item on the database. From the on-line standpoint there are four types of reservations:

1	Local	That is a reservation for an item which is already in the stock of the requesting branch.
2	Global	Where the requirement is to trap an item somewhere else in the system or to satisfy the reservation with the first copy to pass over a counter at any on-line branch.
3	Flagged	That is to target a particular copy which is located at another on-line branch. The copy is immediately reserved, will show

		on a daily listing of flagged items, and should be available on the shelf for picking by a member of staff. Items remain on this list until one copy is put through a screen which allocates flagged items (C9,3) and removes flags from other copies.
4	Designated	Effectively the same as Flagging but targets a copy located to an off-line branch. The copy will become reserved at branch level immediately the next download of data takes place.

Making a reservation at an on-line service point simply requires the reader number and ISBN to be entered on the Reservation Screen (C3). If the required item is in the local stock then entering 'L' completes the transaction. If there is no local copy, or for some reason another copy is required, then entering 'V' will show all copies in the system together with their locations and status. The choice of copy or copies to reserve is then a matter of personal decision by the operator.

At off-line branches the making of reservations is intrinsically simpler than at an on-line branch. Reservation procedures for items in the local stock are identical to on-line branches and are self-contained within the off-line software. Reservations for non-local but in-stock items are entered on the Reservations Screen and are included in the next transaction upload to the central database. Each morning, or at such other interval as may be determined, a list of all off-line reservations are printed out at Headquarters. A library assistant then progresses the reservations by making the human decisions regarding the optimum utilization of stock to satisfy those reservations in the most efficient and effective way. This intervention is particularly important in a rural library authority where the problems of geography and those of communications do not necessarily mean that the most distant branches are those which are going to be slowest to supply requested items. The supply of requested items to off-line branches is, in most respects, similar to the on-line multi-site version of the software.

In order to deal with multiple reservations for bestseller type stock on a centralized basis and thereby make most effective use of stock, a pseudo site – 'HQ Requests' was created. This site contains pseudo locations for every regular service point. In this pragmatic way a considerable number of unnecessary book movements have been avoided whilst maximum use is made of a limited bookstock to serve reservations on a regionwide basis.

Loan renewals – Circulations module

The number of loans generated by a busy public library produce a demand for a facility to handle loan renewals in a simple way. The number of telephone renewals received by Dumfries and Galloway and the requirement to be able to confirm, or less frequently refuse, renewals in as short a telephone call as possible meant that the existing BookshelF procedures had to be enhanced. Loan renewal is an option within the Issue screen (C1). One key stroke produces a list of items on loan together with return dates and other relevant information regarding reservations etc. One further key stroke will renew all items or, if required, an individual item or combination of items can be renewed by line number. As a matter of library policy overdue items cannot be renewed automatically. This parameter can be overriden by a member of staff with the necessary authority.

Receipt of bar-coded stock – Acquisitions module

Most of Dumfries and Galloway's stock is acquired in shelf ready condition from library suppliers. When received into the Bibliographic Services Department each item of stock already has a bar-coded accession label which has been applied by the supplier. In order to receive these items and add them to stock in the most efficient manner a 'Receipt of Bar-coded Stock' facility (screen A 7.2) was created. This screen requires the order number to be input followed by the ISBN of the item in question. Wanding in the bar-code from the accession label then ties the accession to the main catalogue record. Wanding the ISBN straight from the dust jacket is being developed to make this repetitive task a simple two swipes of the light pen operation.

Budget control – Year end roll forward – Acquisitions module

The basic budgetary control system within the Acquisitions module was judged to be very suitable for public library use. The only enhancement required was for a financial year-end roll forward facility to take account of the traditional 'problem' area of the outstanding order file. In even the smallest public library this can amount to several thousands of pounds worth of outstanding orders which will not be supplied in the correct budget year. The requirement was to ensure that material on order, but not delivered, at 31 March each year became a debit against the incoming financial year and a credit to the outgoing year. The BookshelF solution was to add a 'Next Budget' field to the Budget screen (AR2). Running a heavily passworded program at the appropriate point in the financial year carries out the complete transaction.

Audit and financial control – Acquisitions module

The provision of a complete audit trail from point of order to point of disposal *and beyond* was another mandatory requirement in the Dumfries and Galloway specification. This was met by incorporating an 'Invoice Number' field onto the 'Receipt of Barcoded Stock screen' (A 7.2). The invoice number can either be globally added to the whole order, can be individually specified for each item on the order, or, for absolute flexibility, can be a combination of both. A withdrawals facility was implemented to meet the need for archival recording of withdrawn stock. The functionality of this program allows the notification of 'last copy' information before the withdrawal process is carried through. The provision of user-specified withdrawals information to the regional inter-lending bureaux together with comprehensive management information are two further features of this program. It is envisaged that certain files will eventually be run-off to tape for archival storage and in this way it will be possible to maintain a complete record of all orders, accessions and withdrawals, more or less in perpetuity.

Standing orders and subscriptions – Acquisitions module

The provision of a facility to handle subscriptions and standing orders is essential to any library management system designed for public libraries. The BookshelF solution was to strip out various components from their comprehensive Serials module and add them into an expanded Acquisitions module. The Serials module itself was considered by Dumfries and Galloway to be too sophisticated for public library use. The solution which evolved was for a skeleton main catalogue entry to be created. A dummy standard number is applied from a previously defined stream. This dummy number is then used for the first and subsequent orders. An order is placed against the dummy standard number. A 'Next Order Date' field allows a date to be entered which should correspond to the expected date of the next edition or subscription renewal. Each month a program is run to generate orders for the standing orders expected that month. A status of 'Hold' is automatically applied to the order. A list of expected titles is then produced for Bibliographic Services Department use. At the same time the 'Next Order Date' is reset. As each item is received into stock the dummy standard number can be changed to the correct ISBN and this information is written back to the main catalogue record. Chasers can be produced for items which are not received when expected.

Public Lending Right module

The requirement to be fully integrated with the requirements of the Public Lending Right Registrar (PLRR) was yet another mandatory requirement within the Dumfries and Galloway specification. The need for implementation arose in late 1989 when an approach was made by the PLRR with a view to Dumfries and Galloway being the first library authority to provide loan data to PLR on a 'whole authority' basis. The necessary legislative changes were laid before Parliament on 6 December 1990 and came into force on 27 December 1990. Three service points were specified initially, Ewart (Dumfries), Lockerbie and Stanraer and an implementation date of 1 July 1991 was set. The PLR module was installed during late Spring 1991 and extensively tested prior to live running. The data, drawn from the Circulations History file, is processed according to the *PLR Loans Data Specification* and the results run off onto magnetic tape for forwarding to the PLRR. The facility is subject to a regular PLR audit procedure to ensure the integrity of the data supplied. The BookshelF PLR module is designed to allow service points to be added to or deleted from PLR sampling as required. Mobile libraries can be included on the same basis as any other branch library. Once again the programs have been designed to require minimal operator intervention and are extremely user-friendly.

Statistics module

The need for the computer system to provide statistics, both in terms of day-to-day management information and in terms of the annual CIPFA questionnaire and the hundred-and-one other similar surveys meant that the provision of such a facility was considered extremely important in the system evaluation process. Although an impressive array of statistics could be provided using the INFORM query and report generator SCSS undertook to develop a Statistics module which would automatically process the necessary information and present it on demand. The Circulations portion of the module can provide issue statistics very flexibly by user-defined parameters – either daily, weekly, monthly, quarterly or annually; by a selected site or for all sites; with a separate report for each site, date, location, class, media type, reader category or none of these options; by time period within the day – by half hour or any combinations of half hour periods within the day. A retrospective comparison is also provided as standard. Other statistics provided on a very similar basis include Reservations taken, supplied, cancelled or uncollected; Current Loans; Readers; Overdue Letters; and Reservation Letters. The Catalogue Statistics Report Generator (CATGEN) is currently undergoing extensive beta testing on site by both library staff and SCSS programmers and is proving to be an equally flexible and impressive product.

Bookstock software

Many public and other large library systems use the showroom and stockroom facilities of major library suppliers to select stock directly from the shelves. This system of stock selection has advantages in that the purchase decision is effective immediately the book is physically acquired. A further advantage is the ability to select within subject areas – book in hand. The principal disadvantage is the inability of library staff to memorize their stock catalogue and thus risk duplication in purchasing. The BookshelF answer is a laptop computer equipped with Bookstock software – in effect a copy of the library's catalogue stripped to ISBN's and number of copies. A quick check, eventually by wanding the ISBN straight from the book's dust jacket, reveals the number of copies, if any, already in stock.

Conclusion

In retrospect the acceptance of BookshelF as the answer to the automation of Dumfries and Galloway's Library Service may, in one light, be seen as a bold step by the Library. The promise of enhancements, of developments, of programming and of new modules made so easily might not have been carried through – so often promises do not translate into reality. As the software stood in 1988 it was the basis of a solution, the core was there and the rest could follow.

The reality of the situation, in the cold light of day, was that no other system supplier had the complete solution either. During the evaluation process we failed to find a system supplier who could demonstrate a fully working multi-site integrated library management system capable of handling everything from potential record to beyond withdrawal with a combination of static and mobile service points, both off- and on-line.

The decision to go BookshelF and to develop the product in partnership with the supplier has proved beyond doubt to have been the correct decision. It has provided Dumfries and Galloway with a first class bespoke library management system and SCSS with a product which is consistently outselling its rivals. The BookshelF of 1991 is the product we searched for without success in 1988. It is the result of vision and committment on the part of SCSS – I wish it every success!

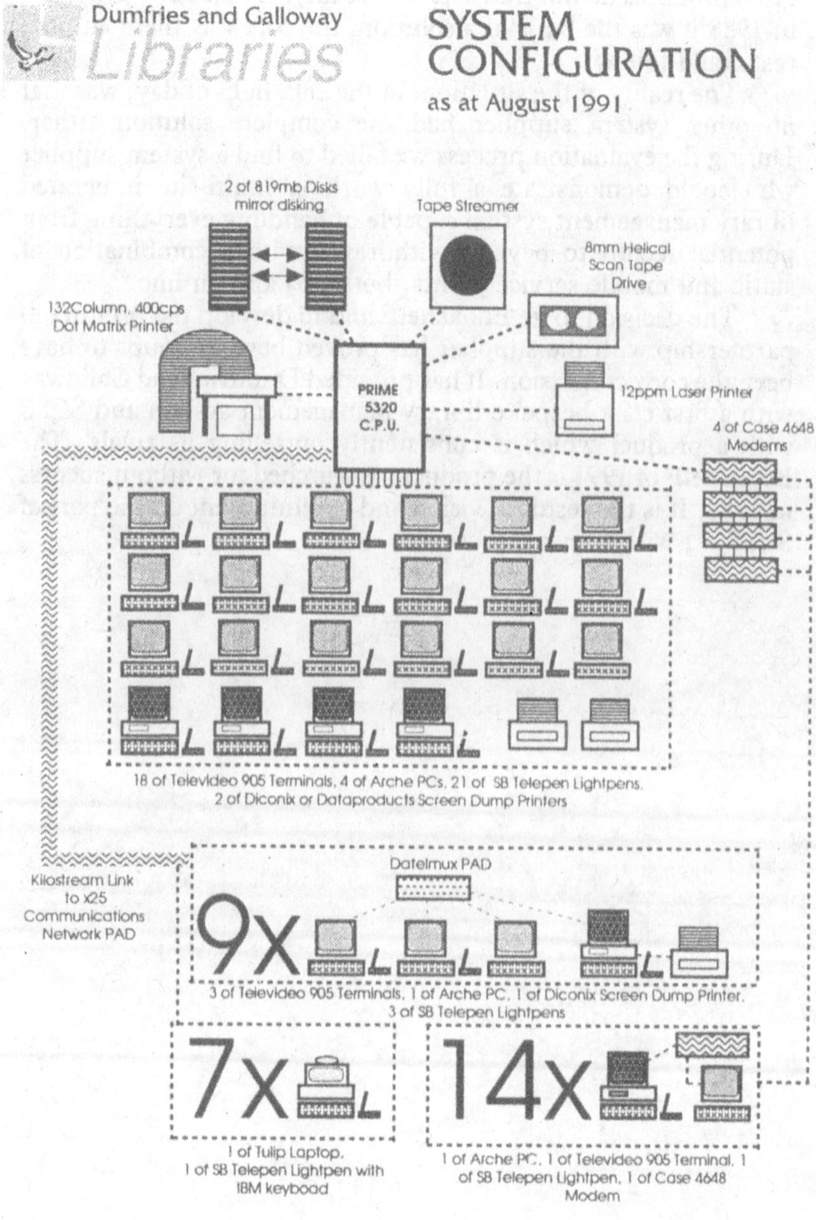

Figure 13.1 Dumfries and Galloway system configuration

```
BOOKSHELF                    10 JUL 91

                        STOCK TRANSFER MENU

  1  Change location within site    5  Requested Item Receipts

  2  Transfer to another site       6  Items for transit

  3  Allocate flagged items         7  'K' status program

  4  List flagged items

  1  Catalogue Menu                 F  Finish

  C  Circulation Menu

                        Please select an option
```

Figure 13.2 Screen print – stock transfer menu

```
SCSS                     BOOKSHELF                      09 NOV 91

                         Catalogue enquiry

HITS     No.    Search command
6069     1.     S* DUMFRIES
3870     2.     S* GALLOWAY
2848     3.     S* 1 & 2



------------------------------------------------------------------
*********************WELCOME TO BOOKSHELF*************************

The program you are now using allows you to ask the computer if
the library has any items that may be of interest to you.

If this is the first time you have used this facility or you're
not sure what to do next, please press the key labelled 'NEXT'.
This will take you to the next help screen.

Press the NEXT key to see the next help screen.
```

Figure 13.3 Screen print – OPAC

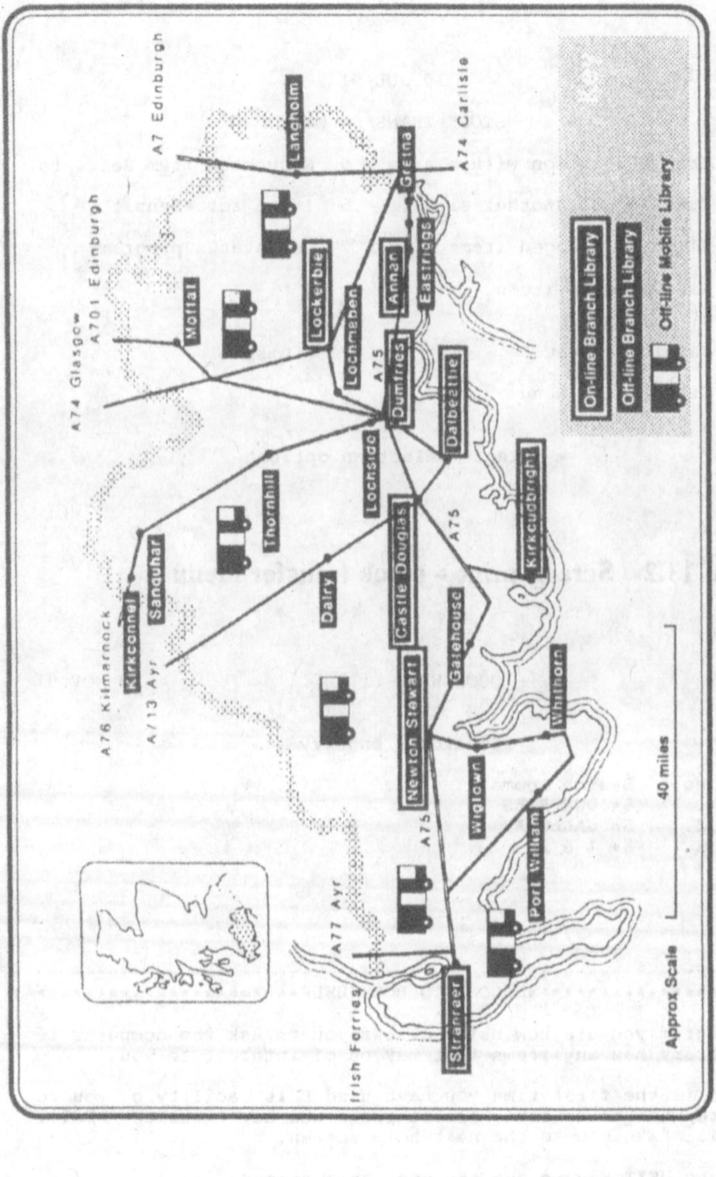

Figure 13.4 Dumfries and Galloway – service points

14 BookshelF in the special library: Equal Opportunities Commission

Pat Darter

The Equal Opportunities Commission and its library

The Equal Opportunities Commission came into existence at the end of 1975. It was set up as a result of the passing of the Sex Discrimination Act 1975 (which also incorporates the Equal Pay Act 1970). It is charged with three main functions and these are set out in Sec.53 of the Act, namely:

i. to work towards the elimination of discrimination.
ii. to promote equality of opportunity generally between men and women.
iii. to keep under review the working of the Sex Discrimination Act and the Equal Pay Act 1970 and when . . . they think it necessary draw up and submit to the Secretary of State proposals for amending them.

It is thus a statutory body and although funded by government it is an independent agency which can, and does, criticize the government itself for those of its actions which we see as being discriminatory either to women or to men.

It was not until 1977 that it was acknowledged that the growing individual collections of books and pamphlets would be much better organized on a central basis. Dermot Englefield, then deputy, now librarian, of the House of Commons was asked to do a report on information provision within the Commission and as a result of his report the Information Centre was set up.

From this somewhat inauspicious beginning the EOC Information Centre has grown to be a unique collection of information on equal opportunities and the rights of women. The book and pamphlet collection now numbers some 22,000 volumes and in addition we subscribe to some 350 current serial titles (as well as maintaining an archive collection of journals which have ceased publication). There is also a collection of newspaper cuttings which is in the region of *c*.50,000 items and on the audiovisual side there are posters, records, videos, badges etc. We produce a weekly in-house news bulletin and deal with *c*.5000 enquiries a year from all over the country (as well as a number from abroad). This is yet another sign of the national importance of the collection and the way in which equal opportunities is now seen as an important aspect of so many areas of life. GCSE project to post-doctoral research, caring employer to aggrieved employee, service delivery or the denial of services may all have their enquiries answered from a collection which covers both the law enforcement aspect of our work as well as the more wide-ranging research and promotional activities of the Commission.

The road to computerization

As the collection grew the inadequacies of the card catalogue became more and more apparent. The more so since we had also started an index of periodical articles and for very obvious reasons decided that we would have to limit our indexing terms to two or at the very most three, per entry. Computerization was the only answer.

However as our need for a computer system increased, the likelihood of the Commission finding the money with which to buy one decreased. More and more demands were being made on our legal budget with the result that all other budgets in the Commission were drastically cut. As far as the Information Centre was concerned this meant that in an attempt to preserve as many periodical runs as possible book buying dropped to little more than an on-demand procedure.

In spite of this however we decided to continue to aim for computerization and to this end ensured that we remained up-to-date as far as new systems coming on the market were concerned through professional reading, demonstrations at exhibitions and even free seminars put on by the suppliers. Even unsubtle remarks to senior managers when searches for information took longer than they anticipated, 'Well if we were computerized . . .', played a part. One problem which we faced was that apart from some word-processing facilities in the typing pool the Commission was a very 'unautomated' place and although gradually coming round to the idea of computerization it was very much by way of a few individual PCs on a few favoured individuals' desks. My talk of a specialized library system costing in excess of £20,000 was enough to set management twitching. Small beer I know, but for that money a significant number of Amstrads or Apple Macs could be purchased. Yet I was determined not to be 'fobbed off' with anything less than what I considered to be the proper solution to our needs. I had a firm conviction that adapting an ordinary database management system was not the answer as far as libraries were concerned and especially not for a specialized information unit like the Information Centre of the EOC.

At last however our persistence paid off and at the end of January 1990 I was informed that since there was a forecast of an overall surplus in the Commission's budget I could have my computer. There was only one snag however, even if not actually installed, the equipment had to be purchased and delivered by 31 March. This was where my policy of keeping up to date paid off because had we been starting totally from scratch there is no way in which we would have been able to meet that deadline or if we had met the deadline we might well have had a system that we very quickly came to realize was not adequate for our needs.

Three priority areas very quickly became apparent:

i. to see and assess the various systems on the market;
ii. to draw up a specification of our needs;
iii. the need for all staff in the Information Centre to feel comfortable about the impending changes.

As far as arranging demonstrations is concerned this is generally not a problem, any supplier will be only too pleased for prospective customers to visit their offices where they will not only demonstrate under ideal conditions but also ply you with an excellent lunch all carefully calculated to influence your choice. However bearing in mind that I wanted my staff to be involved as much as possible I invited the suppliers to come to us. In fairness most responded very favourably and one or two insisted on coming back a second time when various bugs and domestic problems meant that their demonstrations were not as good as they would have liked them to be. Over a period of some two to three weeks we saw demonstrated about eight automated library management systems. We were all on a very steep learning curve and although this may have meant that the first demonstration got off very lightly compared to the much more detailed questions by the time we reached the last, each one left us sufficient literature so that it was possible to go back and re-assess in the light of our rapidly acquired knowledge.

The question of a specification was rather more difficult. At that time we had no one on the Commission staff with any expertise in computer systems let alone the more rarified area of library applications. Again this is where keeping in touch comes in and knowing which libraries of a similar size or type to your own have recently gone through this same process is so important. I was able to obtain specifications from three colleagues all of whom expressed shock, horror and amazement when told of the timetable to which we were working. The document which we then proceeded to put together was nowhere near as lengthy and complex as those I had received. Again time was a factor in this but neither did we have anyone with the technical expertise to assess the answers. In retrospect this is one area where we should have put in more work and allowed ourselves more time. I am not saying that our final decision would have been any different but a number of points have arisen which came as a bit of a shock and which could have been anticipated had our specification document been more detailed.

As far as staff involvement was concerned, I ensured that they were all able to see demonstrations of the systems we were considering. This in itself however does not make people any the less frightened of hitting the keys or indeed apprehensive as to what computerization may mean in terms of the tasks which they themselves carry out. In this respect we were very fortunate in having a library school on our door step with a good range of IT equipment and it was arranged that they would run a computer appreciation course for all the staff of the Information Centre. We did this in two shifts, half the staff going one week and half the next and this was to prove a very valuable investment indeed. Staff were able to get some reassuring hands-on experience and those with good old-fashioned typing skills rapidly realized that they were as good as their younger colleagues whom they had thought to be more computer literate.

After two months of frenetic activity, on March 31st we had a cupboard full of cardboard boxes labelled BookshelF.

System implementation

As far as software was concerned we had decided to make an initial purchase of three modules: Catalogue, Thesaurus and Serials. We hoped to add Acquisitions in about a year's time with Circulation to follow at some unspecified time in the future – we have no great volume of loans and so I felt that we needed time to work out the comparative merits of the cost of all the preparatory work as against the possible benefits of implementing this part of the system.

One major factor in favour of the BookshelF tender was the offer of retrospective catalogue conversion. As I said earlier, this purchase was, at the time, a major investment for the Commission and I felt that in order to maintain any sort of credibility whatsoever for the Information Centre we needed to demonstrate that they were getting good value for their money. We could have gone for the very easy option of retaining our card catalogues and just building up the computer database from a certain date, but this seemed to have very little merit particularly since one important plank in our arguments had been the improvement in information retrieval. Given our current rate of additions to stock it would have taken far too long to build up any meaningful database in this way, nor was I confident that we would ever have the staff resources to make any meaningful impact were we to attempt the retrospective conversion ourselves.

As this part of the exercise proceeded, I was conscious that from time to time I was being asked to make snap decisions which I might well regret within 12 months but on the whole things have not worked out too badly. Yes, we still have some tidying up to do on the database, and it is by no means perfect but we do have an adequate working tool with which we were able to impress all of our customers, Commission staff and public alike from the very moment when we went live.

We were very fortunate in already having our own Thesaurus and had been using this for about two years, mainly in the periodical article index. Inputting the 2,000 or so terms was a very simple task which a relief typist was able to complete in a matter of days. This now forms the backbone of our information retrieval system and in addition to the periodical articles all new documents added to stock have one or more thesaurus terms in the keyword field. We are still left with the problem that the older material, and that still means the bulk of the stock, is not key-worded. This is something which is currently under discussion as we consider whether using our subject index to provide at least one keyword per item by means of 'decoding' the classification number would be an adequate solution or not.

In terms of searching for information and obtaining really up-to-date results the inclusion of the periodical articles has been a success. What has not been so successful however has been displaying the results of those searches. We soon realized that entering the full and correct citation on the Journal Definition screens does not result in this information appearing in the same way as does the imprint information from the catalogue maintenance files. In order to display or print this information we have to use D6 display format which obviously takes more time and space than we would like.

In any of our files the 'W' section of the alphabet takes up more space than librarians usually allow so we realized from the beginning that to search on the terms 'woman' or 'women' would not only take a considerable amount of time but also result in an unmanageable number of hits. But it is surprising what other words also turn out to be no-go areas. For us one example of this was 'social' not in the sense in which the word immediately springs to mind, but social as in 'social security', 'social welfare' and of course, more recently 'social charter'. The result of this is that one develops a curiously convoluted logic when the only information given is the title of a book. Which word in that title is least likely to appear in any other title? I suppose that for us the ultimate nightmare would be a request to find a book called 'Equal opportunities for women in social security'. Fortunately, given the discrimination which still exists, there seems little likelihood of such a title ever appearing in print! In fairness however I must add that the slowness of searching for certain words and also for phrases is comparative and that for the vast majority of our searches the speed is impressive – very impressive to those of our colleagues in the Commission who although familiar with standard database packages had not come across a text retrieval system before.

When any of the automated library management systems currently on the market were developed the very last module to appear has always been Serials Management. There is no doubt that this is a very complex area indeed; setting up all the data certainly took far longer than we had anticipated. Coding sheets were prepared for each title since the various elements required were scattered around a number of manual systems. Finding ISSNs was a major problem and not just for the irregular newsletters of which we seem to have more than our fair share.

Given that ISBNs are now regularly accepted and their importance understood throughout the publishing world, those same publishers seem very coy or forgetful when it comes to their serial publications. Having assembled all the required data there was then the question of the staff time required for input because just at the point when things seemed to be going very well – too well perhaps – we were struck by one of our recurrent staffing crises which meant that in attempting to keep our basic services going any development of the computer system came to a complete halt. Consequently we have only just started to implement this module and for the time being we are running both our old visible index and the computer system side by side. However all the signs are good and in spite of some initial hiccups I do not think it will be too long before we are sufficiently confident of, and conversant with, the module to rely on it completely.

Where are we today?

So eighteen months on from delivery where do we stand?

Although progress has not been so quick in some respects as we had hoped, on the other hand we seem to be light years away from the unautomated and demoralized state in which we entered 1990. We still have a long way to go, our database still requires some attention to bring it up to the standard we would like, there is further work to be done with the Serials module as far as obtaining budgetary information is concerned and we need to look at the whole area of management information and what even our existing system can provide in this respect. Beyond that we need to think about bidding for the resources to purchase the remaining modules and not only cash resources but given the experience we have gained from our current installation a realistic timetable based on either our existing staffing resources or whatever extra ones we may be able to obtain.

There are however many pluses. A demoralized staff who saw themselves as becoming unskilled compared to even ordinary office workers are now much more happy. The speed with which we can answer basic enquiries and produce 'instant' reading lists has increased out of all proportion and because of this our standing with the staff of the Commission has gone up as well. The number of external enquiries still threatens to engulf us but even here we have at least been able to keep pace with the increase in volume and overall there is no doubt that the quality of our responses has improved as well.

15 BookshelF in the special library: Institute of Personnel Management

Barbara Salmon

Introduction

The IPM library currently serves 45,000 members throughout the UK. Most of the work is conducted over the telephone and the service handles up to 170 calls per day requesting anything from a simple address and telephone number to extremely detailed literature searches. In response to enquiries, material is sent out by post in the form of books and photocopied journal articles. The library has a team of 10 full-time professionals, four part-time and seven clericals. In addition there is a part-time abstracter employed on a short-term contract.

The library was established in 1968 and has grown from a staff of six (half of whom were employed on a part-time basis) to its present dimensions. Library holdings currently stand at 14,000 book titles, 1,155 catalogued company documents and 7,113 journal articles all of which are held on the BookshelF database and some further 15,000 journal articles which have been retained on a manual file.

It was in 1969 that the library first began to index individual journal articles storing the information on a system of 5″×8″ cards. Each card was allocated a specific subject heading and on to it were typed the details of appropriate journal articles. Articles were added to the system at a rate of a thousand per annum with an average of three subject entries per title. By 1985 not only had the volume of cards physically outgrown the index storage unit, but staff were finding that to maximize retrieval it was necessary to assign more than three entries per title, thereby increasing both indexing and typing time. The field of personnel management was evolving rapidly, many subject headings demanded revision and some re-indexing was required so that staff could promptly retrieve items in response to members' enquiries. An improved indexing system was needed with the capacity to retrieve material by author and title (something rendered impossible by an index that was purely subject based.). In addition it was thought that a computerized system would allow for the efficient production of SDI bulletins for headquarters staff and current bibliographies for members. As a result, an investigation of software packages suitable for library retrieval was undertaken.

A report produced at the end of 1985 reviewed the merits of nine library packages and recommended only one as suitable for the computerization of the index. However, although the package was appropriate in terms of design and supplier back-up it lacked any form of thesaurus and it was finally decided not to purchase pending the investigation of alternative software on the market.

However, there were other developments. The Institute had undergone a large expansion in membership. In 1979 the Institute had 21 647 members, by 1986 this had increased to 27 356 members and along with this growth came a rise in the volume of library enquiries which had jumped from 7 992 in 1979 to 15 103 enquiries in 1986. As a result the clerical staff in the library were under pressure to handle an increasing number of loans and photocopies with a highly labour intensive manual circulation system.

For every pack of material sent out borrowers slips had to be typed and filed, parcels labelled and postage charges noted. Where photocopies of journal articles were required items had to be copied and declaration/invoice forms completed. Both reservations and overdues increased in number as the volume of library loans grew.

At the same time growing numbers of enquiries increased the daily workload for the professional staff at the information desk making it increasingly difficult to turn around all enquiries within 24 hours. In 1986 professional staffing was around 40 per cent of current levels and appeared unlikely to increase in line with volume of work. Consequently the professional staff found that they were spending a disproportionate amount of time on answering enquiries to the detriment of cataloguing, classification and indexing of library material.

Many enquiries involved quite specific and detailed searches of the information files. However the book catalogue and journal index operated independently of each other and to answer one enquiry it was necessary to search each system with a different set of subject headings. There was a need for a thesaurus of personnel management terms which could be used to index both books and articles thereby enabling retrieval of all types of documents by the same keyword search. If this were transformed into a computerized database it would become a very efficient tool for information work.

By 1986 it was becoming apparent that there was a need to improve the operation of various functions within the library not just the journal index as had been originally thought but also the circulation system and the catalogue.

The computerization of the catalogue meant a huge change to library practices. The bookstock was (and still is) arranged according to the London Classification of Business Studies with a catalogue comprising a classified listing and a combined index of authors and titles with cross references. Cataloguing procedures were very labour intensive. The professional staff handwrote everything onto slips from which catalogue, subject index and cross references were typed. As a result of the faceted classification one item might require four classification cards, one title and up to three author entries all of which had to be typed and manually filled. It was therefore clear that computerization would be beneficial in terms of increased efficiency, less paperwork and a reduction of storage space, added to which staff would be able to retrieve information more quickly by the creation of a database resulting in a more effective response to enquiries. A review was undertaken of packages on the market suitable for library computerization.

Reasons for choosing BookshelF

Five library packages were examined, two of which were immediately discounted after demonstration. The remaining three were evaluated in terms of their relative costs, benefits and problems and as a result BookshelF was selected as the package which best met IPM criteria.

BookshelF, which had been in business for two years, had installed seven other library systems and gave the most coherent demonstration of any software supplier. The demonstration explained how the software operated and detailed the level of support that the library could expect from the company. Back-up facilities were a matter of prime concern to IPM. The majority of library staff had little or no previous experience with computerized library systems and with no in-house computer technical staff the library needed a reliable supplier that would provide good support and maintenance.

BookshelF was a turnkey system with the capacity to accommodate IPM's bookstock, journal index and projected growth. The company offered a Help Desk facility with librarians and programming staff, Help screens and the prospect of a user group starting up by mid-1987. Training was provided by librarians, targeted at specific modules and there was a staff of technicians to provide hardware support. The level of maintenance was thought to be in line with IPM's potential need and there was the additional prospect of a modem link which meant that programmers could dial in and attempt to solve any software problems that arose.

Like other systems on the market at that time, BookshelF had the capacity to add further functions in the future but where the system was deemed most appropriate to IPM needs was in terms of its enquiry facility. BookshelF was essentially a menu-driven system but with an expert facility that could be used by information staff. It enabled the user to tag displayed items and retain searches for future use, two functions necessary for effective telephone enquiry work and had a straightforward command structure which would be relatively easy to learn. In addition BookshelF enabled the operator to use an unlimited number of search statements and as these were numbered, previous ones could be recalled and used in conjunction with new search criteria. Catalogue Enquiry offered the facility to display more hits per screen than other packages and although the display by fields option was not available in 1986 the existing range of five display formats were considered sufficient for viewing data. Of the packages reviewed BookshelF emerged as most suitable for enquiry work over the telephone.

Apart from Catalogue Enquiry the other area of major concern was BookshelF's suitability as a circulation system. Like all library packages reviewed, BookshelF was based on the premise that users would visit the library to borrow and return books. In the case of IPM this was true of only a small percentage of its members the vast majority of whom were remote users who borrowed and returned their books by post. Whatever package IPM purchased needed to have some mechanism for recording postage and photocopy charges and some system for allowing payment.

There was also a problem of addresses. Most members wanted the material sent to their work address because of the difficulties of receiving parcels at home. Some members wanted material sent to their home address and consultants often wanted the information posted to the company in which they were working and this changed with every change of assignment. The concept of a reader record with one fixed address for all correspondence was not feasible in IPM's case. Added to which a member might request information one year and then not use the service for another 12 months having changed jobs in the meantime. The practice of taking down at the enquiry stage the address to which the material was to be sent was clearly the only means of ensuring that material was posted to the correct destination. There was therefore a need to build into the system a method of checking and amending addresses at the issue stage.

The other area of concern was reservations. Clearly, members would not be able to collect reserved items so there had to be some system whereby users would be notified that books had been reserved for them and would be posted to them as soon as available. Obviously no off-the-shelf library package was likely to perform all these functions without modification to the software. However BookshelF considered it possible to make the necessary alterations in order to meet IPM's specification.

There were other reasons for choosing BookshelF. The Journal Article Definition screen was particularly suitable for IPM's needs. The fields corresponded exactly with the information on the library's manual indexing system and the transfer of information looked to be a straightforward clerical operation. In addition there was space for abstracts should the library wish to add them at a later date. The format of the cataloguing screen was straightforward, logical and easy to understand and appeared on the surface to present no problems for the input of library data. In addition, BookshelF were developing an on-line thesaurus package which would be linked to the catalogue and would enable IPM to create the kind of database it required.

Installation took place in November 1987 based on nine Visa link 125 terminals connected to a Prime 2350 minicomputer. The IPM purchased the Catalogue, Acquisitions, Thesaurus and Circulation modules. Two printers were also required: a Wenger 4/1 line printer to handle output from the catalogue and an LBP/8A1 Canon laser printer which was to be used for order letters. The hardware was organized by SCSS in conjunction with a consultant employed by the IPM.

There then followed a three-day training period with the BookshelF librarians during which the system was set up and explained. At this time two of the professional staff spent many hours gaining a practical understanding of how the system operated, particularly in terms of its capabilities and limitations in order that they were sufficiently competent to train the rest of the staff at a later date. In 1987 there was only one manual for the entire system and it was very far from complete; it was therefore necessary to get a great deal of 'hands on' experience before embarking on the conversion project.

Conversion procedures

The conversion project fell into four stages, namely the Catalogue, Thesaurus, Acquisitions and finally Circulation.

Firstly, the Catalogue. It was estimated that there were 10,000 titles in the lending stock (including company documents) to load and retrospectively keyword. In addition the journal index comprised some 20,000 indexed articles which would require inputting and keywording. It was decided to bring in a cut-off date of 1985 for journal articles. This was agreed on the basis that loading articles between 1985–87 would create a sizeable database of 3,500 articles alone and it was doubtful that articles as far back as the late 1960s were required on the system given that members were interested predominantly in more recent material. In addition the logistics of retrospectively keywording and possibly later abstracting upwards of 3,500 items were difficult to contemplate.

The next priority was staffing. On the clerical side it was decided to utilize existing staff to input data rather than recruiting typists from outside. IPM staff were already familiar with library cataloguing procedures and would require less training, were competent typists and providing strict guidelines were established as to the information to be input in each field, might hope to complete the project in nine months. The clerical team consisted of one full-time library secretary, one part-time library secretary and a full-time departmental personal assistant. On the professional side IPM recruited one extra assistant librarian for the information desk so that the remainder of the professional staff could devote more time to the training of the clerical staff, retrospective keywording and general management of the system.

Inputting of journal data presented no difficulties whatsoever. The IPM had maintained a master file of all articles in the index. Each time an article had been added to the system it had been allocated a running number and a complete and in effect chronological list had been built up. The existing numbering system was therefore utilized for control numbers and prefixed by the letter 'J'. Details were taken from the masterfile (from 1985 onwards) and simply loaded onto JAD 1, leaving the keyword field empty in preparations for re-indexing. It was a straight clerical operation and was completed by March 1988.

Loading book material was a little less straightforward. Guidelines were drawn up for the clerical staff as to what information was to be entered in each field. Book material was to be allocated a GMD of T and company documents were to be entered as C. The IPM does not hold audiovisual material so only two GMDs were set up. The clerical staff could easily distinguish between the two media as all company documentation carried a '77' suffix in the classification number. Staff used the catalogue masterfile for data input which was a system of 5″×3″ handwritten slips arranged in classified order. These were the original slips from which the old catalogue cards had been typed and staff proceeded to input the entire catalogue via Catalogue Maintenance, recording standard numbers on the appropriate slips in preparation for bar-coding. All the details were input apart from keywords. This field was left empty in readiness for indexing with the new thesaurus terms later on.

The process was not without a couple of problems. The first difficulty which arose concerned standard numbers. IPM had never used ISBN numbers as over 10 per cent of the stock consisted of catalogued, internal company documents which were not 'published' as such. The solution was to allow the computer to generate its own standard number by inputting a letter and pressing return. This led to a problem of screens 'locking' when more than one person attempted to input data at the same time. Terminals had to be logged out from the system console to release the lock and the problem was solved only when each member of the clerical team was allocated her own individual prefix.

IPM also had a slight problem with the publisher field which was not of sufficient physical length to accept for example trade union names as publishers. Staff preferred to avoid the use of abbreviations as this caused difficulties with lesser known organizations and with no adequate system of cross referencing on BookshelF, IPM had made it a policy to enter corporate names in full. As a result, the IPM publisher field on Cat 1 has a physical length of 39 characters and the screen was reformatted to accommodate this.

The only other modification was to the Corporate Author field. When Cat 1 was originally designed the Corporate Author field was single value to be searched in the same way as the Title. IPM stocked a large number of items with up to three corporate authors, namely trade union and company agreements and required the facility to retrieve this material by company or trade unions involved. At IPM's instruction the Corporate Author field was made multi-value to be searched in the same way as the regular Author field.

Data input of the Catalogue and Journal Article index took only eight months to complete and was finished by the end of the summer of 1988. The second stage of the project was the Thesaurus. There was no commerically available set of Thesaurus terms for personnel management so IPM were forced to develop their own. Work began in mid-1986. Utilizing existing journal article index terms, subject headings and with knowledge of the 'state of the art' in personnel management the structure of a thesaurus was pulled together incorporating broader, narrower and related terms. Scope notes and definitions were added and a network of synonyms to provide adequate cross referencing was devised.

The development of an in-house thesaurus proved a useful exercise for various reasons. Firstly, it was an opportunity to look at existing subject headings and replace them with more up-to-date terminology that reflected the changing nature of personnel management. Secondly, it was a chance to introduce new and more specific concepts and thirdly, it made us think about our users, the terminology they used and how they would be best served by the database created.

A pilot scheme was run over several months whereby all recent acquisitions were manually indexed with the new terms. The pilot was quite successful. The indexing staff found the new terms easy to use and very flexible although it was understood that many areas would require substantial expansion and that some of the terms would need refining as the indexing process progressed.

The thesaurus was stored on a manual system of 5″×8″ cards with one card per heading. Beneath each term was entered the relevant broader, narrower and related terms and when at the end of 1987 IPM obtained the Thesaurus software, the information was simply typed into the relevant fields on Thesaurus Descriptor Definition. It was a straightforward clerical exercise.

IPM was the first library to make use of the BookshelF Thesaurus software. The Thesaurus option did not appear on the main menu and was not linked to Catalogue Enquiry. Access to the software came via the colon prompt. However in the early months of 1988 the programmers updated the software in terms of its capacity and capabilities. The Thesaurus appeared as an option on the main menu, became linked to Enquiry and more importantly vocabulary control was incorporated.

Having loaded the Thesaurus the professional staff began the process of re-indexing. All new material from January 1988 was input directly onto the system and indexed with the new keywords. The re-indexing of journal articles dated between 1985 and 1987 began in March 1988 and was completed by September 1989. The re-indexing of the bookstock began in mid-1988 and to date has not yet been completed.

The thesaurus is still developing and requires a good deal more work, particularly in the area of industrial relations. All indexing staff have an input into it. New terms entered in the Keyword field of Catalogue Maintenance and Journal Article Definition go into a holding file (Thes.Entries) and one member of the professional staff updates the Thesaurus and positions the terms in the structure. Thes.Entries lists new keywords and relevant standard numbers so if a problem arises with the context or meaning of a term the original document can be retrieved and consulted.

All members of the information team have hard copies of the Thesaurus which are printed out via an Inform statement and updated regularly. The Thesaurus can also be accessed on line via Catalogue Enquiry. After completing a search of a specific keyword the user hits the return key and is taken into the Thesaurus. The screen displays all the broader, narrower and related terms and gives the user the option of widening or narrowing the search by simply keying in the appropriate line number. The operator is then taken back into Catalogue Enquiry where the number of hits is displayed. Should the user key in a term which does not appear in the Thesaurus, the screen displays Zero hits and there is no facility to browse the Thesaurus. Staff need therefore to be aware of relevant keywords before they can use Catalogue Enquiry effectively, hence the use at IPM of hard copy thesauri. This inability to browse the thesaurus at the time of inputting a keyword is the one drawback to the system as it stands at present.

The third stage of the project was Acquisitions. There was never any specific intention to computerize IPM's ordering system. The library only adds to stock some 150 to 200 items per month and this had never presented any major administrative difficulties. However, given that Acquisitions updated the Catalogue it seemed logical to computerize the ordering system rather than maintain a manual file.

IPM began to use the Acquisitions module in the early months of 1989. It was the least problematic part of the system to introduce as it required no special modifications. New titles are ordered via option one of the menu – Order Requests and Catalogue Update. As IPM does not use ISBN numbers the user types in an alpha 'O' presses return and BookshelF generates the next available number. The 'O' prefix appears on the catalogue denoting an Order Record and distinguishing it from other alpha prefixed standard numbers on the system.

The library orders the vast majority of its material from individual publishers, consequently the library has 315 suppliers set up in the reference data. After details of orders are input the order requests are processed by selecting option two of the menu – Process Order Requests. It is IPM practice to accept order numbers generated by the system rather than input alternative numbers. As soon as orders have been batched into suppliers the user then prepares orders for printing by selecting option four of the menu – Prepare Orders for Printing. Once into 'Process Orders for Sending' the user notes down the batch numbers for the orders about to be printed. This number is then used in a specially written programme that enables IPM to print out order slips. Output is to a Canon laser printer which is loaded with letter headed stationery.

Material is received using options two of the Receipts/Claims menu – Receipt of Bar-coded Stock. A location of 'PROCESSING' is entered for all copies being received. IPM use pre-printed bar-codes which are read in with a telepen. Invoice numbers and amended prices are not entered as the budgeting facility on the Acquisitions module is not currently in use at IPM. The library maintains a manual record of all library expenditure as a large amount of material is paid for by postal order or proforma invoice and the current budgeting facility on BookshelF is not as flexible as IPM requires in accommodating this.

After receipt the majority of accessions are acquired from labelling using option seven of the Catalogue menu. However, any items which have been received and for which reservations have been placed are acquired from labelling via the Returns Program of the Circulation module as it is not possible to use option seven for reserved materials.

Reference books are again treated differently at IPM. When a new item has been received via Receipt of Bar-coded Stock and where it is known that the item is for reference only, the material is acquired from labelling in the normal way and then the status of it is changed again to one of 'Hold' via option two of the Catalogue Menu – Accession File Maintenance. All reference material at IPM has a status of 'Hold' to distinguish it from lending stock.

Material is then catalogued by the Assistant Librarian – Acquisitions who also amends the standard number from an 'O' prefix to the appropriate standard number prefix for that year. New standard numbers are entered in the books and the material is passed for classification and indexing. All unordered items or material which comes by gift or exchange is added to stock directly via Catalogue Maintenance. Reserved items are always given priority in the system.

After classification and keywording, material is processed. IPM buys in book labels and these are manually typed by staff. Book processing is then checked and the location of PROCESSING is changed to that of 'L' denoting lending or 'LR' indicating a library reference copy. Originally the acquisitions staff entered a location of 'L' or 'LR' at the receipt of bar-coded stock stage but brought in a location of 'PROCESSING' when they discovered that staff were wasting time searching the shelves for material which on the catalogue was 'available' but was in fact awaiting processing. Having amended Location codes material is shelved in the normal way.

Acquisitions has been the least problematic module to implement at IPM. Library procedures are now established in the use of the module and staff training has been greatly facilitated by the compilation of an in-house manual giving a step-by-step guide to IPM's use of Acquisitions. IPM is only using the module in its most basic capacity but in fairness the software has proved 'bug-free' and the transition from a manual ordering system to a computerized one has been relatively smooth.

The final stage of the project was Circulation. This module underwent large-scale modifications in order to meet IPM's needs. The software modifications were completed in 1989 and the system went live at the end of September the same year. The bookstock was bar-coded in a mammoth two week exercise in October 1988 during which the library was closed to telephone enquiries and visitors. Using pre-printed bar-codes the library staff worked solidly in order to complete the operation within the allotted time. The staff organized themselves into two teams. Material was systematically pulled off the shelves and the standard numbers written in the books (standard numbers were taken from the old cataloguing slips). The books were then bar-coded and added to a stock using telepens via Accession File Maintenance. Any items on loan were bar-coded on return and those records with no bar-codes were assumed missing and deleted from the catalogue.

Circulation was not an easy module to implement. Because of the customization much of the software was new and largely untried. Staff needed to acquire an awareness of how the system worked, its potential and limitations before the module could be fully operational. Staff began with the issuing and returning of books and the reservations programme was phased in after a few weeks. Reader details were input from enquiry forms at the issuing stage and a database slowly developed. By Christmas 1989 Circulation was up and running and the staff were familiar with the system and equipment.

There are two terminals assigned to the Circulation module. One terminal at the circulation desk is used purely for issues whilst reservations, returns, overdue etc. are carried out at a terminal in the main office. Output is to a DL3400 Fujitsu printer and books are discharged with a micropen (bar-code reader).

Loans are currently running at 400 per month, photocopies at approximately 1,500 per month and there are upwards of 7,500 readers on the system.

The circulation desk is manned by five clerical staff who work on a rota basis. Telephone enquiries come in at the information desk. Professional staff complete enquiry forms detailing the nature of the research to be undertaken, name of the member, membership number and address to which the material is to be sent. Material is then selected out in response to queries and passed with relevant enquiry forms to the circulation desk. The clerical staff discharge the books, photocopy any specified journal articles, completed invoices/declaration forms and send the packages out in the post.

At the issuing stage staff are prompted for a reader code. This is the IPM membership number; an eight-digit number which is quoted by the member and checked against the membership list on a terminal by the information desk. Input of the reader code takes the user directly into the Reader Screen to check the address with that of the enquiry form. If the address differs amendments are made so that material will be sent to the destination specified by the member.

The user then presses return and is taken back into the issue screen. Books are discharged in the normal way by running a telepen across bar-codes. After the first book is issued to a reader the user is prompted to enter a postage charge and then any charges for photocopying. This having been completed the user may issue any further material to that reader in the normal way. Should a reader not require photocopies the operator simply types in zero i.e. no charge. The operator then places the material in a packing envelope on which he writes the reader's surname. Twice per day the user selects an option on the Circulation menu called – Print Address Labels and adhesive labels are run off. These labels are attached to the appropriate parcels which are then sent out in the post. The operator then returns to the colon prompt and enters Clear.File Data Address.label. This clears down the file in preparation for the next label run.

The return of material is carried out in the normal way via option two on the Circulation menu. After reading in a bar-code the user presses return and is alerted to any monies outstanding and then invited to enter payment. It is at this point that any remittance accompanying the loan is input into the system.

Details of all money transactions are held on the Credits/Debits screen. This is a separate screen accessible via the Issue screen which appears as an option after pressing the Help key. The format of Credits/Debits resembles that of a bank statement and is an itemized listing of charges incurred for loans and photocopies. Where a charge was made for postage the title of the first book issued is displayed on the screen. Details of any payments are also recorded on the screen together with total amounts outstanding.

Members may borrow up to five items at any one time. This total may consist of any combination of books and company documents and the circulation rules are set up accordingly. All items are loaned for a period of four weeks from issue and postage is charged at a flat rate depending on whether a parcel is sent by first or second class post. The library opens Monday to Friday, closes between Christmas and New Year and the calendar in Reference Data is appropriately set up. IPM reserves items for members and the system produces letters which explain that readers have been placed on a waiting list and that material will be posted out as soon as possible. Reservation Priorities is used only for checking the number of members waiting for an item as there is rarely a need to amend the waiting order.

After material has been overdue for 14 days members receive a reminder. This is followed 14 days later by a second reminder and should the material fail to appear an invoice is despatched for the replacement cost of the books plus an administrative charge. The invoice is sent out ten weeks after the books were originally issued.

Four weeks later if the loans have not been returned members receive a final letter which indicates that their loan privileges have been suspended. At this point the message 'Suspension of Loan Privileges' plus the date of the letter is input into field twelve of the reader record and a loan and reserve stop placed upon the reader.

All the letters are produced from BookshelF but in the case of invoices any replacement costs are inserted manually from current price lists. Following the suspension letter the system is set up to produce a further letter three weeks later for the Assistant Librarian – Acquisitions who considers possible replacement of the material.

All library letters (apart from invoice/declaration forms which are printed by the Institute) including order and reservation notifications are carried out via a special programme. The operator logs into the system as reserve, overdue, order etc. and is then prompted for a batch number. This will already have been obtained from the screen of the appropriate function or by typing in at the colon prompt: List Overdue Letter, List Order Letter etc. The user is then prompted to designate a printer for the operation. Having input a printer code (PR1 or PR2) the user then presses return wherupon the system will spool and then automatically log out. Letters are produced at the specified printer.

Although Circulation performs broadly the functions that IPM requires there is still a problem when a member requests photocopies or a fax but no loans. The credits/debits screen is attached to the issuing of book material and there is currently no way of accessing it to input other charges where a loan is not involved. As a result when a payment is received if the amount is not outstanding on BookshelF staff need to consult manual files of invoices to explain the remittance. This can be time-consuming particularly when a member sends payment covering two or three enquiries at the same time. IPM and BookshelF are currently looking into further modifications to solve this problem which may involve direct access to the Credit/Debit screen to input charges.

Since the installation of Bookshelf in 1987 library staffing has increased significantly and there are now 20 terminals in the library connected to a Prime 2450. The 2450 had previously been in use by the Institute to run a membership package and other housekeeping software and when in October 1990 it was upgraded to a Prime 2950 the BookshelF software was loaded onto the 2450 and the two machines networked together. As a result back-ups now take place for the entire Institute system in the early hours of the morning by virtue of a helical scan magnetic tape sub-system. Prior to this, library staff performed their own back-ups after 5 pm which restricted access to the database in the evenings.

From September 1989 onwards the IPM has employed a part-time abstractor to retrospectively abstract all the journal articles on the database. This exercise is now complete and since 1990 any articles added to the system have been abstracted and keyworded as a matter of course. The re-indexing of the bookstock is still ongoing although it is hoped to complete this by the end of 1991.

In conclusion although BookshelF was thought to bring a large number of benefits to the IPM and perform many functions that the manual system was failing to do, it was never fully appreciated what implications computerization would have for the structure of tasks, skills of individuals, physical location of personnel and training. All these have changed beyond recognition in the last four years as BookshelF has taken on more functions and staff have become more computer literate.

16 The use of BookshelF in teaching students of Information and Library Management at Manchester Polytechnic

Introduction

The Department of Library and Information Studies at Manchester Polytechnic offers a comprehensive programme of courses, both full-time and part-time at undergraduate, postgraduate and masters degree level, in order to meet the fast developing needs of the library and information profession. A major strand of the Department's activities is focussed on state-of-the-art information technology teaching and facilities. Such facilities are continually under development. An important step forward has been possible in the past academic year (1990–1991) with the implementation of BookshelF, the multi-user library system from Specialist Computer Systems and Software Ltd. The BookshelF software has been sponsored by its suppliers and is available in the Department on both the Polytechnic's Prime computer system and on a small local area network.

This chapter describes the way in which the use of BookshelF software has been integrated into the curriculum and identifies the learning objectives which have been achieved through the use of the software.

BookshelF was installed in the Department early in 1990 and throughout the academic year 1990–91 has been used extensively in the teaching of Information Systems and Information Access, which are two of the core components of the BA(Hons) Information and Library Management.

BookshelF provides students with the opportunity to experience a fully integrated library system including modules for ordering, circulation control, cataloguing, OPAC, thesaurus and serials control. The system is installed on a 64 Mb Prime 6350, running under Information and is linked to the Departmental computer terminal laboratory. This facility houses 18 Volker-Craig VDUs linked by a Gandalf 24 port multiplexer to the Polytechnic's Prime network and to JANET and PSS. The system is supported by the Polytechnic's central Computing Services Unit. The network also provides access to other software applications such as INFO (a relational-type DBMS text-retrieval system) and to statistical packages such as Minitab and SPSS-X.

Departmental IT facilities

The Department has a tradition of developing teaching methods in tandem with opportunities afforded by new IT-based resources. The use of INFO (Doric) in teaching database design and information retrieval was documented in 1987 (Rowley, 1987 a,b,c). Since then the IT facilities in the Department have been considerably extended. A dedicated Information Access laboratory now contains 18 Mitac PCs which can be used as stand-alones, as part of an Ethernet Isolan LAN, and as intelligent terminals to access the Polytechnic's Prime system through this gateway access to PSS and JANET. The Information Technology laboratory provides 16 Tulip 1 Mb AT COMPACT 2 286 EGA workstations, each with a 40 Mb hard disk. A 3 Mb Tulip AT 386 SX 160 Mb hard disk machine acts as a file server on an Isolan Ethernet LAN, supporting Novell Advanced Netware v.2.15, linked to the workstations. Several networked applications software packages are currently installed including dBASE IV, Framework III, Lotus 1-2-3, and Wordstar 5.5. A second integrated library system, Datatrek (sponsored by the distributor) was installed on the network in 1991. It is intended that the use of the system be integrated into the syllabuses in the next academic year.

Courses

The Department runs a full programme of undergraduate and postgraduate courses in full-time, part-time and mixed modes. Central components to the programme are:

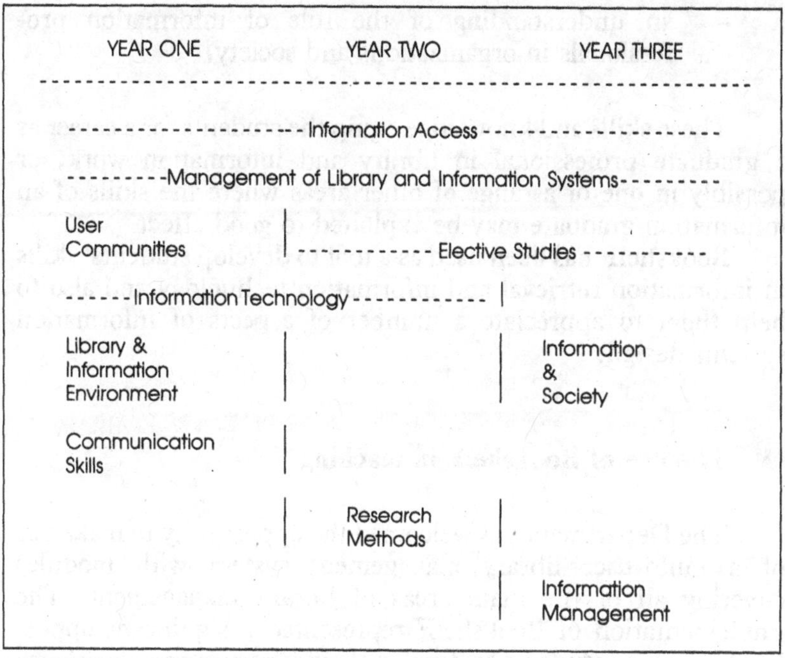

Figure 16.1 BA(Hons.) Information & Library Management course outline

- BA(Hons.) Information and Library Management
- Postgraduate Diploma/MA in Information and Library Studies
- MA Strategic Library Management
- MPhil/PhD Research Degrees

The applications of BookshelF described in this article are on the BA(Hons.) in Information and Library Management, which is the main undergraduate programme in the Department. This course includes the components shown in Figure 16.1.

The course aims to help students to develop their intellectual, social and personal abilities. By the end of the course students should have:

- an understanding of the needs of information users;
- an ability to organize information for retrieval;
- an ability to locate information in electronic and printed sources;
- an appreciation of the role of management;

- an understanding of the role of information professionals in organizations and society.

These skills and knowledge equip the students for a career as a graduate professional in library and information work, or possibly in one of a range of other areas where the skills of an information graduate may be exploited to good effect.

BookshelF has been used as a tool to develop students' skills in information retrieval and information technology and also to help them to appreciate a number of aspects of information systems design.

The use of BookshelF in teaching

The Department has welcomed the opportunity to make use of a multi-user library management system with modules covering all of the main areas of library management. The implementation of BookshelF represented a significant opportunity to allow students to develop their expertise and experience of computerized library systems and computerized systems generally. The package gives us the opportunity to develop different teaching objectives for different groups of students. Before elaborating on these, perhaps one objective which we do **not** have, which needs to be stated is that we have never used BookshelF, nor do we ever foresee using BookshelF to train students in how to use a specific system. We do, however, expect them to learn a lot about how BookshelF works but we expect them to use this as a basis for comparison and analysis. This means that our teaching emphasizes principles, operations and approaches and the applications (often in the form of projects which mirror real life) for which the students are using the software. These objectives are explored more fully in the next section.

This academic year, 1990–91, has been the first year in which we have had the opportunity to exploit BookshelF in teaching. We have started by using it most extensively with Year 2 undergraduates on the BA(Hons) in Information and Library Management. These students follow a Year 2 course that includes Information Access, Information Technology, Management of Library and Information Services, Research Methods and Statistics, and an elective chosen from Information Systems

Design or a focus on a user community and its needs such as Local Community, Children and Young People or Business Community. We have made use of BookshelF in 2 of these components – Information Access and Information Technology as described below. It is important to appreciate that both of these subjects are also studied in Year 1 and that all students have participated in a course that lays down the principles of information retrieval, cataloguing, information resources, indexing and classification. Year 1 Information Technology develops a general awareness of IT and offers students experience in the use of standard business software for word processing, spreadsheets and databases.

In addition to the use of BookshelF with Year 2 undergraduates, which is discussed in more detail below, the system has also been used with a smaller group of Year 3 undergraduates who choose to pursue the Library Housekeeping Special Study.

The use of BookshelF in teaching Information Access

The Year 2 Information Access course aims (1) to provide an integrated approach to the design, use, management and evaluation of information resources and services and (2) to provide a flexible framework for the study of access-based strategies to information resources.

The BookshelF system gives students practical insight into methods of organizing and accessing information. It also provides a mechanism for the assessment of individual student's efforts and depth of understanding. Indeed, this latter aspect has been a major breakthrough in the use of such a system for teaching when a more usual method of instruction has been to demonstrate the features or, at best, hands-on experience of a shared data-file (meaning that all data held in the system can be accessed by all users – this being one of the primary advantages of an integrated library system). This is inadequate for assessment of individual student's input. Students at Manchester, however can access their own individual BookshelF systems which are located via personal Prime directories. Programmers in the Polytechnic's Computing Services Unit have created a 'Virtual BookshelF Environment' i.e. have set up pointers in 65 student Prime directories to the BookshelF programs so that each student appears to have access to their own versions. This means that students, working simultaneously, can create catalogue entries, index them, create thesauri etc. and print out their work for assessment purposes without accessing any other student files or using other students' data.

The BookshelF catalogue database is at the heart of the system, supporting the Circulation and Acquisitions functions. The control number of a bibliographic record (ISBN or in-house) is the key identifier to which order, accession, issue, return, reservation etc. is attached. The creation, retrieval and display of bibliographic information in the system is therefore experienced in the context of the total system. The students undertake two projects in Year 2 Information Access which focus on (a) bibliographic description, access points and headings and (b) indexing, retrieval and thesaurus construction. BookshelF provides a two-page formatted screen which allows the input of bibliographic data into variable-length multi-value fields. For the first project, students are required to provide bibliographic descriptions for a set of book and non-book items in accordance with AACR2 Rules and then transpose this information into the BookshelF Catalogue Maintenance screen.

What do students learn from this exercise? Firstly, they have had the opportunity to evaluate the role of AACR2 in non-MARC based computerized cataloguing. The problems of accommodating non-standard data in a standardized database record format (which is primarily book-oriented) is examined. Although BookshelF provides a field for a coded General Material Designation, there is no designated field or sub-field for scale and projection (maps), running time (videocassettes), material specific designation, provenance, manufacturer (3-D artifacts), distributor (software, motion pictures) and so on. Conversely, a free-text IR system such as BookshelF demonstrates that in retrieval terms, the record format is of secondary importance when all data elements are indexable and are entered somewhere in the record e.g. the notes field. Secondly, students are able to explore through practical experience, the issues concerning the value and use of main headings and added entries. There is no uniform heading field on the version of BookshelF used for teaching this year. The personal author and corporate author fields are multi-value. Multiple authors therefore have equal status in BookshelF when creating a record or searching for a known item. The student submission for assessment includes a print-out of their set of catalogue entries (a hard-copy catalogue) arranged by author. Multi-value personal and corporate author fields are automatically 'exploded' to provide a listing which includes all authorbased access points. Author headings are in fact modified statements of responsibility. Where there is no identifiable statement of responsibility for a document, the field is left blank so there is no filing element for that particular record on the hard-copy catalogue. This emphasizes the value of headings in computerized cataloguing, especially for hard-copy listings and for the order of items appearing on an OPAC enquiry screen. Students are also required to submit a written discussion of the role of the main heading in computerized cataloguing systems, based on their practical experience of data entry, searching and output from the BookshelF system.

The second Information Access project focuses on subject indexing and thesaurus construction. For this project, students create bibliographic records for 14 journal articles, using the Journal Article Definition formatted screen. In addition to standard fields (author, title, source, class number), two further fields allow for subject enhancement of the record. The inclusion of an abstract, in a designated field allowing up to 999 lines of text and a free-text search facility, gives students the experience of retrieval using natural language. A 'keywords' field is linked directly to the Thesaurus program, and therefore a controlled indexing language. Students create their own thesauri, in a specified subject area, and assign relevant controlled terms to the records in the keywords field which automatically checks whether a term is in the Thesaurus. In addition to print-outs of assigned index terms and thesaurus relationships, students are required to submit an analysis which compares the effects of searching the database globally (using natural language) and restricting the search to the keywords thereby invoking the Thesaurus (using a controlled vocabulary).

What do students learn from this project? Firstly, the principles of vocabulary control are reinforced on an experiential basis by using these BookshelF facilities. Secondly, the complexities of recall and precision ratios (always difficult for students when taught in the abstract) become meaningful in a practical application working with a limited set of documents. The effects of using primary and secondary concepts as index terms on recall and precision is demonstrated at close quarters.

The use of BookshelF in teaching IT

The Year 2 Information Technology course has the following general objectives: (i) to enable the student to develop foundation skills in systems analysis and design and (ii) to enable the student to select software for a particular library or information environment. The focus for the course is systems analysis and implementation.

The course is taught through a one-hour lecture and one-hour workshop or seminar sessions each week throughout the academic year. The lectures give an introduction to a range of aspects of systems analysis and implementation as might be appropriate to the information professional who may be responsible for specifying and implementing computer systems. Topics which are explored include systems theory, systems methodologies, data gathering techniques, data analysis and modelling techniques, software and hardware evaluation, implementation, security and training. Lectures are complemented by seminars or workshops where students are working in smaller groups. Some seminar sessions have been used to develop various themes, but most of them have been devoted to workshop sessions which develop the skills necessary for the student to be able to complete successfully their assessed coursework. As outlined above, students come to this project with experience of other database packages and already having used BookshelF in the Information Access component to build a cataloguing database and a thesaurus and investigate retrieval from the database. This IT project constituted the first opportunity to examine BookshelF as a system. In summary, the aim of the project was twofold: to familiarize students with the functions of a computerized library housekeeping system, and to help students develop skills appropriate for systems specification.

Preparation for the project involved the following stages:

i) examination of the Circulation Control module of BookshelF;
ii) students work on the responses to the specification for Circulation Control, under the guidance of the tutor and are finally given the model response;
iii) examination of the Acquisitions module of BookshelF;
iv) students work on the response to the specification for acquisitions. This is handed in for assessment.

Students are given the opportunity to explore both the Circulation Control and Acquisitions modules of BookshelF and are required to analyse their operation in some detail.

Once a basic familiarity with the module has been achieved, students are able to begin to write a response to the specification. The specification used this year was written for Sandwell Public Libraries in 1990 when they were seeking tenders for their (then proposed) computerized library management system. The sections on circulation control and acquistions were extracted and made available to students. The specification asks a range of questions concerning how basic library operations, which reflect practices at Sandwell, can be executed and integrated into the use of a computerized system. Once students have experimented with the provision of answers to these questions they are provided with the answers in the form of a model response. This model response also acts as a model for the format of the responses that students need to prepare for their assessed coursework.

For Acquisitions, appropriate reference data must be established. This includes data about suppliers, budgets, countries and currencies. The Acquisitions module is explored by starting with the ordering process and taking an item through all of the stages necessary before the item is available for loan, including ordering, receipting, accessions file maintenance and finally issue and return. Claims and standing orders are also explored, as are a number of reports.

Future developments

BookshelF has facilitated the implementation of plans and allowed us to achieve our teaching objectives more effectively than might otherwise have been the case. Work this year has, however, been focussed on certain modules and on two groups of students. We envisage making more extensive use of BookshelF in the future. Areas for development that are currently under investigation are:

1. Use of the serials module to examine the issues and problems of serials management.
2. Comparative student projects between BookshelF and Datatrek (recently mounted on the Departmental PC network).
3. Use of BookshelF with students on our other courses (MA, PG.Dip., full and part-time, BA, part-time) and in other components of the full-time undergraduate programme. For example, Information Management is

a theme on all of the courses in the Department and the use of management information from BookshelF could be examined in this context.

4. Use of the BookshelF/MARC facility which allows records to be downloaded from BNBMARC files and converted to BookshelF format by linking tagged fields and sub-fields and running the BookshelF conversion program.
5. Examination of different classification schemes for subject retrieval in an on-line context.

References

Leggate, P and Dyer, H. (1987) *The development of a microcomputer facility for small libraries* (LIR Report; 42), British Library.

Rowley, J.E. (1987a) 'Information technology at Manchester Polytechnic', *ITs News* (12) May, 17–19.

Rowley, J.E. (1987b) 'The use of INFO, a database management system in the teaching of library and information studies,' *Education for Information*, 6, 456–69.

Rowley, J.E. (1987c) 'Teaching information systems analysis and design,' *Library Association Record*, October, 528–9.

Appendix 1 Further reading

'BookshelF: an integrated modular package for the smaller library,' *Vine*, **54**, June 1984, 37–8.

Beetham, Joy (1987), 'BookshelF – available off the shelf,' *Library Micromation News*, **17**, Aug, 3–6.

Butterwick, S. (1990), 'The academic library on the school campus,' *School Librarian*, Feb.

Haynes, E.M. (1988), 'Harwell Library's SPARC,' *Program*, **22** (4), Oct., 317–36.

Hunt, C. and Dyer, H. (1989), 'Automated serials control: a view of Microlinx and BookshelF,' *Computers in libraries*, **9** (5), May, 18–21.

Johnston, A. (1988), 'BookshelF in Dumfries and Galloway,' *Vine*, **73**, Dec., 9–14.

Leggate, P. (1984), 'Cairns medical library's online system: a first look,' *Vine*, **55**, Oct., 23–7.

Leggate, P. and Dyer, H. (1987), *The development of a microcomputer facility for small libraries* British Library, (Library and Information Research Reports, 42).

Leggate, P. (1988), 'A multi-user microcomputer system for small libraries,' *Information Services and Use*, **8** (1), 31–8.

Manson, Pat (1985), 'Housekeeping systems for small libraries,' *Library Micromation News*, **7**, Jan., 11–18.

Powne, Clare (1987), 'First experiences with BookshelF at Fife Health Board,' *Program*, **21** (3), July, 260–72.

Wilson, Ruth (1991), 'The BookshelF thesaurus: treasure or trauma?' *Library Review*, **40**, (6) 42–9.

Appendix 2
BookshelF customers in the United Kingdom

Academic libraries

Askham Bryan College of Agriculture and Horticulture
Barony Agricultural College, Dumfries
Bath College of Higher Education
Bell College of Technology
Bilston Community College
Birmingham College of Food, Tourism and Creative Studies
Blackburn College
Bolton Institute of Higher Education
Bradford Grammar School
Bretton Hall College of Higher Education, Wakefield
Bridgwater College, Somerset
Brighton College of Technology
Bristol – Multi-cultural Education Centre
Brooklands Technical College
Brunel College, Bristol
Carlisle College
Chester College
City of London School
City of London School for Girls
Coleg Meirionnydd, Dolgellau
Craigie College of Education
Crawley College of Technology
Dudley College of Technology
Dumfries and Galloway College of Technology
Dundee College of Further Education
Edge Hill College of Higher Education
Farnborough College of Technology
Filton College
Godolphin and Latymer School, London

Grimsby College of Technology
Henley College of Further Education, Coventry
Homerton College, Cambridge
Huddersfield Technical College
Hull College of Further Education
Isle of Man College
James Allen Girls School, London
Kent Institute of Art and Design, Maidstone
Kidderminster College of Further Education
Kilburn College
Kingston College of Further Education
Kirkland High School, Fife
Lancaster – St. Martin's College
Liverpool Institute of Higher Education
Manchester College of Arts and Technology
Matthew Boulton College, Birmingham
Mid Warwickshire College of Further Education
Northbrook College Design + Technology, Worthing
North Lindsay College of Technology, South Humberside
Paisley College of Technology
Pershore College of Horticulture
Peterborough Regional College
Preston College
Ridings High School, Bristol
Royal College of Nursing
Runshaw College
Schiller International University, London
Scottish Agricultural College, Ayr
Sevenoaks School
Somerset College of Agriculture and Horticulture
Somerset College of Arts and Technology
Southall College of Technology
Spurgeon's College, London
St. Marys College, Middlesex
Strode College, Somerset
Suffolk College of Higher and Further Education
Tile Hill College of Further Education, Coventry
Waltham Forest College
West Cheshire College, Chester
Weston super Mare College of Further Education
Willesden College of Technology
Wolverhampton MBC, Jennie Lee Community and Professional Centre

Yeovil College, Somerset
York College of Arts and Technology

Government libraries

ACAS
Employment Department
Employment Department – The Training Agency
Royal Naval Engineering College
Scottish Office

Public libraries

Bearsden and Milngavie District Council
Dumfries and Galloway Regional Library Service
East Kilbridge District Council
Llanelli Borough Council
Newport Borough Council
North East of Scotland Library Service
Orkney Library Service
Sandwell Metropolitan Borough Council
Wigan Metropolitan Borough Council

Medical libraries

Bolton School of Nursing
Bradford School of Nursing
Broadmoor Hospital, Berkshire
Cairns Library, Oxford
Charles Frears College of Nursing, Leicester
Combined Training Institute, Cardiff
Fife Health Board
Hellesdon Hospital, Norwich
Hospital for Sick Children, Great Ormond Street
Kettering General Hospital
Leeds College of Nursing and Midwifery
Leicester General Infirmary
Milton Keynes General Hospital
Norfolk and Norwich Hospital
Northampton Health Authority

Salford School of Nursing
South West Manchester School of Nursing
Stoke on Trent, City General Hospital
United Midlands College of Nursing and Midwifery
University of Wales College of Medicine
York District Hospital

Special libraries

Barnardos
British Telecom Research Laboratories, Ipswich
Equal Opportunities Commission
Institute of Directors
Institute of Personnel Management
Institution of Structural Engineers
John Innes Centre for Plant Science Research
London Borough of Tower Hamlets
Museum of Mankind – British Museum
Royal Institution of Chartered Surveyors, Edinburgh
Royal Institution of Chartered Surveyors, London
Science Policy Research Unit, University of Sussex

Northern Ireland

Altnagelvin Medical Library, Londonderry
Bloomfield Collegiate School, Belfast
Sacred Heart Grammar School, Newry

Eire

Cert Ltd. (State Training Board for Hotel and Catering), Dublin

Appendix 3

Enhancement of computerized operations in Paisley College Library

Specification

21st March 1985

Preliminary note

The title of this document relates to the 'Enhancement' of computerized operations in the College Library. The College Library already has a database of about 25,000 items at SCOLCAP.

While tenders are being sought for complete computerized library systems which could run without the support of SCOLCAP Cataloguing and Acquisitions Services, tenders are also being considered for computerized circulation systems which could be linked with SCOLCAP services or with similar cataloguing and acquisitions services provided by another database supplier.

Introduction

After consultation with the HMI of the Scottish Education Department, the College has decided to put forward a submission to the Scottish Education Department for an enhancement of computerized operations in the College Library, with a view to implementation in the summer of 1986.

The College is most anxious to ensure that this approach to SED bears fruit. The performance of the College Library cannot match the performance of the English polytechnic libraries without extensive computerization of library routines.

To minimize the risk of failure, the HMI has advised the College to submit more than one tender, leaving the Department to make a final choice in the light of its financial resources at the time.

The College will arrange the tenders received in groups which are broadly comparable in terms of cost and will select one from each group for submission to SED. The number of groups, and therefore the number of tenders submitted, will be decided by the College.

Systems offered by 13 suppliers have been considered, but the offer to tender is being issued only to the seven who seem most able to meet our requirements. An eighth contender, whose system is still very much at the design stage, may be considered if it matures before the end of the current calendar year.

All those invited to tender will have already supplied the College with considerable detail about their systems. A specification has been constructed, on the basis of the information supplied to us, which should not exclude any of the recipients of this invitation from submitting bids. If, therefore, there is some mandatory condition which appears to exclude a potential tenderer, he should consult us. Any relaxation of the conditions of specification for one tenderer will, of course, be communicated to all others.

Systems offered need not be complete at the date of tender, but should be fully operational by the end of the calendar year.

The specification contains both mandatory and desirable characteristics at both the basic and 'advanced'* levels. The distinction between mandatory and desirable characteristics should be apparent from the language employed. The distinction between basic and advanced levels is not easy to define, except in terms of expense. Generally speaking the basic system is cumbersome and slower and requires a lot of operator intervention, but it still represents a significant improvement on manual systems.

All advanced systems must offer a computer with 32 or more ports. Requirements which are mandatory at the basic level are also mandatory at the advanced level. The absence from this specification of any statement regarding a feature which is standard in the supplier's product is not to be interpreted as an invitation to excise it from the contract. Please consult with us first.

Information already supplied to the College about the product range of the tenderers concerned, about installations already made (together with reports from the operators of such installations), about downtime and about maintenance arrangements, will all be taken into consideration by the Committee.

The proposal

1. It is anticipated that some tenderers will find that their systems do not match the specification in a few details. The proposal should state the points of difficulty and include

* Advanced system requirements are preceded by an asterisk.

estimates of the cost of remedying the deficiencies individually.

2. The proposal is required by 22 April, 1985. Tenderers unable to meet this date should advise us.
3. The proposal should ideally give an item by item reply to the specification.
4. The costs to be itemized include:
   (a) The Central Processing Unit, its controlling equipment and disk drives.
   (b) Mainframe line printers.
   (c) Magnetic tape drives.
   (d) Terminals.
   (e) Mini printers or screen printers.
   (f) Modems/line drivers and telephone links.
   (g) Software and customization cost.
   (h) Running costs.
   (i) Maintenance of hardware.
   (j) Maintenance of software.
   (k) System back-up equipment.
   (l) Database costs, where access to a database is provided by the potential supplier.

1 System general requirements

1.1 All files to be created must take account of the provisions of the Data Protection Act.

1.2 All equipment supplied must comply with the relevant British Standards and Health and Safety Regulations.

1.3 Increasing concern about the physiological effects of prolonged exposure to the radiation emitted by monitors now makes it important that suppliers should provide an additional quotation for alternative equipment, either of the LED type or simple but silent terminal keyboard-printers, though such solutions will not be practicable for all operations.

1.4 Any equipment not capable of operating between 5°C and 35°C is to be advised as to its limits, as special arrangements for its housing may have to be taken into consideration.

1.5 Public access terminals at least should be of robust construction. Metal casings, where available, should be preferred to plastic.

1.6 The system must be operable by library personnel. The presence of computer personnel should only be necessary in the event of system failure.

1.7 The supplier is expected to provide training facilities for library staff in the induction period within the terms of the tender. Facilities thereafter will be available on mutually agreed occasions by negotiation.

1.8 The system must be capable of handling the following transaction flows and accommodating stock and user files as indicated below.

Collections	
Monograph titles	68,000
Monograph volumes	79,000
Serial titles	1,400
Serial volumes	21,000
Reserve book collection (vols)	2,000
Accessions per annum	
Monograph titles	4,500
Monograph volumes	5,200
Bound volumes of serials	750
Circulation	
*Issues per annum	40,000
*Discharges per annum	40,000
*Reserve book transactions per annum	60,000
Max. No. of items on loan at any one time	14,000
Peak circulation transactions (per day)	
General collection (incl. reservations)	3,000
Reserve books	1,200
Peak circulation transactions (per hour)	500
Reservations made per annum	1,600

Cataloguing
Current throughput: see Accessions
Retrospective throughput: As at present funded, zero. About 54,000 titles still not machine-readable.

* These figures may be expected to increase by a factor of 2.6 upon reduction of the loan period from the Session to 14 days.

Special funds hopefully forthcoming to deal with 18,000 of these in four months.

Catalogues
PAC intended as normal usage, but facilities needed to produce a COM catalogue to provide for UDC, Author/Title and Title sequences. If ever produced, they would be produced for outlying departments.

Acquisitions

Orders placed per annum	7,000
Library funds maintained	31
12 Serial	
19 Monograph	
– and likely to rise (both figures)	

Inter-library loans

Requests handled per annum	5,000
Items received per annum	4,800

Serials

Issues received per annum	13,000

1.9 The supplier is required to ensure that hardware is maintained under contract.

1.10 A call-out delay of more than 8 hours between the time of reporting a fault and the appearance of a mechanic on site would be regarded as unsatisfactory, transport not being affected by strikes or fuel shortages.

1.11 All software is to be maintained under contract. The supplier is to state in his proposal the nature of the software support.

1.12 No credence is given to the statements of suppliers that their systems are invulnerable to subversion. Many of our students are trained as computer technologists or programmers and would have no difficulty in subverting a standard operating system. Non-standard operating systems will simply take longer. Nevertheless the system must make it as difficult as possible for any but approved members of the library staff to gain access on a write or read/write basis, to *any* file within the system. The combination of badge *and* password is particularly favoured for protecting files, but double password protection will also be regarded favourably. Time locks to prevent access to the computer out-of-hours, without impairing its performance of any batch functions it may be called upon to perform, would also be helpful.

1.13 Partly for security reasons, and partly for management statistics, it would be highly desirable for the system to record all circulation transactions on tape as well as on disk.

1.14 There must also be facilities for creating and updating a master bibliographic data tape to enable the data base to be reconstituted in the event of disaster.

1.15 The system should allow for the future connection to it over the proposed College Ethernet system of a wide variety of terminals which will be used to consult the catalogue, make reservations, and place tentative orders with the Acquisition section.

1.16 Adequate documentation for the initial system and for future enhancements will be provided.

1.17 The supplier is expected to have a programme of continuous improvement to the software and to state in the proposal financial policy on availability.

1.18 No system will be considered that does not offer at least 18 ports for the connection of printer, modem, Ethernet and terminals (*With advanced systems at least 32 ports must be available.)

1.19 No system will be considered that does not offer a disc capacity of at least 120 megabytes.

1.20 Acceptable response times under conditions of peak usage will be:

Registering a loan or return	2 seconds
Retrieving a specific record using one key only	8 seconds

1.21 The system will be basically on-line, real-time, with full service available during the hours the Library is open:

Monday–Friday	9.00 am – 9.00 pm
Saturday	9.30 am – 12.30 pm

1.22 Security back-up and printing will preferably be carried out as a background task during normal opening hours. Tenderers proposing to perform these tasks outwith normal library hours must indicate whether staffing is required and the probable duration of the operation.

1.23 *In advanced systems certain parameters supplied to the system must be variable at start-up time each morning to meet extraordinary conditions that arise. These are to include loan periods, loan entitlements, the initial delay in reminder notices in Acquisitions and the frequency of reminder notices in both Acquisitions and Circulation.

1.24 Help screens must be available at central points throughout the system.

1.25 Tenderers are advised that the following complement of terminals is felt to be the very least with which the College could operate:

Circulation
3 Issue terminals
1 Supervisory terminal

Acquisitions
1 Supervisory terminal

Accessions
1 Supervisory terminal

Public Access Catalogues
3 Terminals

2 External databases

2.1 The normal method of system database construction will be by the adoption and modification of MARC-format records from external databases. The modification may be either by the omission of library-selected levels and/or fields in the MARC record or by complete restructuring to the requirements of the system database. The limits at which any author, title, or author/title field will be truncated are to be indicated if a truncated author or title field will contain less than 100 characters, or an author/title field less than 180 characters.

2.2 The system must also provide software to enable bibliographic records constructed by the library staff to be output in MARC format for integration with external databases. The tenderer should indicate the exchange media possible but quote for the cheapest. The software is to be capable of handling material at both the general and analytical levels.

2.3 The system tender must include all software necessary for the above functions as well as any modem or other hardware required.

2.4 It shall be no part of any contract that the College will be required to draw records from any one specific database.

2.5 Where the supplier of a system also offers access to an external database, the costs of using such an external database are to be explicitly and separately stated.

2.6 External databases which incorporate files of British Books in Print and of Current Government Publications will be of particular interest.

3 Acquisitions

3.1 The system must permit the production in-house of a tentative catalogue record *prior* to its use for order purposes.

3.2 The system must permit the adoption from an external database of a tentative catalogue record *prior* to its use for order purposes.

3.3 At the basic level the Cataloguing module would compose the catalogue records and write them to file as the first operation; and in a second operation they would be called serially by the Acquisitions module and used to produce printed orders.

3.4 *In advanced systems, at the end of input for the cataloguing record, there should be a prompt from the system enquiring whether the item is now to be ordered. An affirmative response should produce an automatic transfer to the Acquisitions module, with automatic reversion at the end of the order input for that item to the Cataloguing module.

3.5 Not all items catalogued will require to be passed through the Acquisitions module. Donations will pass to the Bibliographic Database directly. So will dummy catalogue entries, intended to save staff time by informing readers that we do not have a specific title but that they can consult it in a named library. The listing of Desiderata in the Biblographic Database could also offer a similar advantage, but there are also strong arguments for assigning such materials to a separate file.

3.6 Items which do not require to be immediately ordered will be held on a Potential Requirements file whence they may be retrieved for order purposes serially either by ISBN or by author/title or *by any or most of the fields normally available to users of the PAC system.

3.7 *In advanced systems, working within the Acquisitions module, it should be possible to recover the catalogue record for order purposes automatically in response to a system prompt for the identifier in an index field selected at the beginning of the Acquisitions Session (but capable of reselection), that is, without operator transfer to the Cataloguing module and return to the Acquisitions module.

3.8 *To prevent accidental duplication of library materials the system is to advise the operator, preferably by flashing highlights, of the existence of copies within the system. However, ordering is not to be inhibited.

3.9 The Cataloguing Data in the Bibliographic Record are to be immune from alteration, save by members of the Cataloguing Section or by Senior Library Management.

3.10 Equally, the Acquisitions Data in the Bibliographic Record are to be immune from alteration, save by members of the Acquisitions Section or by Senior Library Management.

3.11 Acquisitions Data is to be input in response to system prompts and is to include:

(1) Status of order (*perhaps automatically adjusted)
(2) Order number (*perhaps automatically generated)
(3) Originating department (code); name of requester
(4) Number of copies to be ordered (*up to 19 preferably in WORDS rather than Arabic numeral)
*Default value ONE.
(5) Type of binding of edition
(6) Optionally, but preferably, the estimated cost (total of all copies)
(7) Supplier code, failing which –
(8) Supplier name and address
(9) Date of order (*perhaps automatically inserted)
(10) Special instructions

(11) Reports of suppliers
(12) Actual cost (total of all copies)
(13) All invoice and credit note numbers associated
(14) Date of receipt or cancellation.

3.12 *A currency conversion module would be advantageous, especially if on-line updating facilities are available.

3.13 The system is to provide an on-line file of the names and addresses of frequently used suppliers, with facilities for insertion, amendment and deletion. Irregular suppliers to be inserted in the Acquisitions Data in response to system prompts and recorded with the other acquistions data for the order. **Note**: System suppliers should indicate the number of entries possible in the file.

3.14 Allocation of materials to suppliers will continue to be made normally on an item-by-item basis.

3.15 The printing of orders in the basic system will proceed in batch after library opening hours.
*In more advanced systems printing would be under the control of a command file for printing at slack times during opening hours, or may even proceed concurrently with other operations.

3.16 The system must produce automatically reminders for material undelivered within specific time limits.
*The more advanced systems should either vary the time-limit according to country of publication or permit item-by-item time-limit assignment.
*The more advanced systems should permit suppression of reminders on individual items.

3.17 It must be possible to issue cancellations of orders.
*Advanced systems may have an automatic cancellation facility.

3.18 Acquisitions Data is to be amendable only by Acquisitions staff of Senior Library Management.

3.19 Acquisitions Data is to be retrievable (for amendment) by order number, ISBN or control number, title, author/title or,
*in an advanced system possible also by author/title acronym.

3.20 The system is to allow for part receipt of orders.

3.21 At the receipt stage accession numbers will be the subject of prompting.

*In an advanced system there may be an option for automatic supply.

3.22 If there is no separate Serials module, the Acquisitions functions for Serials are to be included in the Acquisitions software.

3.23 *It should be possible to transfer items ordered but undelivered in one year to the subsequent financial year by a simple command.

3.24 *It is to be impossible for the Acquisitions staff to delete an entry where payment has been made unless the item has been received or a credit note supplied for the full value. Only Senior Library Management are to be able to delete entries for such items.

4 Budgetary control

4.1 The system must be able to handle at least 24 separate departmental or subject funds, but, if serials are included in the Acquisitions system, the number must be doubled. ***NOTE**: System suppliers should state the number of funds their system will handle.

4.2 All funds are to be automatically adjusted for current invoices and credits.

4.3 Expenditure, both committed and incurred, against each fund is to be ascertainable on request.

*In advanced systems either a free balance is to be shown for each fund as each item is charged against it, or, alternatively, a warning of fund depletion, preferably with flashing highlights or audible tone, should be available.

4.4 Over-expenditure is to be advised, but not inhibited, though *in an advanced system orders over a specified value may require confirmation by Head of Section or Senior Library Management.

4.5 Itemized print-outs of expenditure, both committed and incurred, are to be available for each fund for the current year, and for the previous year separately.

4.6 For the current year these statements are to be available monthly and on demand.

4.7 Printed listings must also be available by order number, ISBN or control number, author/title *supplier, date or order, *fund, *UDC shelf-mark, and possible also a *course code, each giving the final cost, if available, otherwise the estimated cost.

The listings are to be available for all orders in the current financial year, for all orders in the previous financial year, possibly for active orders in the current year, possibly *for orders placed on or after a certain date, and possibly *for orders placed within a certain time-frame.

4.8 There is to be permanent archive storage for security reasons, preferably off-line, of all the acquisitions data, including *preferably details of failed purchases.

Transfer to archive storage should occur for records of the year (X-2) at the commencement of the year X.

The software that produces the printed listings mentioned in 4.7 above must be capable of extracting similar information from archive tapes. As this might, however, put excessive demands on disk space for sort purposes, it should be possible to omit the sorting stage and proceed directly to printing in random order.

4.9 If there is no separate Serials module, the Budgetary Control functions for Serials are to be included in the Acquisitions software.

5 Bibliographic database and cataloguing

5.1 The software is to permit the incorporation of records, received from external databases in MARC format.

5.2 Addition of a record to the database must not imply (1) that it has been through the Acquisitions process, or (2) that it will go through the Acquisitions process, or (3) that the item it represents will necessarily be circulated, or is even available in the College Library.

5.3 The software is to allow the transfer of records from the Acquisitions process to the Cataloguing process, with subsequent updating and revision of fields by the Cataloguing staff.

5.4 The software is to allow local input of cataloguing records in real time in response to a series of system prompts. Fields supplied by MARC but not supplied by the system should be indicated.

5.5 *In advanced systems the input of fields relating to authors, class-marks and subject headings is to take place under the control of authority files set up, expanded and corrected by the system by interaction with Cataloguing staff.

5.6 *Records derived from external databases are to be subject to the same semi-automatic indexing procedures.

5.7 The software is to create analytical records if present on the MARC tape.

5.8 Analytical cataloguing is also to be available for in-house cataloguing.

5.9 The software is to permit the real-time amendment and deletion of records already on the database.

5.10 Such amendment and deletion is to be open only to Cataloguing staff and Senior Library Management.

5.11 The software is *not* to inhibit the creation of records which do not meet the full MARC standard.

5.12 Acquisitions data is *not* to be lost, but is to be ultimately preserved on archive tape.

5.13 Acquisitions data is *not* to be open to amendment by the Cataloguing staff, but only by the Acquisitions staff or Senior Library Management.

5.14 The local cataloguing data to be added will include: (1) UDC shelf-marks (at least two will be required); (2) UDC class-marks (at least two will be required); (3) Alphabetical subject headings; (4) Local public notes; (5) Local private notes; and, (6) *possibly keywords.

Accession numbers are indicated in Section 3 as being allocated by the Acquisitions process, but might be part of the Cataloguing process.

5.15 The database should accommodate dummy entries for items not in the stock of the library to provide, in a local public note, information as to where a copy can be consulted.

5.16 The database should also incorporate entries for items on order but not yet received and should provide readers consulting the public access catalogue with the latest supplier's report.

5.17 The database will eventually be called on to accommodate entries for non-print material.

5.18 The basic system should update the Bibliographic file in real time.

*More sophisticated systems may have a catalogue review file where records may first be *Reviewed* by Head of Section.

5.19 Software should be available within the terms of the contract to permit printed listings of COM tape output of the entire bibliographic database or of delimited sections of the database indexed by the names of authors, by titles, by UDC class-makes and/or shelf-marks, by subject headings, by ISBN, by accession numbers, or even *by keyword.

5.20 Software should also be available to enable print-outs to be made of selected indexes to the Bibliographic database.

5.21 Items should not be deleted from the database simply because they are missing.

5.22 It should also be possible to make a complete dump of the Database from time to time for security purposes. If this dump does not take place daily, then there should be daily copying to tape of all changes to the Bibliographic database.

6 Circulation control

6.1 At the basic level issues, discharges and reservations may be effected by keyboarding book numbers and borrower numbers in response to system prompts.
*Advanced systems must normally carry out all loan and return transactions by means of light pens and bar-coded labels, but keyboard back-up should be available.

6.2 Software and equipment is to be provided to enable the bar-coded labels to be produced in-house. The software is to provide for the production of individual labels or for runs of labels between upper and lower limits. All labels to bear the accession number not only in coded form but also as Arabic digits.

6.3 All circulation terminals are to be capable of all circulation transactions: loan, return and reservation.

6.4 At least one of the terminals in the circulation department, and preferably more than one, is to be capable of registering borrowers.

6.5 At least one of the terminals in the circulation department, and preferably more than one, is to be capable of ensuring that searches can be made of the online files to discover (1) which items are charged against a particular borrower, or (2) the transaction details of all copies of a particular book, including any borrowers and issue dates.

Issue/Return

6.6 The system must have some means of attempting to prevent claims of erroneous charging, e.g.

(1) the presence of a machine-readable borrower's card;
(2) software which requires the circulation assistant to confirm that successive items are to be charged against the same borrower;
(3) printed output for signature by the borrower;
(4) keypad input of a confidential code by the borrower to ratify each transaction, with audible or visible confirmation of acceptance to the Circulation assistant.

Solution (4) is preferred to solution (3) which is preferred to both (1) and (2).

6.7 The equipment is to signal to the circulation assistant the success or failure of a transaction.

6.8 The due date for return is to be displayed against each transaction.

The due date for return is to be printed on a slip preferably with the accession number for the convenience of the reader.

6.9 On discharge a receipt is to be printed upon request.

6.10 Skeleton records for both stock and borrower are to be acceptable to the system.

6.11 The system is to indicate to the staff that:

(1) the item is overdue;
(2) the reader has overborrowed;
(3) the reader owes money for fines, losses, etc.
(4) the reader has failed to return a wanted book;
(5) there are inter-library loans or reserved books awaiting collection by the readers;
(6) the reader has lost his loan privileges;

(7) there is a message for the reader;

(8) the item presented for issue is already recorded as being on loan or missing;

(9) the item presented for issue has been reserved for another borrower;

(10) the item returned is wanted by another reader;

(11) the reader's card presented has been notified as lost or stolen;

*(12) the reader's card presented has been notified as stolen.

*At advanced level the above responses should be inserted and made generally automatically.

6.12 Each of the default conditions indicated under 6.11 (6.11.3) to be overridable by either the circulation assistant or circulation supervisor.

6.13 Each of the default conditions indicated under 6.11 (except 6.11.3, 6.11.10) to be individually erasable by the circulation assistant.

6.14 The conditions excepted under 6.12 and 6.13 to be overridable and erasable only by the circulation supervisor and other senior library staff or, during evening hours, by the library captain for that night.

6.15 *The system to permit the temporary adoption of inter-library loan items for circulation purposes.

6.16 It should be possible for Circulation staff to override the status of Reference Books and issue them on short loan.

Fines

6.17 A fines module is not essential at the basic level. *Fines will be calculated and displayed, and part-payment will be possible.

6.18 *The system to recognize that selected categories of borrower are not subject to fine.

Loan periods

6.19 At the most basic level there must be five different periods (including a short-loan period). *The loan period may be fixed at will for each item.

6.20 *The loan period to be modifiable by borrower status.

6.21 Loan periods to be variable at the discretion of the circulation assistants.

6.22 * The number of renewal periods should be limited and variable by the library.

6.23 Re-issue to the same borrower is to be possible immediately following return and cancellation.

6.24 Telephone renewals should be possible despite the absence of any borrower's machine-readable card.

Short-Loan collection

6.40 A facility must exist for issuing selected items for loan periods of one hour, or multiples of an hour, from the precise moment of issue.

6.41 The facility should permit overnight loans or weekend loans. This means that all items issued after a certain time need not be returned until 10.15. am on the next operational day (excluding Saturdays).

6.42 * The facility should permit special adjustment of the overnight and weekend loan periods for readers on certain courses or living at a distance from the college.

4.43 It must be easy to transfer items from the ordinary collection to the short loan collection.

6.44 The number of short-loan items permitted to each borrower should be restrictable.

Security systems

6.45 The system will require to operate compatibly with a 3M Tattle-Tape detection system.

6.46 *An advanced system will be expected to be programmable to restrict the availability of services to persistently troublesome borrowers. This can range from denying further loans to such borrowers, to denying them access to the catalogues, or even access to the library.

6.47 With public access catalogue terminals, and even more so with external on-line catalogue consultation facilities, there exists a danger that data will be deliberately corrupted by readers. To guard against this, transactions should not only be written to disk but also to tape, and software should exist to enable the library to identify from this tape the last-known borrower of a specific work, or to identify all the undischarged works issued to a particular borrower. This need not be a real-time activity.

Membership database

6.48 The file must comply with the requirements of the Data Protection Act.

6.49 The information to be recorded for administrative use in the database is as follows:

(1) Library borrower number
(2) Surname/forename/initials/title
(3) Home address
(4) Term-time address
*(5) Other address
(6) Telephone no. at home address
(7) Telephone no. at term-time address
*(8) Telephone no. or telex no. at other address
(9) Department/course being followed
*(10) Tutor's name and department
(11) Date of registration
(12) Date of expiry of registration, with flag for final year students
(13) Message and trap facilities as recorded in 6.11
(14) Status
(15) Locality code (for short loans system)
*(16) Historical information of library use, disputes, etc.
*(17) Customer relations field
(18) Borrower entitlement
(19) Number of items currently on loan
*(20) Fines outstanding
*(21) Total borrowings in current year
*(22) Total borrowings since first joining
*(23) Notes

6.50 The borrower file must be updateable in real time.

6.51 The system is to offer at least five different grades of borrower entitlement.

6.52 The system is to permit transfer and amendment of the relevant fields of student records from the College computer system (currently a Prime configuration) by direct line, magnetic tape, or floppy disk.

6.53 Data on all patrons to be able to be keyboarded by Library staff in response to prompt displays. Amendment and deletion facilities to be available.

6.54 Borrower traps will be made automatically for programmed circumstances, but traps may also be set at the discretion of the circulation staff.

6.55 The software will automatically advise members, about a fortnight before the date of expiry of their registration, either to apply for a summer extension or to return the borrowings listed.

6.56 The system will automatically provide a daily print-out of:

(1) those users whose membership has now lapsed;
(2) all current defaulters, with reason for their default.

7 Public access to the database

7.1 Library patrons will be able to obtain read-only access to the catalogue file or files from dedicated terminals in the library.
*Such access to be restricted to readers not in default by prescribing insertion of a library membership card or by keying in the borrower's secret code. Any secret code should not be displayed at the terminal.
*Though the cost of printers is not to be included in the current tenders, tenders should be made on the assumption that screen printers can be attached to the relevant terminals if they themselves are not in fact printing terminals.

7.2 *Library patrons passing security checks are to be able to obtain read-only access to the file of their borrowings, the listing giving author and title as well as accession number.

7.3 *Borrowers are to be able to make tentative reservations at the dedicated terminal for items already on loan from the library. Such reservations are to expire after 24 hours if not confirmed by the library staff.

7.4 Access to the databases is to be menu-driven and is to permit the following modes of information retrieval:

(1) By accession number
(2) By the names of authors, including corporate authors
(3) By author/title
(4) By title
(5) By specific UDC class-mark or shelfmark
(6) By subject heading
(7) By series title (optional)
(8) By ISBN or control no. and for advanced systems by as many as possible of the following:
*(9) By 'keyword'
*(10) By acronym
*(11) By any indexed field
*(12) With the option of using Boolean methods
*(13) With facilities for search entry error correction
*(14) By free text

7.5 *In addition to normal speed access for inexperienced users, the menu system should allow faster access for experienced users.

7.6 *Help screens must be available to users lost in the system.

7.7 The basic display facility required is that of a single record at a time giving full bibliographic information and loan/order status of all copies.

*A briefer optional display should be available giving author/title/edition/date/location/availability.

*A single-line entry facility should be available for rapid search purposes. When the required entry has been found it should be possible to display a full entry for the item without restarting the search.

No display on public access terminals is to give the names of actual borrowers, only the fact that the work is on loan.

*It should be possible for readers to obtain print-outs on screen printers, though these are not to be included in the present contract. (May require to be a chargeable facility.)

7.8 Readers should be able to examine the files of index fields to determine search parameters.

7.9 *Patrons should also be able to access in read-only mode the record of their borrowings and reservations, the display giving author/title and date due.

7.10 *Patrons should also be able to effect a limited number of reservations at public-access catalogue terminals. The facility should be capable of being withdrawn by the library staff.

7.11 *College staff should be able to place tentative orders with the Acquisitions section, through the system.

7.12 *The software to be supplied should permit members with a home computer to perform the operations listed above from their homes. The supply of hardware for this purpose is not part of the present tender, as no immediate application is foreseen. However, it is assumed that all that is required will be a fairly inexpensive modem.

8 Serials control

8.1 A Serials control system is not regarded as an essential part of the system for which tenders are invited. Nevertheless, tenderers who have such systems available should include a separate quotation for the supply of the necessary hardware and software. (Two terminals required.)

8.2 If the financial control of serials is not handled by the Acquisitions package, then that is an essential part of the Serials package.

8.3 *As noted under Acquisitions (Section 3) the provision of an automatic currency conversion module could be helpful.

8.4 At the basic level the system should be capable of handling up to 24 different funds; *48 different funds would be required.

8.5 Listings should be obtainable

(1) alphabetically by title
(2) by supplier
(3) by fund
(4) by UDC shelfmark and, optionally, by class-mark as well
(5) – within specific ranges
(6) by subject heading

The data to be printed in such listings to be variable, and to include title, supplier, fund, UDC shelfmark, subject heading, price, renewal date.

8.6 The information to be recorded against each subscription for each title is to include:

(1) subscription agency
(2) subscription period
(3) renewal date
(4) price
(5) payment required in advance?
(6) payment date
(7) invoice and credit note numbers
(8) index to be claimed
(9) Circulation schedule
(10) Holdings, if possible differentiating between bound, unbound, at binders
(11) receipt of parts, with dates of receipt

8.7 System is to allow for the issue of extraordinary supplements at extra charges.

8.8 In a basic system the formal orders are to be produced either at the end of the order session or in batch after closure of the library. *A more sophisticated system should enable their production under a command file at a time when the library is less busy.

8.9 Claim forms for missing issue are to be generated automatically for overdue issues:

In a basic system either on receipt of the next issue or after a set time interval;

*In a more advanced system the interval is to take into account the country of origin of the periodical and/or its previous receipt history.

An added recommendation would be to permit the serials librarian to suppress recalls on his own intuition.

8.10 A facility must exist for recording the reports of suppliers.

8.11 In the basic system it must be possible to retrieve individual entries for amendment by order no., ISSN or title.

*In more advanced systems access should also be possible by supplier, fund, issuing body or keywords.

8.12 Only unbound stock will be issued on the package. Issue machines should have both light pens and keyboard.

Initially journals will require to be identified by keying in an acronym or the ISSN, with part numbers also being keyed in.

*Advanced systems will also permit identification by the bar-code printed on some journals, leaving only the part number to be keyed in.

8.13 *Modem access to suppliers' files, for the extraction of bibliographic information, for the placing of orders, and for the registration of claims is desirable.

8.14 A module to handle binding operations is not an essential part of any serials system offered, but if available it should provide accounting facilities and generate binding instructions.

9 Management information

9.1 Not all these facilities are expected of every system. Tenderers should advise facilities not provided within the tender.

A = Annual	W = Weekly	R = On Request
M = Monthly	D = Daily	I = Exceptional Requirement

9.2 Acquisition (excluding periodicals)

		Frequency
(1)	Number of items ordered	A/M
(2)	Number of items received	A/M
(3)	Number of items ordered from each supplier	A/M
(4)	List of items outstanding, by supplier, where time elapsed since order greater than x (British) or y (foreign) days	A/M/R
(5)	Total commitment and expenditure per fund with total allocation to fund	A/M/R
(6)	Total commitment and expenditure by supplier	A/M/R
(7)	Analysis of additions according to format (perhaps 12 formats)	A/R
(8)	Average cost of items received by UDC category	A/R
(9)	Average for each supplier of delay between ordering and delivery	A/R
(10)	Average for each publisher of delay	

between ordering and delivery A/R

9.3 Acquisition (periodicals)

(1) Number of subscription periodicals A/R
(2) Number of gratis periodicals A/R
(3) Total commitment and expenditure, by fund A/M/R
(4) Total commitment and expenditure, by supplier A/M/R
(5) Total commitment and expenditure, by span of UDC shelfmarks A/M/R

9.4 Cataloguing

(1) Number of new titles added A/M/R
(2) Number of volumes added A/M/R
(3) Number of copies added A/M/R
(4) Number of titles withdrawn A/M/R
(5) Number of volumes withdrawn A/M/R
(6) Number of copies withdrawn A/M/R
(7) The same information as (1) to (6) but related to individual types of non-book materials (perhaps 12 formats)
(8) Report of penultimate and last copy withdrawals W
(9) Total number of titles, volumes, copies in the collection by UDC mark or ordering department R
(10) Total number of non-book items in the collections by any of 12 formats R

9.5 Binding (where Serials module covers)

(1) Number of periodical volumes sent to binding, total – and by up to six binders A/R
(2) Number of periodical volumes returned by binders, total – and by up to six binders A/R
(3) Average cost on return basis per binder and overall A/R

9.6 Circulation

(1) Number of issues, returns,

	renewals, reservations as logged by the system every 10 minutes with daily, weekly, monthly and annual cumulations	D/W/M/A
(2)	Number of issues, returns, renewals, reservations, by course for undergraduates, by department for staff, and others	A/R
(3)	Number of items on issue	A/M/W
(4)	Number of items on issue, by variable UDC categories	A/R
(5)	Listing of total issues for items circulated in the current year	A/R
(6)	Last date on which a specific item was returned	
(7)	Listing of all items in stock that have not circulated since a variable date	R
(8)	Lists of all items more than x days overdue	D
(9)	Number of borrowers registered for as many categories as available under circulation	A/R
(10)	Listings of readers persistently late in returning recalled or overdue books	A/M/R

10 Miscellaneous

10.1 It should be possible to set up a Desiderata file to record out-of-print items to be sought in antiquarian lists.

10.2 Facilities must exist for purging the databases periodically of records no longer required, if deletion under Cataloguing does not in fact have this effect.

10.3 The possibility of creating a local Community Information File is interesting, but would only be required if it did not add to the overall cost of the system.

10.4 The possibility of recording interest profiles for members of staff and using these to disseminate information is again interesting, but only provided that it does not add more than 1 per cent to the VAT-free cost of the system.

10.5 The availability of general statistical analysis packages and a word processing package should be intimated, but such do not form part of the items under present tender.

10.6 A message facility for staff would be advantageous.

Index

Routledge Revivals

The Shakespearean Metaphor

First published in 1978, this book represents a study of the ways in which Shakespeare exploits the possibilities of metaphor. In a series of studies ranging from the early to the mature Shakespeare, the author concentrates on metaphor as a controlling structure — the extent to which a certain metaphoric idea informs and organises the drama. These studies turn constantly to the relations between symbol and metaphor, literal and figurative, and examine key plays such as *Richard III*, *King John*, *Henry V*, *Romeo and Juliet*, *Troilus* and *Cressida*, and *Coriolanus*. They also provide a key to *The Tempest* which is analysed in terms of power and possession — the dominant motif.